THE REAL U

Ujamaa: familyhood, African s̲ ____
From Kiswahili *jamaa* (origin Arabic): family,
   kin, comrade, colleague, gathering, co-operation.
The *u* adds 'hood' or 'ism' as in: brotherhood,
   socialism.

With national independence in 1961, President Julius Nyerere of Tanganyika (later Tanzania) urged farmers to take the lead in economic development. Villagers could work the land collectively on traditional African principles where all worked and all benefitted. Tanzania could thus bypass capitalism with its exploitation of the many by the few.

In 1962 President Nyerere coined the Kiswahili word that summed up this strategy: *ujamaa* or African socialism.

Some people in the Ruvuma Region were inspired to put this into practice – the village of Litowa was born and soon after the Ruvuma Development Association (RDA). By 1969 the RDA had seventeen *ujamaa* villages, which transformed all aspects of their rural society.

President Nyerere was supportive in every way. But the leaders of his party were deeply hostile and banned the RDA.

Defeated by his own party, Nyerere opted for "villagization": a form of State farming. In the mid-1970s the rural population was moved by diktat, creating large bureaucratically managed villages. Bigger *ujamaa* villages were swamped with resentful newcomers; people in smaller villages were forced to join other villages.

Villagization increased neither co-operation nor agricultural production. It was abandoned in 1985.

Villagization was the opposite of *ujamaa*. Yet it came to be known as Tanzania's *ujamaa*, hiding what *ujamaa* had been and what the RDA had achieved.

This book rights this wrong. It tells the inspiring story of the RDA, the socialism created by African villagers.

Dear Alishia

Thank you so much for everything!

UJAMAA

The hidden story of *Alina*
Tanzania's socialist villages

by

Ralph Ibbott

Introduction by Selma James

Ϯ

CROSSROADS Books

Published 2014 by *CROSSROADS* Books
Crossroads Women's Centre, 25 Wolsey Mews,
London NW5 2DX, England
sales@crossroadsbooksonline.net
www.crossroadsbooksonline.net

ISBN 978-0-9568140-1-2

Editors	Selma James and Nina López
Formatting	Nina López
Typing, scanning, proofreading	Cristel Amiss, Claire Glasman, Fanny Weed and others
Printing on 100% recycled paper	Polestar Wheatons Ltd, Devon
Cover design	Nina López
Cover photo	Brian Rée 1964

The cover photograph is of the villagers of Litowa, including
Noreen and Ralph Ibbott and their four children. (Full photo
pp 10-11.) Other photos from the Ibbotts' private collection and
their contacts. Map of Tanzania from *Shamba Letu* 1970

Thanks to the Barry Amiel and Norman Trust for its financial
contribution to this project.

To the memory of
my wife Noreen Ibbott
and of
Ntimbanjayo Millinga and
all the people of the
Ruvuma Development Association

CONTENTS

Litowa 1964

INTRODUCTION
Selma James

It's not often that an important moment in history is rediscovered. This book is about one of these. It is the story of the Ruvuma Development Association (RDA) of Tanzania[1] and its seventeen *ujamaa* – or African socialist – villages.

The RDA was built from scratch from 1961 by farming families – men, women and children – most of whom had little or no formal education. The villagers were developing their economy and in every way transforming their rural society, demonstrating what can be achieved with even the slenderest of resources by determined people working collectively. The self-governing RDA was the continuation in Tanzania of the great movement for colonial liberation and the hope and energy it generated.

Yet the RDA was destroyed after eight years, at the very moment when the success of its collective self-reliance was beginning to be taken up by many other Tanzanian farmers. Although *ujamaa* had not (yet) involved millions, the story of its creation and destruction can tell us much of what we need to know about the mid-twentieth century liberation movement from which it sprang, and perhaps also about present movements for sovereignty and justice, their exciting potential and the social forces that stand against them.

Ralph Ibbott's book is also unique because it is written by a deeply committed participant and one who is extraordinarily aware of what the villagers did and how they decided to do it. The book has no resemblance to an academic speculation. Rath-

---

1   Tanganyika was renamed Tanzania in 1964 when it united with Zanzibar – the only two African countries that united, and stayed united.

er, from the description of events and people, we get not only the history but how it was made.

People today have little awareness of the movement of many millions which chased the European imperialists out of countries they had colonized and subjugated for centuries. Yet this was a major turning point for most of the world, since most of the world had been colonized.

The first to gain national independence, from Britain, was India in 1947, after a struggle over generations. Clement Attlee, prime minister of the 1945 Labour government – itself a victory of those who were determined never to go back to pre-war depression and class degradation – proclaimed soon after the landslide election that tossed out arch imperialist Winston Churchill, that Britain was getting out of India.

But the catastrophic Hindu-Muslim split led to the partition of Pakistan from India. Mahatma Gandhi, India's internationally respected leader, opposed partition with all in his power, but he could not stop it. It cost millions of lives, and dimmed the triumph of Britain's departure.[2] This should have warned us that political independence was not enough to ensure a compassionate future.

Nevertheless, when on 6 March 1957 the British flag was lowered on the colony of the Gold Coast and Ghana's Black Star flag replaced it, anti-imperialists everywhere were ecstatic with triumph and hope. Black Africa, maligned, demeaned and brutalized in every way, was lifting itself up, able finally to show its own worth and determine its own future as much as any single country can – and maybe even to unite as a continent. The scourge of imperial occupation, a major source of the racism that justified the theft of great wealth in human labour and natural resources, was ending in Africa.

That the anti-colonial movement is largely unfamiliar now reflects the (mis)education we all receive, including from the

---

2   Britain had experience of partitioning colonies that wanted freedom; they had done that in 1921 in Ireland, their oldest colony.

media. The history made by unknown millions, when silenced people speak with action, is usually distorted when it is not censored. Such massive involvement of people on their own behalf is truly subversive, threatening a tide of change even in retrospect.

But the achievements of the anti-colonial movement could also be wiped from view by the dictatorships, proxy wars and excruciating poverty that followed. How could such enormous tragedy be its outcome? The implication often lurking behind political and academic diagnoses is that more could not be expected, that people who have little can only accomplish little.

The RDA's history helps right this racist wrong.

The story begins with the extraordinary Julius Kambarage Nyerere, socialist and pan-Africanist who in July 1954 formed the Tanganyika African National Union (TANU) to spearhead the struggle for independence from Britain.

Nyerere had lived in the village of Butiama until he went to school at age twelve. He was the son of a chief of the Wazanaki tribe which had not been distorted into a steep hierarchy by the colonial administrators, as had some tribes. Shaped by traditional communal village life, he never ceased to see the world from the point of view of villagers. It was a crucial component of his leadership, an unalloyed and unique strength.

Nyerere was the first Tanzanian to go to university abroad (Edinburgh, 1949-52 where he got a master's degree). It is known that in 1944 at Makerere University in Kampala (Uganda) he wrote a paper on The Freedom of Women. He later commented: "My father had twenty-two wives and I knew how hard they had to work and what they went through as women."[3] Not too many men, African or not, acknowledged the hard work of women at that time. Or even today. This awareness ensured a more accurate view of who "villagers" were.

---

3   Interview by Ikamba Bunting, *New Internationalist*, Issue 309, 1999.

He returned from post-war socialist Britain to teach. This was when he gained the title of Mwalimu, or Teacher, how he was known from then on. A year later, earlier than he had planned, he threw himself into organizing for independence.

For Nyerere, political independence from any imperial power did not by itself ensure independence from Western economic, political and military power. Describing independence as "the preliminary goal"[4] made clear that it was crucial but not the movement's only aim. This perspective was way ahead of the prevailing unrealistic view that all a colony had to do was win political independence for everything to change. How, when resources were so meagre? The wealth that had been stolen over centuries (including the wealth in people via the slave trade) was gone; the profits accumulated by those who had dominated were a power for them to continue to dominate. The forces ranged against "new countries" were formidable, especially dangerous when they were not acknowledged.

How to cleanse the society emerging from colonialism of the structures the imperialists left behind? What should and could replace them given the level of skills of the population who had been deprived even of literacy, let alone technical and scientific training?

We should remind ourselves that even people in the West who were committed to colonial liberation rarely considered that the form of government they lived under and often challenged should not be imposed on ex-colonies. The movement itself, blinded by euphoria at the moment of its greatest power, also seems to ignore the power of capitalism to recover and reconquer. As early as 1897, James Connolly, Irish socialist leader, told the nationalist movement:

> If you remove the English army tomorrow and hoist
> the green flag over Dublin Castle, unless you set about

---

4   Introduction to *Uhuru na Umoja/Freedom and Unity*, Oxford University Press, Dar es Salaam, 1966, p 1.

the organization of the Socialist Republic your efforts would be in vain.

England would still rule you. She would rule you through her capitalists, through her landlords, through her financiers, through the whole array of commercial individualist institutions she has planted in this country and watered with the tears of our mothers and the blood of our martyrs.[5]

It is a lesson which has proven hard for anti-capitalist movements to learn.

The solution often proposed to all problems was Africanization – for local people to step into the posts the British were vacating. But it is those who fight for personal advancement who usually take charge, including of expatriate salaries that had always fleeced the population. They change little but the colour and accent (and nowadays also the gender, sexual preference, etc.) at the top.

A power-hungry elite was emerging, in other newly independent countries. In 1961 agronomist René Dumont, committed to colonial liberation, reported on the response to this danger in formerly French colonies:

In May 1961 a number of farmers north of Brazzaville said to me: 'Independence isn't for us; it's for the city people.' I heard the same criticism that year in Dahomey and Madagascar . . .[6]

He quotes the mayor of Ngongsamba, Cameroon:

. . . the masses have the impression that national sovereignty has created a privileged class which has cut itself off from them . . . a good number of our officials,

5   Socialism and nationalism, Shan van Vocht, 1897, reprinted in *James Connolly: Selected Writings*, P Beresford Ellis (ed), Pluto Press, London and Chicago, 1997, pp 121-124.
6   Introduction, *False Start in Africa*, Sphere Books, London, 1966, p 20.

scorning a real sense of public office and duty, are only
interested in the advantages and privileges of their positions . . . at the rate we are going now, we are headed
towards a worse colonialism, that of class.[7]

Dumont also considered independence as a preliminary
goal and knew that what was essential was for the farmers to be
enthusiastic enough to make "a massive effort". Ibbott reports
that Nyerere read his book *False Start in Africa* and ordered copies to be distributed to his ministers.

Also in 1961, Frantz Fanon, a psychiatrist from Martinique
in the Caribbean, drew vital lessons from the Algerian revolution against France, of which he was part. He was one of the
earliest to identify even before independence the counter-rev-
olution driven by the ambitious new elite. They were "a little
greedy caste, avid and voracious", and the party heading the
movement was "transformed into a trade union of individual
interests . . . a means for personal advancement."[8]

TANU was the same. Already in February 1960, nearly two
years before independence, Nyerere told a TANU conference:

> I have seen TANU officials getting drunk with power
> and scheming to undermine one another . . . Too many
> big TANU officials seem to spend most of their time
> talking about their positions. To what sort of govern-
> ment would that lead when responsible government
> comes? You and I must reform because if we do not,
> we will be blamed by the 200 million in Africa. If we
> cannot reform, then we must destroy TANU because it
> will be of no use to this territory.[9]

(Note: for him pan-Africanism was a political principle; they
were accountable to all in Africa for what they did in Tanzania.)

---

7   *False Start*, p 21.
8   *Wretched of the Earth*, Penguin Books, England, 1967, pp 136, 138.
9   Quoted by Cranford Pratt, *The Critical Phase in Tanzania 1945-1968*,
    Cambridge University Press, 1976, p 110.

Nyerere called it on the opportunistic use of race; it was "racialism". Merely replacing Europeans with Africans could not change the nature of the State that imperialism had carefully left behind, whose structure aimed not to liberate but to discipline and repress.

A profoundly radical alternative strategy was needed.

He spoke in Kiswahili, the language that almost everyone understood, irrespective of region or tribe. (Local languages were often spoken in the villages, especially by women.) Mwalimu, the teacher, spoke to the people via the transistor radio.[10] No electrification needed and relatively inexpensive, it was a way of organizing which brought town and country much closer. Change depended on the 96% of the population scattered in the countryside. He informed his audience about the independence struggle, and about the profound problems they would face once the colonizers had gone.

> . . . we are free already. What is freedom? It is the power
> we have to decide what is going to happen in Tanganyi-
> ka and when it is going to happen and that power we
> have. All that remains is hard work . . . We must spend
> our brains, we must spend our sleepless nights to see
> how we are going to give our people the water they
> need, to give them the schools they need, how are we
> going to give the people the health they require.[11]

Tanzania became independent in December 1961. Nyerere was its first elected Prime Minister. TANU's commitment to socialism was enshrined in its 1962 constitution: "To establish a democratic and socialist form of government . . . "[12] What did this mean in practice?

10 Kate Wenner who worked in Litowa for a year, says: "Millinga . . . sometimes brought his [radio] along to *ujamaa* meetings . . . When the news came on everyone hushed . . . They wanted to hear news of Tanzania and the world." *Shamba Letu*, Houghton Mifflin, Boston, 1970, p 205.

11 Tanganyika, *Legislative Council Official Report*, 36th Session, vol 1, cols 390-1, 20 October 1960, quoted in *The Critical Phase*, p 85.

12 *The Critical Phase*, p 173.

Nyerere's strategy for economic and social development began not with academics or planners but with African farmers.

Brought up in "tribal socialism", as he called it, Nyerere had found, in fact invented, the Kiswahili word which both named and explained his alternative strategy:

> *"Ujamaa"* . . . or "Familyhood", describes our socialism. It is opposed to capitalism, which seeks to build a happy society on the basis of the exploitation of man by man; and it is equally opposed to doctrinaire socialism which seeks to build its happy society on a philosophy of inevitable conflict between man and man.
>
> We, in Africa, have no more need of being "converted" to socialism than we have of being "taught" democracy.[13] Both are rooted in our own past – in the traditional society which produced us. Modern African socialism can draw from its traditional heritage the recognition of "society" as an extension of the basic family unit.
>
> . . . Our recognition of the family to which we all belong must be extended yet further – beyond the tribe, the community, the nation, or even the continent – to embrace the whole society of mankind. This is the only logical conclusion for true socialism.[14]

This was far from a narrow State plan; national, but also internationalist. People in industrial countries had fought class exploitation and privilege by voting socialists into power so the State would act for them. It was a triumph, despite drawbacks, when welfare states were created with free national healthcare and education, affordable housing, and benefits. In Tanzania there were hardly any doctors, nurses, teachers, hospitals,

---

13 He is referring to the policy of delaying independence until "the natives" were "ready for self-government" having learnt parliamentary democracy as practised in Westminster.

14 *Ujamaa – the Basis of African Socialism*, a TANU pamphlet, 1962, republished in *Freedom and Unity*, pp 170-1.

schools, money – little to nationalize. But it did have a rich tradition of a communalist society, which took responsibility for
the care of its people.

With *ujamaa,* the population rather than the State would
take charge of development on the basis of the communalism
they already knew. While traditional society was generally pre-
sumed to be limited and limiting – what development overcame
– Nyerere saw both its social value and its possibilities precisely for overcoming underdevelopment. Rural people using not
an import but a native framework could develop their society
without capitalism – in fact while bypassing capitalism as an
economic and social system. He was not applying any socialist theory, Marxist or otherwise,[15] but adapting the communal
foundation of traditional society to modern needs, aspirations

---

15 Nyerere was sometimes criticized or even dismissed for not being a
    Marxist. Responding on one occasion, he is reported to have said, "If
    Marx had been born in Sumbawanga, he would have probably come
    out with the Arusha Declaration rather than *Das Kapital!*" (Issa G Shivji,
    The Mwalimu in Nyerere, 16 October 1999.)
    The joke had an element of truth. Nyerere was closer to Marx than
    even he may have realized. They both were convinced that in the pro-
    cess of collectively transforming society people transform themselves.
    The strategy of *ujamaa* is based on that.
    Marx's 1870s *Ethnological Notebooks* contain his research into pre-class
    and more recent societies with many communal or collective relation-
    ships. In his famous 1881 letter to Vera Zasulich he says that in some
    circumstances these societies could bypass capitalism to become "the
    fulcrum of social regeneration". (See T Shanin [ed], *Late Marx and the
    Russian Road*, Routledge and Kegan Paul, London, 1983.)
    Nyerere lived in a continent with many such societies; they had of
    course changed but their communalism had still not been destroyed by
    imperialism. His strategy of *ujamaa* presumed that in the circumstances
    of that time the communal African village could become the fulcrum of
    Tanzania's social regeneration.
    Marxist historian Walter Rodney, who worked for some years in
    Tanzania (and later became leader of a mass movement in his native
    Guyana), also notes the similarity between Nyerere's African socialism
    and Marx's view of the anti-capitalist potential of communal societies.
    Rodney dismisses the reduction of "African socialism" by Senghor
    and other African politicians to a "permanent co-existence of capitalist
    and supposedly socialist relations". (Tanzanian Ujamaa and Scientific
    Socialism, *African Review*, Dar es Salaam, 1:4, 1972.)

and developing personalities. It was socialism without money, rooted in the soil that had shaped Tanzanians, most of whom had lived outside of the money economy. His strategy was bold; it was a strategy for a poor but sovereign country determined to pull itself out of poverty and remain sovereign.

In April 1962, a few months after independence, Nyerere resigned from the government to use the impetus and energy of the movement that had just won the "preliminary goal" to build the movement for *ujamaa* within the party and among the population. His resignation made clear that building the movement was his priority over governing: if the people had to do it, then the people had to be informed and inspired and mobilized. Already, he said, "there had been a general acceptance of the social attitudes and ideas of our colonial masters" and of the false promise of a quick route out of poverty via the money economy. The elite which had emerged in the party and the new State was ready to use this drift to the cash nexus to secure its position. There was not much time; Nyerere had to act before the movement receded further and "tribal socialism" was swept away. African socialism – the people themselves building a communal agricultural economy – was in a race with the elite's gold rush for wealth and power.

> I have taken this action [of resigning] and won the support of my colleagues for it after a long debate that has gone on for days because of our firm belief that this is the best way to achieve our new objective, the creation of a country in which the people take a full and active part in the fight against poverty, ignorance and disease.[16]

He put running the government in the hands of Rashidi Kawawa, a government minister, and travelled throughout the country meeting with TANU members and with the public. He

---

16 *The Critical Phase*, p 117.

published three pamphlets. His *Ujamaa – the Basis of African Socialism* made the case against capitalism and for socialism, urging Tanzanians:

> to re-educate ourselves; to regain our former attitude of mind. In our traditional African society we were individuals within a community. We took care of the community and the community took care of us. We neither needed nor wished to exploit our fellow men.
>
> . . . It is up to the people of Tanganyika – the peasants, the wage earners, the students, the leaders, all of us – to make sure this socialist attitude of mind is not lost through the temptations to personal gain (or the abuse of positions of authority) which may come our way as individuals . . . [17]

Integral to the strategy of *ujamaa* was self-reliance. They had to do without loans and aid from abroad; both had strings attached. "For a community, self-reliance means that [Tanzanians] will use the resources and the skills they jointly possess for their own welfare and their own development." They would be neither wage slaves nor exploiters; rather, they would reshape their own society so that it ended poverty, ignorance, disease.

There are not many political leaders who can tell their voters who had just won independence that to stay that way they had only their own hard work to rely on. Nor was his view of traditional communalism in the least romantic. There had to be changes to overcome "two basic factors which prevented traditional society from full flowering".

The first was that women suffered from "ill-treatment and enforced subservience".

> It is impossible to deny that women did, and still do, more than their fair share of the work in the fields and

---

17 *Freedom and Unity*, pp 116-7.

in the homes. By virtue of their sex they suffered from inequalities which had nothing to do with their contribution to the family welfare.[18]

The second was poverty.

Certainly there was an attractive degree of economic equality, but it was equality at a low level. The equality is good, but the level can be raised.[19]

. . . there is an almost universal belief that life in the towns is more comfortable and more secure – that the rewards of work are better in the urban areas and that people in the rural parts of the country are condemned to poverty and insecurity for their whole lives.[20]

Increasing the scale of farming by families working together and using more modern methods of agriculture could increase yields. This was vital not only to attack poverty but to transform rural life so that it did not suffer the deprivation of the services and facilities available only in cities:

The land is the only basis for Tanzania's development; we have no other. Therefore, if our rural life is not based on the principles of socialism our country will not be socialist, regardless of how we organize our industrial sector, and regardless of our commercial and political arrangements. Tanzanian socialism must be firmly based on the land and its workers. This means that we have to build up the countryside in such a way that our people have a better standard of living, while living together in terms of equality and fraternity. It also means that, in the course of time, the advantages of town life in the way of

---

18 Socialism and Rural Development, *Uhuru na Ujamaa/Freedom and Socialism*, OUP, Dar es Salaam, 1968, p 339.
19 *Ibid*, p 339-340.
20 *Ibid*, p 341.

services and personal pleasures and opportunities must
become available to those who work in the rural sector
as much as those in urban areas.[21]

Rural society, from which economic change had to come,
had to transform itself into satisfying and rewarding communities, no longer socially deprived backwaters.

The elimination of poverty that would make this possible
required another change.

Women's subordination had wide economic implications.

The truth is that in the villages the women work very
hard. At times they work for twelve or fourteen hours
a day. They even work on Sundays and public holidays. Women who live in the villages work harder
than anybody else in Tanzania. But the men in the villages . . . are on leave for half their life.

If men pulled their weight, this "could contribute more towards the development of the country than anything we could
get from rich nations."[22] Men had to change as a socialist principle but also as an economic necessity. It is extraordinary how
neglected are these prominent anti-sexist views.

There were no quick fixes, not from him. Government-managed schemes which were relatively well-funded had promised
much but had failed, wasting scarce resources and discrediting
ministers and their managerial methods. The lesson was that
success depended not on investment but on the committed and
collective self-management of the producers.

People's trust in the honesty of their leader enabled him to
speak these truths. He seemed without personal ambition, the
rarest and most vital quality of the head of government and the
movement leader – he was both. He trusted in their ability to

---

21 *Ibid*, p 346.
22 The Arusha Declaration: Socialism and Self-Reliance, *Freedom and
    Socialism*, p 245. Republished in *The Arusha Declaration, Rediscovering
    Nyerere's Tanzania*, Crossroads Books, London, 2008.

understand and consider what he was urging them to do. And he had the patience his strategy demanded in order to steer the whole society away from the imperialists' waiting jaws.

> We are now a poor nation; there is no short cut to prosperity; hard work and a deliberate decision by us to plan for a better future is the only way forward.[23]

> We must not rush this development; what matters is not the speed but the direction in which we move.[24]

On 7 November 1960, Ntimbanjayo Millinga, twenty-one years of age, a TANU Youth League member, and secretary of his branch, set off with fourteen other TANU YL members, to build what later became known as an *ujamaa* village. All left family behind. Though young, Millinga had worked on a sisal estate, and had training as a nurse; he had also been a trade union representative – all valuable experience.

Once they had built a shelter, the men cleared the bush and planted some acres of maize, a staple of the diet. But they had to return home for lack of food to sustain them till the first crop.

Some months later, in June 1961, Millinga tried again with three of the same men and some others. This time they stayed.

During this second attempt, Millinga attended a short course at the new Kivukoni adult education college in Dar es Salaam. Ralph Ibbott had been invited to speak there about his experience on a 10,000-acre multiracial co-operative farm at St Faith's in apartheid Southern Rhodesia. He had worked for ten years with Guy Clutton-Brock, a dedicated, highly regarded anti-apartheid campaigner.

A new priest hostile to such anti-racism had pressed the church that owned the land into telling Ralph, his wife Noreen and their three children (all born in Rhodesia) to leave. The Ib-

---

23   After the Arusha Declaration, *Freedom and Socialism*, p 404.
24   *Ibid*, p 407.

botts were now living at Nyafaru, another multiracial co-operative farm on donated land.

Millinga invited Ralph to their new village of Litowa to advise them on improving agricultural methods. Ralph visited Litowa and met the other men. He saw what they were doing and with what commitment they were doing it. He was deeply impressed, especially with Millinga. This serious young man was clever, energetic and a natural leader (others later described him as charismatic). Ralph wrote soliciting a donation, and a kind English woman sent £50 which ensured the group could survive until the first harvest.

Millinga then spent some time with the Ibbotts at Nyafaru. They discussed Litowa and the Ibbotts' possible move there, and drafted a constitution for the Litowans to consider.

This was Ralph's chance to do the collective development work which apartheid could never allow. He would work with people at the exciting moment when they had won their liberation from colonial rule. Most important, unlike in Rhodesia, the Tanzanian President himself was advocating what they were attempting: that they take charge of the economic and social development of their village. The Ibbotts would have an African point of reference, a talented, determined man, and could contribute to a project to which a whole village was dedicated.

The two men began a strong and productive friendship that lasted until Ntimbanjayo Millinga's death in 2008.

The Ibbotts returned to England as they had planned. On the way, there was a quick visit to Litowa so that Noreen and the children could see where they would be returning to. Now Ralph was in search of funding. War on Want, the UK charity, agreed to give the Ibbotts the £50 a month Ralph had asked for to stay and work in Tanzania. In April 1963, the family made the move to Litowa.

By this time their families had joined the men in Litowa. The women were nervous to leave all they depended on to join this village in the bush; would it be able to feed the family? They slowly but steadily became full participants of the village. Not surprisingly, a decisive factor was that the children flourished.

Litowa was structured to encourage all to participate in decision-making. The key gathering was the *ujamaa* dinner of all the villagers two or three times a week, served by the girls and boys. This was where problems were confronted and decisions made, from how much of each crop to plant, to when they could afford to invest labour and other resources in better housing.

Ntimbanjayo was the compassionate, respected leader, pulling people together while gently but firmly raising criticisms of those who for example did not pull their weight. He in particular encouraged the women to speak up.

Talented organizers emerged, strengthening the collective. The man chosen to plan the field work would present his plan and then take up his hoe along with everyone else. Planners were still field workers; so division of labour did not automatically divide the labourers.

All worked, and all work was respected. Most of the women came later to the field, so they could care for the children and do other household work.[25] Elderly and disabled people who could not do heavy field work often had the job of frightening away the baboons who wanted to share in the lovely food the people had planted. (Later, they might help with childcare.)

And when any of the crop was sold (planting some tobacco as a cash crop was a government requirement), the cash remaining after social needs were met was divided equally among all, women and men, field workers and baboon scarers. The RDA's pay equity was probably among the first anywhere. Not much money was at stake but its equal distribution was in keeping with socialist values. (Equity was growing in other directions. Domestic violence was not approved of by the villagers, which proved an effective deterrent.)

---

25   "An old wheel was struck with a short stick every morning at about 7 am to muster the men for work. The married and older women were given a later time to start work on the farm crops so as to give them time for household chores, carrying water, washing, etc.: they went out about 9 am or later." Noreen Ibbott, from an unpublished manuscript.

There seem to have been constant consultations as there were always expanding or diversifying projects, or villagers were receiving visitors or travelling to other areas to explain what they were doing and how.

Though Ralph could be called on at any time for his opinion or advice, and Noreen was always contributing to village life, the Ibbotts never attended communal decision-making meetings. This was a principle which they at least as much as others were determined to uphold. It had to be the villagers who made and saw themselves making all decisions.

Ralph, trained as a quantity surveyor, had many practical skills. After the years at St Faith's and Nyafaru, he knew something about agriculture in Africa and about working collectively. One stunning contribution was installing a hydraulic ram by a waterfall on the Luhira river to enable water to be piped to Litowa (see Chapter 13). It was a boon especially for the women and children who traditionally transport water. It lifted the whole village.[26] Similar was planned in other villages.

Noreen was one of those creative housewives who, eminently flexible, can make herself useful anywhere, and find or invent practical solutions to most problems. Like Ralph, what she didn't know how to do and thought would be useful to the village, she sent to England to learn about. When Litowa decided to rear sheep, she imported a spinning wheel, taught herself to make yarn, and then trained others. She took her children into the forest to find natural dyes. And she taught people to knit: men as well as women could be seen walking in the village knitting wool garments for the high altitude winter.

It was Noreen who suggested to Ntimbanjayo that the village organize childcare. She saw hungry and cranky children whose mothers hadn't arrived back from the fields. The village could take on feeding and caring for them until their mothers' return. The village agreed. It was set up and was a great success.

---

26 "Life was already becoming more satisfying; when the water came to the centre of the village it was wonderful." Noreen Ibbott.

Nyerere was opposed to Africanization, among other reasons because he was determined that people should have access to the skills and expertise of non-Africans like the Ibbotts who had come to help rather than to dominate or profit. He thought in particular socialists who had little scope in their capitalist countries could put their commitment and skills to work in Tanzania. Others besides the Ibbotts had come and were welcomed by the villagers. One of the teenage Harvard undergraduates who stayed for shifts of one year, wrote a lively book about her year of hard work, learning from Litowans, including about her native US.[27] Because villagers were committed to and in charge of what they were doing, they got the best from working visitors; and the visitors were amply rewarded by the harmonious and expanding life the village offered.

The size of the village helped determine participation. Litowa's population was not to exceed about eighty families, maybe 400 people – a number often discussed. More than that could prevent every individual's participation. Farmers who heard about the success of Litowa (and later other villages) would come to join. But *ujamaa* could only be built by the willing. Interested people were invited to stay and work in the village for a few weeks to ensure that this was the life they wanted. If it was, they would be encouraged to join a smaller village or helped to start their own village (a number of villages were formed this way).

---

27 Kate Wenner was often asked about the Vietnam war: "How come Americans are spending so much money on a war in a country that doesn't belong to them? . . . Why don't they worry about the race riots in America?" She "began to understand why the issue had become America against the entire Third World . . . the villages being bombed . . . were villages like Litowa, Liweta, Luhira and Mtakanini. I knew that the people in the villages of Vietnam like the people in the villages of the RDA had no other source of livelihood but the lands . . . Vietnam, the Vietnamese, their villages and houses, their farms – it became a new reality for me because of what I knew of Africa. It was frightening and senseless." *Shamba Letu*, pp 207-9.

Limiting the numbers but graciously incorporating new people is a widely applicable principle where the aim is involving everyone. It can work even in large factories, offices, hospitals, neighbourhoods. The units can then co-ordinate, as ultimately the villages co-ordinated.

When there were three or four villages, the Ruvuma Development Association came together. It was mutually helpful, sharing skills, practices and resources. A carefully chosen group was formed to help with this, and help newcomers to get started and to integrate. It called itself the Social and Economic Revolutionary Army, or SERA – Chapter 8 describes its great work.

It's hard not to be impressed by the generous caring welcome, despite slender resources, extended by SERA to strangers who wanted to join in building *ujamaa*. It could only spring from the kind of caring society most of us want for ourselves. The thoughtfulness with which people were incorporated helps explain why almost all the villages that started thrived. (One village failed, and Ralph explains why in Chapter 17.)

There was as much consultation and joint decision-making among the villages as distance and difficult transport permitted. Their major joint enterprise besides SERA was the school at Litowa which educated the children from all the villages. Litowa boarded them during term time. It was perhaps the single greatest achievement of the RDA.

Led by a head teacher, the school had student self-government. More important, it had rejected the competitive principle of most formal education as we know it, which prepares the young to compete with each other to move up in the social hierarchy: to rise out of poverty, not to eliminate poverty. This usually results in the child rejecting his own community, especially if it is rural (read: "backward"). The purpose of the Litowa school was to educate children to be part of the development of their rural society. It deserves a book in itself. Certainly those interested in education might want to study the documents included here, especially one in Chapter 11 by Suleiman Toroka, the head teacher of this great and innovative school, who became a member of Litowa village.[28]

No wonder then that when President Nyerere was asked by anyone at home or from abroad what he meant by *ujamaa*, he sent them to the RDA. The RDA, he said, that is *ujamaa*.

He always supported the villagers. He had been confident that what he had proposed would work. But now he had brilliant proof. His key writings, published as *Ujamaa* in both Kiswahili and English, a small popular book "for leaders and educators of the new Tanzania", mention the RDA twice.

> Any model which is drawn up should just be a guide which draws the attention of the people to the decisions which have to be made by them; each village community must be able to make its own decisions. Nonetheless, the experience of existing *ujamaa* villages, such as those now operating within the Ruvuma Development Association, could be helpful, and the ministry of local government and rural development should try to make this experience available to people from different parts.[29]

> . . . nothing succeeds like success! If we can get a few of these village communities working in every area, their success will lead to others also being started. . . . [the] *ujamaa* villages in the Ruvuma Development Association have grown out of a beginning made by ten individuals . . .[30]

Almost from the beginning there was opposition first to Litowa, then to the RDA as a whole. Ralph Ibbott's Epilogue reports that

---

28 Which meant that, as well as participating in decision-making, his salary went to the village where all shared the same standard of living.

29 OUP, Dar es Salaam, 1968, p 143.

30 *Ibid*, p 181.

> ... the antipathy to the RDA ... came from the top:
> from the central committee, government ministers and,
> with rare exceptions, top civil servants – what amount-
> ed to the whole political establishment. The RDA would
> not have been allowed to exist as long as it did had it
> not been for Nyerere's commitment to it.

The villagers sidestepped disapproval, disdain and even sabotage from above as much as possible, often with the President's
help. And since he was unambiguously and publicly on their
side, it never threw them off course. They were TANU. They
were *ujamaa*. And they were growing and gaining in confidence
and reputation.

By the mid-sixties, Millinga had become a member of parliament – the RDA had decided this would represent them nationally, and Nyerere asked for Millinga to work closely with
him. The President tried to use him and other RDA members
to educate party leaders about *ujamaa*. But the problem was not
lack of education; it was hunger for power. They had no wish to
learn from "ignorant peasants" who were autonomous of them.
It was a waste of the RDA's time. That Nyerere continued to try
to persuade them of the value of what they hated – the power of
the people – could only mean he didn't know what else to do.

In February 1967 Nyerere had made a great effort to renew
TANU's commitment to socialism, and to curb ambition in party
and government. He issued the acclaimed Arusha Declaration[31]
calling for the nationalization of some industries for which there
was general support. Part Five (the Arusha Resolution known
as the Leadership Code) limited the wealth politicians could ac-
cumulate – this caused uproar.

Later that year he published Socialism and Rural Development, which he said was part of the Declaration. The clarity of
this renewed case for socialism is breathtaking: more confident
and concrete – as though the people themselves had written it.

---

31 Its original title: The Arusha Declaration and TANU's Policy on Social-
    ism and Self-Reliance.

In a sense they had, since it was informed by what the RDA was actually mastering as he wrote. We must give the RDA the credit they deserve for their contribution to this historic document.

With this Declaration in hand, Nyerere resigned the presidency a second time, again prioritizing the strengthening of the movement over governing. He concentrated on the grassroots of the party, the natural transmission belt to and from the people. He led marches and meetings, celebrating the power of the grassroots as expressed in this great Declaration. It was enthusiastically received by the public and adopted by the party and the government. But changes were introduced to the Leadership Code, blunting its impact on the party and government elite. They were shaken, but not enough.

Nyerere had worked to avoid Tanzania becoming a society torn by the disparity of class power. But the seeds of class conflict were sown from the moment the movement formed to win State power. What had got the British out was a movement of the entire country with all its sectors and tendencies. Once they left, however, the new elite defended the colonial hierarchy and salary scales they were in the movement to collect. As is usually the case, they considered it unjust for them to be denied what the former rulers had, but were oblivious to the injustice they perpetuated against others condemned to work hard to pay for their greed. Few at the top escape becoming psychopaths: insensitive to the pain they inflict on the less powerful, man or beast.

Nyerere had been particularly outraged when in 1966 the university students who had got free education refused to spend time in National Service to the community, and fought to move straight into the high-salary jobs. How could *ujamaa* flourish under or even alongside such avarice?[32]

---

32 "Is this what the citizens of this country worked for? . . . In order to maintain a top level of exploiters . . . You are demanding a pound of flesh; everybody is demanding a pound of flesh except the poor peasant. What kind of a country are we building?" "These damn salaries. These are the salaries which build this kind of attitude in the educated people . . . All of us, we belong to a single class of exploiters." Quoted in *The Critical Phase*, pp 234-5.

Finally, in September 1969 there was a decisive confronta-
tion on the RDA at a stormy meeting of TANU's central committee. Although no vote was taken, twenty-one out of twenty-four
members pressed for the RDA to be banned and TANU to be in
charge of all *ujamaa* developments. The President was defeated.
He was about to leave the country on government business the
following morning. As soon as he was gone, the minister for
rural development and others travelled to Litowa and enforced
the order, destroying years of precious work and equipment.
Ralph Ibbott is convinced that their action was illegal. Nyerere
was shocked on his return; he had not expected that this would
be the outcome of the decision against the RDA, or that they
would move so quickly and so brutally against it. But he did not
reverse their action.[33]

Could Nyerere have done more?

The central committee decision against Nyerere and the
RDA tells us how isolated he was at the top, not only without
a committed core but hemmed in by those who hated the self-
reliant grassroots and the strategy only they could carry out.

For the President to have an open disagreement with his
party and government leaders on behalf of the RDA could have
wide and unpredictable consequences. He had been bold before
in defence of principle, but the RDA was small, the whole national and regional leadership was united against it – and thus
against him. If he went to the people with this split in the leadership, would they support him? Or would they be discouraged
and retreat from active participation? And if they supported
him, would that result in civil war? Would there be opportunistic appeals to tribal, ethnic or religious allegiances and conflict,
especially between Africans and Arab and Asian Tanzanians?

---

33 The geography of Matetereka has helped it to survive as an *ujamaa*
    village to this day. The villagers were on hills where the newcomers
    forced in by villagization could not dilute their purpose and practice.
    In 1992 when the Ibbotts visited Tanzania, Matetereka welcomed them
    with a thrilling speech. See Appendix IV.

Would it trigger a coup[34] or become an occasion for the cold war which he had kept out of Tanzania, to divide the country he had worked so hard to keep together?[35] Could he take these risks?

Nyerere had worked for African unity all his political life, but this had failed. Without unity, African governments were much weaker. Tragedies had already afflicted country after country, the outcome of internal power struggles which the imperialists had seized on or directly organized to regain control and influence, often with the help of local elites. Lumumba had been murdered in Congo in 1961, Ben Bella overthrown in Algeria in 1965, Nkrumah in Ghana in 1966, and the Biafran (Nigeria) war had started in 1967. Nyerere could not take a chance with the power balance in Tanzania and Africa generally.

Nyerere's speech on the fortieth anniversary of Ghana independence explains what stood in the way of unity, not only in Africa. Those of us in the independence movement who fought for the federation of the formerly British West Indies have lived through what he describes:

> . . . too many of us had a vested interest in keeping Africa divided. Prior to the independence of Tanganyika I had been advocating that the East African countries should federate and then achieve independence as a single political unit. I had said publicly that I was willing to delay Tanganyika's independence in order to enable all the three mainland countries [Kenya, Tanganyika and Uganda] to achieve their independence together as a single federated State.
>
> I made the suggestion because of my fear – proved correct by later events – that it would be very difficult

---

34 Nyerere had faced an attempted coup in 1964 based on the military's demand for Africanization and higher wages; it was quickly defeated. The army was disbanded and a new one recruited from the TANU Youth League to begin with.

35 "We shall not allow our friends to choose our enemies for us." The Union of Tanganyika and Zanzibar, *Freedom and Unity*, p 292.

to unite our countries if we let them achieve independence separately. Once you multiply national anthems, national flags and national passports, seats at the United Nations; and individuals entitled to a 21-gun salute, not to speak of a host of ministers and envoys, you would have a whole army of powerful people with vested interests in keeping Africa balkanized.[36]

So much was at stake that he seems to have deluded himself that *ujamaa* could survive the destruction of the RDA which was *ujamaa* in action, the seeds of the *ujamaa* movement. The RDA went to the wall. It destroyed great possibilities and broke many hearts, perhaps also Nyerere's.

In the mid-1970s, Nyerere was asked by a journalist what was his greatest success? He replied, "That we have survived." Asked the same question by the same journalist in 1983, his reply was, "I think I would still give the same answer."[37]

To this day, Tanzania, almost unique in Africa, while still poor remains free of wars or dictatorships, ethnic violence or military coups. President Nyerere's socialism, including his sharp refusal of any opportunistic attempts to introduce racial or ethnic disparity of rights, must take much credit for this.[38] In 2008, when republishing the Arusha Declaration, a Ugandan woman at our women's centre told us about Tanzania's invasion to save them and all of East Africa from Idi Amin who overthrew President Obote, and was murdering and invading. "One of the soldiers asked me please could he have a glass of water. I had never seen respectful soldiers like that. Tanzanians were different." Nyerere was different.

---

36 Kwame Nkrumah and African Unity (Vigour, Commitment and Sincerity), Accra, Ghana, 6 March 1997.

37 Shivji, 1990, referring to an interview with Peter Enahoro, *Africa Now*, vol 32, December 1983, p 101.

38 Socialism is not Racialism, *Freedom and Socialism*, p 257.

This book will with luck interest young people in particular in the anti-colonial movement which is so little known. It has many lessons for those of us in today's sprawling justice movement. Because of the specifics of time and place, the problems faced in impoverished former colonies may not seem relevant to movements elsewhere. But look again.

First, the battle against colonialism and the wars and proxy wars fought for competing imperial interests are far from over. More than five million people have been killed in the Congo, and yet this is hardly mentioned. The genocide of Tamils in Sri Lanka is ongoing. We write not long after the latest (2014) slaughter in Gaza by Israel which has occupied Palestine for almost seventy years.[39] Haiti which gave us the first successful slave revolution is moving towards yet another dictatorship under a brutal US-UN occupation.

Second, the same almost manic energy of those who form the hierarchy in ex-colonies is also a blight on every grassroots movement. Ambition, the great weapon of imperialism, has subverted struggles against all varieties of injustice – war, torture, every form of sexism, racism, exploitation, environmental devastation . . . – turning them into career options at the cost even of the planet's survival.

Ambition may appear to be merely a personal failing, but it is integral to capitalism. We are urged and trained to compete – for money, status, jobs, housing, everything. Nyerere knew that competition, with its few winners and millions of losers, would destroy Tanzanian society (as it has wrecked ours). Usually endemic, at this moment it is epidemic. Yet most of us have still to acknowledge the ambition that subverts us. Nyerere's alternative was *ujamaa*, which rests on the principles of communal equity and mutual accountability. In fact, whatever is the particular context of our organizing for justice, the principles are the same. Indigenous societies today – from Asia to Latin

---

39   See footnote 2 in Chapter 5 for Nyerere's condemnation of Israel.

America – have used similar communal principles to stand up to multinationals and all kinds of exploitation.

The RDA's history and the *ujamaa* principles they upheld can help us anywhere. Ralph Ibbott applied these when working with youngsters in working class Greenock, Scotland, to brilliant effect.[40]

The Ibbott manuscript lay in a drawer for over forty years, read and even quoted by academics, but never published. We discovered its existence when republishing the out-of-print Arusha Declaration on its fortieth anniversary, and Ralph and Noreen wrote to tell us that what we had said about 1960s Tanzania was "not quite like that". We went to Scotland to interview them at length about *ujamaa*. When we read the manuscript we were blown away by the story it tells and by the commitment that illuminates every page. We suspect that the reason Ralph's manuscript had been neglected for so long was that such an optimistic account of what the grassroots made happen, was not in fashion.

In the decades since that more hopeful era, we have been told every day in a thousand ways, some subtle, some violent, that it would be foolish to rely for significant social change on people like those who made socialism in Ruvuma.

Here we glimpse what those of us with least resources, least rights, and least respect, are able to accomplish. It is the single most important truth about our world, which we need in order not only to understand it but to change it.

Solveig Francis, Nina López and I worked with Noreen and Ralph over the years (Noreen was a most gracious hostess to all three of us and our dogs.) This Introduction reflects the views of all three of us. Nina's work editing, researching and referencing was invaluable.

---

40 Mentioned in his biography, it deserves greater attention.

1

THE VILLAGES –
ORGANIZATIONS OF THE PEOPLE

Before starting on a historical outline of the Ruvuma Development Association (RDA), it would be a great help to have a picture of what the villages which were the Association were like. The essential point to bear in mind is that the villages were entirely organizations of the people in them, and that the Association was entirely an organization of these villages.

During the first months – my family and I moved into Litowa in April 1963 – I discussed much with the Litowa people on their organization and sat with them through their first organizational meetings suggesting the sort of things which needed discussion. After those first months I never attended any complete organizational meeting of Litowa or of any other of the villages or of the Association. Many times before a meeting, village or Association leaders would come and ask my views on particular topics which were to be discussed, and sometimes during a meeting I would receive a message asking me to go along when I would be told of the topic under discussion, what had been said on it to that point and then asked my views; I would remain for perhaps part of the further discussion. Invariably at a certain stage I would be thanked for coming and told that I might go to get on with my work. I invariably went.

The Litowa village had what one might have called a custom whereby at every quarterly meeting of their management committee I was asked immediately after the reading of the minutes to attend and express any views I might like to, on the work of the village. After giving a short talk I always left. There were, however, many informal talks with the Association and individual village leaders, and I always made myself available to discuss with anyone whenever they required it, but never would I make suggestions where individuals came to me and should have gone to their own committees. I received reports of the various meetings from numbers of different people attending. Ntimbanjayo Millinga, the undisputed leader who had invited me to come to RDA, understood the necessity of the villages having power to make their own decisions. The one most responsible in the early days of building up the Association, he was most responsible for successfully developing organizations absolutely controlled by the villagers, generally described as controlled "from below" but I never quite see why this should be thought of as below.

In order to give this picture of a village it might be good to use an account of Liweta village as seen by a visitor to Ruvuma in August 1966. Jim Brain had fifteen years' experience in East Africa and had travelled widely in Kenya, Uganda and Tanzania. He had for a time been connected with co-operative attempts at agricultural plant hire and had considerable knowledge and experience of agriculture. He was fluent in Kiswahili – the language of most Tanzanians and the lingua franca of East Africa – and was for a time in charge of the language orientation course run by government at Tongoru for incoming expatriates. At the time of his visit he was a member of the Syracuse University (New York State) Village Settlement Project attached to the Village Settlement Agency. When he heard of the RDA villages he was very sceptical of the whole idea and paid a short visit to Ruvuma when he was able to spend a few hours at Litowa. This very short visit aroused a certain amount of interest so that he asked if he might come and spend a week or two in the villages. The Association said they had no objection to his coming. His writing, which is here in its entirety, is also interesting because there are comparisons with settlements started "from the top" into which he had been researching. The report is dated August 1966.

Village Settlement Project
Syracuse University
PO Box 96
Dar es Salaam

Report on a Visit to the
Ruvuma Development Association Schemes
By Jim Brain

The constitution of the Ruvuma Development Association is still under discussion, but it is not the intention of this paper to attempt to describe the workings of the Association as a total organization, which would require a separate study, but rather to show how one of the villages works in practice, and to try and examine the extent to which this may have relevance to the government pilot schemes or to the projected "new approach" schemes.

To understand these schemes needs something of a revolution in thought which is not always achieved by casual visitors. For instance, visiting political dignitaries are often so enthusiastic about what they see that they wish to show their pleasure by offering large scale financial help, and recently before a visit by the minister of agriculture the local agricultural officer went to one of the villages and told the people to make out a list of all the things they wanted, as he was sure that the minister would be so impressed that large-scale loans would be forthcoming. Both these ideas show a misunderstanding of the philosophy of the schemes. Obviously they need political support, and at times financial help, but the latter is only wanted for some specific project with which it is within the capacity of the people to deal. The enthusiasm of visitors is indeed understandable, for it seems that in these villages the original ideas of the President [Nyerere] have borne fruit. People who previously lived in scattered homesteads have moved together, and the result is an incomparably better life. Moreover, they are showing that it is possible to weld together the best of traditional African society and more modern ideas into something which truly merits the name of *ujamaa*.

Litowa

This is the parent village, where the Ibbott family live together with a VSO [Voluntary Service Organization] mechanic and two Harvard volunteers. Also at this village is a boarding school attended by children from other villages where an attempt is presently being made to build up a syllabus which will have more relevance to the life of rural Tanzania than the more formal one inherited from the colonial era. Litowa seems to act as a pilot area for a variety of activities, and in spite of its own impressive achievements it is not entirely typical of the villages in general. Therefore Ralph Ibbott suggested that after one day's stay there I should move out to Liweta, some eight miles away, where things are entirely under the control of the villagers themselves (not that Litowa is managed by anyone but the people themselves, merely that since there are expatriates around it is not typical). To get to Liweta one goes either by road from Litowa itself twelve miles beyond Peramiho, or goes direct from Songea. In the first case one travels over about six miles of road made by the Liweta people crossing two bridges, in the second one uses five miles of road and two bridges on the other side of the village, all of this the product of the efforts of the villagers.

Liweta

Liweta is an aesthetically pleasing village, comprising a village street, houses sited sixty feet apart in two staggered rows each side of the street, and a central community centre, with a food store on the opposite side of the street from it. Existing trees have been utilized until such time as the fruit and flowering trees already planted have reached maturity. The houses are all constructed on the same pattern, a well-built rectangular traditional mud and wattle type, plastered with a local anthill earth which sets like cement, coloured grey and very attractive in appearance. Each house has a small courtyard and at the end of it another small house which has accommodation for the goats kept by all, and for children and guests. This house plays an essential part in the recruitment process. The community centre built of bamboo with great manual skill is also an extremely important part of the village. The agricultural land adjoins the end of the houses, but each house has a very small garden plot beside it, in which are planted gourds and sweet potatoes. Most people keep pigeons for food and have neat pigeon cotes beside their houses. The village street is swept and tidy, as are the house surrounds. There is a well-kept vegetable garden not far from the houses near the river. Not far from the upper end of the village, a reasonable football pitch has been made and is in constant use by the young men.

History

They started in 1961-62 hearing the call of the *Baba wa Taifa* [Father of the Nation] to move in together, but really did not know how to set about it. At first there were only seventeen [people] and one of them was a cripple, and in 1963, encouraged by the area commissioner, Mr Hinjuson, and the AO [agricultural officer] Mr Mchau, they began to plant tobacco, but they only made 274 shillings [£13.7] in all and were becoming discouraged. In 1963 too they began to get some advice from Ibbott and were given some clothing and hoes, both of which items were most encouraging (it is very cold in Songea at this time of year and warm clothes absolutely essential). In 1964 things began to move a bit, and in 1965 many more wanted to join and rules of conduct were drawn up. The original "manager" resigned in a huff, basically because he wanted to be too much of a boss. Until 1965 they were still living in isolated homesteads and just cultivating in a sort of block, but in this year they built the present village, which is still growing as more members ask to join.

At present the number of adult males is about forty, and women about the same number. There are a few more women than men because of some widows who live with their relatives. It is hoped to expand until there are about eighty males and their families.

Organization

All adults are members of the society. The recruitment of new members will be dealt with below. There is a democratically elected manager and assistant manager, a *bwana shamba* and assistant, a secretary, a treasurer, and part-time dresser, and a storeman who doubles as chairman of the biweekly meetings. None of these persons is in receipt of a salary, nor do they live and work in any different way from any of the settlers. This is most important to realize. They only become manager or *bwana shamba* when this role is appropriate, e.g. the *bwana shamba* is the person who rules what the day's work is to be in accordance with the needs of the season, and having so ruled, takes up his hoe or *panga* [cutlass] like everyone else. Each person holding office does so for one year, but presumably is eligible for re-election, since the number of those having the necessary characteristics for these posts is limited. It is significant that a few of the older men who form the core of the office holders were members of the KAR [King's African Rifles] and have worked on sisal estates. The major office holders meet daily in an informal manner, and of course, it must be realized that because of the planning of the village everyone meets face to face every day.

Quite the most important function in the running of the village is the twice-weekly *Chakula cha Ujamaa*. This is a communal meal taken every Tuesday and Thursday evening, when all bring their own *ugali*[1] and are issued with beans cooked in bulk by women who take turns for this chore, and then sit down on mats in the hall. The young girls and unmarried men wait on the others with water, etc., and then after the meal the chairman

---

1   Cornmeal dish.

calls the meeting to order and asks for statements from the various office holders, who can be questioned by any member after gaining the chairman's permission to speak. Any problems or difficulties are raised, and there is quite an element of mutual criticism. The women are encouraged to speak and give their opinions. It is at these meetings that policy and plans of work are thrashed out. The traditional method of gaining a consensus by discussion is used, rather than vote-counting. Any person who has strayed is brought to book and allowed to defend his actions, and if in the wrong made to feel thoroughly despicable, a most effective sanction. The meeting always closes with lengthy prayers.

Working Organization

Work starts daily at 7.30 when a bell is rung. Women are allowed until 8 am to finish their household chores, and usually return home about 11.30 am, when they cook and do necessary work round the household, or possibly go and work in the two-acre individual plots which have been operated up to date for extra food (it is hoped to eliminate these finally). Men work through until about 4 pm or later if there is a need, sometimes arranging for food on the job. In the evenings they perform odd jobs round the village, sometimes play football or gather round the scheme radio. A muster roll is maintained and any man who misses a day without adequate reason will have three shillings taken from his income at the end of the season, and this is actually done, not merely said to be done.

All work according to their ability, for instance one old man who has only one arm acts as a game guard, some of the very old women do bird and baboon scaring, a highly necessary task which in other circumstances can tie up able-bodied persons who might be more gainfully employed. Another man not too strong works as permanent gardener in the vegetable patch, which supplies tomatoes, cabbage, *mchicha*,[2] etc., most of the

---

2   Spinach.

year. Unless there is other urgent work, such as tobacco grading, there is a permanent gang of sixteen men on bush clearing, which is a continuing process that can go on indefinitely. Other than two-acre plots, all work is done communally, apparently without any problems, and obviously with a much more efficient use of labour than would be the case if individual holdings were operated. Settler selection and the moral atmosphere of the scheme have much to do with this, it is thought.

Income

Food from the individual plots is stored in granaries at the people's houses, but is not thought of as being purely personal property. Food crops grown communally are stored in the food store, and issued or sold as required. Any cash income obtained is shared equally between all adults, regardless of age, job or sex. All insisted that this is fair, just and acceptable. Man and wife get equal shares of any revenue.

Agriculture

The main cash crop is fire-cured tobacco, and this year a harvest of about three tons was obtained from fifteen acres, most of which was first and second grade, only sixty-six pounds being in fourth grade. For the first time this year the crop was transported direct to Ngomat [Ngoni-Matengo Co-operative Union] instead of passing though the small local co-operative. This is clearly better, but it would be much more advantageous financially, according to Mr Myers, for them to sell directly to B.A.T. [British-American Tobacco] which, contrary to popular belief, needs and is prepared to pay a good price for fire-cured tobacco. It will be recalled that it was noted last year that Ngomat was giving an extremely unfavourable deal to its members as compared to the prices given to growers in the lake area.

The other cash crop grown is peanuts, and this year a surplus has been obtained which will be sold.

The total acreages were:

Tobacco	15	Cassava	6
Maize	20	Soya	3
Groundnuts	6	Pigeon peas	2
Beans	9	Haricot	1
Sesame	2	Eleusine	10
S/potatoes	1/2		

There is about half an acre planted to banana, and in addition to the vegetable garden, the women have a plot of onions, etc., and each family has two acres of maize and eleusine.

The general standard of the cultivation was quite the best I have seen anywhere in Tanzania. All crops were grown on ridges and ridges followed the contours. All the crops seen were free from weed growth. The maize looked like a demonstration plot, and well-constructed cribs have been made for the maize and groundnuts. Both goat dung and artificial fertilizers are in use. Satisfactorily constructed curing barns have been put up and it is intended in the future to build them from burnt brick, as is already being done at Litowa. The grading experts at Ngomat commented that the crop was the best lot which had come in, both in quality and grading.

Recruitment

When a new settler wishes to join he is first invited to come for about three days to stay. If at the end of this time he likes things and the members are prepared to accept him, he is told to go home and then after thinking about it for a while to return if he still wants to, this time to stay for up to six months on probation, bringing his wife if he wishes. During this probationary period he is fed free by the scheme members, and is housed in one of the guest houses in someone's courtyard, and must join in all work and communal activities. At the end of the period both sides consider the case, and if both are satisfied then the new settler moves in and is given a plot of land on which to build, following certain specifications, and with a fixed period in which to complete his house.

Expulsion

Two persons have left the Liweta village so far. One was the first manager, who was not prepared to abide by the rules. The other was a young man whom it had been hoped would be the tractor driver, and who was undergoing training to this end, but was found to be selling the fuel. Such a severe view of this was taken that it was decided to expel him from the community. Just as in a family, a certain amount of human failings can be condoned, but at the same time the very closeness of relationship acts as a most effective sanction on deviant behaviour, since it would be so shameful to be found out.

Establishment of New Villages

Since there are now eleven villages in existence it is clear that there must be some organization for spreading the idea. Like most things of this nature, it will evidently snowball progressively faster, but it is one thing having an idea and another implementing it. For instance, as this report was being written a visitor from Kilosa to Bwakira Chini was telling about how 300 people in the Kilangali area, where there is a big block farm, want to start a village but have no idea how to set about it, and have been told by the area commissioner to draw up laws for a society, which probably they will have no idea how to do. Were this the Ruvuma Region the answer would be simple – not to wait for the government to do something but to send for SERA. This is not as one might suppose from the name some miraculous female, but the rather grandiosely named Social and Economic Revolutionary Army of the Ruvuma Development Association. What this means is a group of dedicated young people who are prepared to go to such an area and advise on how peo-

ple should go about setting up a village, based on their experience at Litowa. It must be emphasized that such persons cannot
be produced in a three-week course on how to set up villages.
It is said that it takes at least nine months for them to acquire
not only the necessary expertise, but also to absorb the needed
moral character. It is this latter which is almost of more importance than the physical skills. Clearly this has a marked bear-
ing on Mr Nellis's area of interest, the feeling that the spiritual
side of the settlement schemes is basically of more importance
than the physical achievements, at least in the early stages. On
the skills side the Association operates a scheme whereby existing villages send members for extended periods to new ones
to teach techniques. For instance, during my stay at Liweta a
man returned from a five-month stay at two new villages near
Mbamba Bay where he had gone to teach tobacco growing. During his absence his place had been taken by a man from the host
area so that his home village would not be short-handed.

The importance of the moral atmosphere of the schemes
cannot be overstressed. There is a mixture of motives involved
and it might be instructive to try and isolate some of them. First,
there is tremendous faith in the President and his pronouncements. This is combined with a belief in TANU [Tanzania African National Union] as a force, but a distrust of most politicians
as persons: a belief in socialism as a principle but operated as a
private enterprise and not bogged down with the red tape of a
government enterprise. There is a belief in the validity of African tradition for establishing *ujamaa* while rejecting those parts
of the traditional culture which hinder progress or conflict with
the rulings of moral conduct laid down by Christian teaching
(Islamic teaching could be equally valid in this context). The
size of the villages is highly important, the maximum size being considered to be eighty families, since anything over this
size would be unwieldy and it would not be possible to impose
the moral discipline which is so much a part of the whole project. The village acts somewhat like a lineage group in the tradi-

tional society, though in a more democratic way and indeed in
many cases the families are related by ties of blood or marriage.
There is a very marked contrast in behaviour to the government
schemes where the presence of temporary civil servants tends
to lead to series of casual liaisons between them and local unattached girls. Within the Ruvuma villages family and marriage
are stable and moral, and the strongest sanction on behaviour
is the fact that everyone is part of a large family. Prayers are
held after the communal meals and a service each Sunday, a
priest visiting once monthly to say Mass. At first the whole Association was regarded with grave suspicion by Peramiho as being probably of communist affiliation, but now the church has
come to recognize that these villages represent the best possible
hope for the family life which seems to be disintegrating in so
many spheres of present Tanzania. The superior has sent a letter
to all parish priests in the region ordering them to co-operate
with such schemes to the maximum. Bishop Huddleston,[3] too,
at Masasi is hoping to see similar developments in his diocese,
and there has been a recent visit by Lutheran authorities from
Ulanga District interested in the whole idea.

One of the most important aspects of Liweta, at least from
a sociological viewpoint, is that it is a real and not an artificial
community. That is to say, it has persons of every age grouping
from the youngest to [the] oldest, and there are several persons
who are partially crippled. The presence of old and middle-aged
people exercises a restraining influence on the young people,
and the latter by their presence ensure that there is a constant
supply of new ideas. The government sociologist who did research in labour migration among the Ngoni showed that most
of them were little interested in good working conditions; their
sole aim was to make the most money in the shortest possible
time and then to return home, in many cases having as their aim

---

3   Trevor Huddleston was an Anglican priest well known as an anti-
     apartheid activist. He was bishop at Masasi for eight years.

the acquisition of adequate money for the marriage payment, which in this area tends to be high (5-600 shillings). Most sociologists are agreed as to the undesirability of a migrant labour situation for stable family life, but under the poverty-stricken conditions which obtained in Ngoni, men had little alternative. The village provides an answer to this, providing the bride-wealth payments for a young man who wishes to get married, if the bride meets with the people's approval. This means that the village has assumed some of the functions of the family and lineage group, and there can be little doubt that the obligation incurred by a young man in this way will be a powerful deterrent to moving to the towns. From a girl's point of view the fun of life in a village such as Liweta with its constantly increasing standard of living and provision of amenities such as a piped water supply (already in operation at Litowa), its social occasions and sense of belonging to something solid and enduring, must provide the best alternative yet to the bright lights.

I was interested in the degree of political interest and sophistication among the settlers who I found to be well up on both national and international affairs in very marked contrast to my findings at Bwakira. People listened to the radio a lot, and it was noticeable that they generally went much later to bed in consequence.

It may be that none of the above has relevance to the government pilot and is only suitable for operation by local societies and voluntary agencies such as churches, since it is essentially "private enterprise socialism", which relies on small family-type scale, lack of bureaucracy and on autonomy for its success. Unless there is a radical change in present government policy for settlements it can have little relevance to the present pilot schemes, since an essential part of them as they exist is the hierarchy of salaried staff living in superior-type housing, earning greater salaries than the settlers are ever likely to make by farming, with their wives taking no productive part in the life of the village and, moreover, with the possible exception of Kitete, a tendency to move towards individual holdings. It is this class society which exists on the government schemes which is in such marked contrast to the Ruvuma schemes. Clearly, when there is a large and expensive scheme, government must put in a competent manager, who must expect a reasonable salary in accordance with his ability, but it is suggested that this should be a charge against the government in the same way as is the salary of any other extension officer, and should not be charged to the settlers, to whom such a salary must prove an intolerable burden. It is the presence of the rest of the staff that one must question. If we take the example of Bwakira Chini, we find in addition to a manager: three settlement assistants, two clerks, five drivers, one dresser, two storemen – all of these drawing salaries which bear little if any relation to the production of the land. All this for eighty settlers; whereas at Liweta we find forty settlers with not one salaried staff member, and those who are office holders all working with their hands as do their wives, and who will draw equal shares in any proceeds with all the other scheme members, male and female. If the principle of individual holdings is pursued, then the former situation seems inevitable, since if one recruits a tractor driver among the settlers, who then cares for the driver's land? If, on the other hand, the principle of communal work were adopted then it would prove quite possible to utilize the existing skills for the settlers without having to pay them any salaries. For instance, once more taking Bwakira Chini as our example, my research showed that among the settlers are men who have been drivers, turnboys who have unofficial experience of driving, clerks, storemen, and even a man who was a ward orderly. Furthermore, if one uses settlers for the specialized tasks it is quite possible to mobilize them in moments of crisis to take part in farm activities such as weeding or picking, which it is not possible to do with the existing staff, especially if one has individual holdings, and of course settlers' wives would be productive members of the village, which present staff spouses are not.

One essential feature of the Liweta village is that it is a village, and not a collection of homesteads, as are most of the government schemes. In other words, everyone meets face to face daily and it takes a matter of minutes to call everyone together or for someone to walk through all the houses to make an announcement. Since it has been more or less decided to re-plan Bwakira somewhat on these lines one can hope that a greater degree of community spirit will result. It might be possible to obtain advice from a member of SERA on new ways of running things, though whether SERA members would be able and willing to undertake work so far removed from their original object is rather problematical. This is clearly a matter for discussion at the seminar to be held later this month. It must though be realized that the Ruvuma methods are no easy short cut to rapid taxable income, and to be successful such schemes have to be a slow organic growth. They cannot be used as a place for employing out-of-work politicians, nor can members hope for quick cash returns. The aim is only secondarily for a better income, the primary aim is to build a better life and better citizens. We cannot expect the results of the Ruvuma schemes unless we are prepared to use their methods, which means that there must be a spiritual change in both settlers and staff, between whom on pilot settlements there now exists what amounts to a class war. If we give up the principle of communal work at Mlale because the people will not work co-operatively, and yet ten miles away the very same people are working with energy and enthusiasm in a communal fashion, it would appear that the fault lies not in the people, but in the way in which their affairs are run.

There can be little doubt that the Ruvuma schemes have great relevance to the "new approach", in which it has been said that traditional villages displaying initiative will be sought out and assisted. I am sure that enthusiasm could be aroused in many parts of the country for this type of scheme, but it must be properly directed. It is my strong conviction that such schemes should be as informal as possible, and should have the very minimum of financial assistance. Something like SERA would have to be created, and in view of the undoubted success of Peace Corps[4] in Latin America in community development work, and in settlement work in Kenya, serious consideration should be given to using Peace Corps for such an operation. It is thought that their enthusiasm, coupled with the fact that they are known to be present only for a two-year period and not trying to create a permanent job, would be in their favour. Until the seminar to be held at Kivukoni [College][5] has discussed these matters it would probably be presumptuous of me to make further suggestions, but that Tanzania should profit from this amazing example would seem imperative.

---

4   The Peace Corps is a volunteer programme of the US government.
5   TANU's adult education college.

2

SETTING OFF FOR LITOWA

In 1960, between the time of internal self-government and independence in Tanganyika,[1] Ntimbanjayo Millinga became the
secretary of the Peramiho branch of the Tanganyika African National Union Youth League (TYL) in the Songea District, part of
the Southern Province. During this time he heard radio reports
of speeches by the party leader and president of TANU, Julius
K Nyerere, insisting that the people of the country work hard
and work on farming together. As a result of hearing this, Ntimbanjayo and fourteen of his fellow Youth Leaguers founded the
village and farm at Litowa. On 7th November 1960, they strug-
gled across the Luhira river using the branches of trees, at a
point nine miles as the crow flies to the north of Peramiho, and
selected a spot on the opposite ridge to build their first shelter overlooking the fertile Litowa valley beyond, just before it
joined the Luhira river. They named the project the TYL Farmers' Scheme, Litowa.

The original pattern they aimed at came from the experience of the people. Men left Songea to work on the sisal estates
on the coast. For six months in 1959 Ntimbanjayo had been
in Dar es Salaam as a union agent of the Sisal and Plantation
Workers Union and visited such sisal estates. If large estate

---

1   The process of moving to independence in most of the British colo-
    nies was first internal self-government: increasing the number of
    "Native"members of the legislature who managed national affairs,
    while international relations and the police remained in the hands of
    the Colonial Office that governed all the colonies. Only at the moment
    of independence, when the British flag went down, did full self-gov-
    ernment begin.

farms could be developed in Songea by the people, they would no longer need to go away to the coast to work. The fifteen in the original group who arrived at Litowa, after discussing on these lines, had as their aim the development of a "modern scientific" farm on which they would work together. When they crossed the river they had a few hoes and axes, a little food and the clothes they stood up in.

Some dozen years before, Litowa, on the eastern side of the Luhira river, had been occupied. Largely because of trouble from lions, the villagers there had then crossed to the western bank, where they still are, in the village of Luhira Goliama. The lions were also a worry to the newcomers to Litowa and contributed to the failure of this first attempt. In February 1961 the last of the Youth League group gave up the battle and left what crops were planted to be harvested by the baboons, wild pigs and monkeys. Apart from the fear of lions, the main cause of failure was the lack of adequate food. Every weekend most of the members had gone back to their homes looking for enough food to bring to Litowa for the next week. One by one as they were unable to get food, the members dropped out until Hambisa Komba, the last to stick it, found that he too was forced to leave. (He was later to become manager of the scheme for a time.) Ntimbanjayo obtained employment as district secretary of the Transport and General Workers Union in Lindi on the coast.

While in this work Ntimbanjayo decided that to progress with the ideas of Litowa he needed to know more about economics and so applied for the first course at the new Kivukoni College in Dar es Salaam. He was interviewed by Colin Leys, the first principal of the college, who was impressed by his thoughtfulness. After the interview Ntimbanjayo had thought further on the questions he had been asked and in the evening he sought out the principal in his hotel room to let him know of his additional thoughts. The application was successful, and Ntimbanjayo returned to Songea in July 1961 to visit his home at Lituhi, and also the Youth League at Peramiho, before going on to Dar es Salaam.

In the previous month a fresh start for the TYL Farmers Scheme had been made by the Youth League at Litowa. Much of the work of getting people together this second time was done by Wilfred Sanga, the local agricultural field worker of the Department of Agriculture who had visited Litowa after everyone had left and collected samples of the crops before the baboons completed their harvesting, hoping to encourage people to return. He was most useful to the group, and later to other groups which started in the neighbourhood. From this second start there began a continuous settlement at Litowa and a steady – if at first slow – development of the farm and village.

This time it was members coming in ones and twos over a number of months, only two of whom had been amongst those of the original 1960 group: Ntimbanjayo and Mateso Mhagama, one of the Litowa carpenters. Most of those joining Litowa had had only four years of formal schooling but amongst them were those with a higher education: Ado Mgimba who was standard IX, Wayakile Sangu, standard VIII, and Bwanaliko Matupa, standard X.[2]

It must be noted that all of these and some others were people who were in employment, which they gave up to join the Litowa village. Ado worked in the police and prison service and later in the trading store run by the mission at Peramiho. He later said that it was largely the songs sung by the Youth League members at Litowa that attracted him away from this work. Also in the trading store was Ntotera Nyoni who later became manager at Litowa. Leaving his employment was no easy decision for him as both his family and his wife's family were very strongly opposed to his giving up paid work for Litowa. Wayakile was also employed by the mission in their bookstore at Per-

---

2   Standards I to VII indicate primary school (age seven to thirteen); standards VIII, IX and X secondary school.

amiho. Bwanaliko was employed by an Asian trading company. Ngomathy Nungu, who was afterwards the chairman of Litowa, worked for seven years in the mission printing press.

It was encouraging that men were ready to give up employment as the trend was very much the other way, with most people trying desperately to find paid employment. After this first influx of people with a little more formal education and paid work, it was not until 1969 in the months immediately before the Association was disbanded, that such people again came to join. A rural medical aide who had been for seven years employed by the Tunduru district council joined Litowa; a government surveyor who had previously worked on the survey of the land for the Liweta village applied for membership of that village; almost the entire teaching staff at the Association school at Litowa either had or were preparing to become village members. This meant giving their salaries to the village and receiving back from the village the same services as the other villagers, in addition to meeting certain special needs because of their work in the school. It is not easy to be certain why this was so but I felt that, resulting from the independence struggle, there were a certain number of people with ideals; in Peramiho these were the ones who gave up their jobs to develop their country. When it was then seen that most political leaders, government officers and so on were seeking their own ends, these potential idealists were disillusioned, only to reappear after a number of years as they realized that their real struggle was against the oppressors amongst their own people. This was at a time when President Nyerere felt in a position to push out the most ruthless of those in positions of power and was putting before the people ideals which gave them a pattern to work to. But this was in the future.

The Songea District was large in area and with a low population density, where it was easy enough to procure land for new villages. Nevertheless there were difficulties and the first movement to Litowa in 1960 precipitated a dispute with the people of Luhira Goliama, who considered this land on the eastern side of the river, which they had previously worked, as also belonging to them. This dispute was settled by Hinjuson, the district secretary of TANU, together with Chief Zulu, the Ngoni chief, and the people of Luhira Goliama. The people of Luhira Goliama promised sixty acres of land for the new people at Litowa for their use.

Hinjuson, who later became the first area commissioner for the Songea District, was always friendly, co-operative and helpful during his short tenure in that office before becoming area commissioner elsewhere, and maintained his interest and friendliness when paying visits back to Songea, which was his home area. It was he who later encouraged Millinga and me to visit other groups of people beginning to work together in other parts of the district. When the chiefdoms were abolished in 1962,[3] the people of Litowa made an application to the executive officer of the district council which then became responsible for land allocations. This officer, in consultation with the area commissioner, authorized the council to allocate any available land to the Litowa village and farm, and 12,000 acres have since been set aside.

There was a further small dispute with the people of Luhira Goliama in 1963. The wide fertile valley of Kidigidigi on the Litowa side of the river and to the north had been cultivated by the people of Luhira Goliama. The early members had in fact been rather belligerent about this, claiming that it was on their side of the river. On discussing it with the Litowa people, they changed their attitude considerably and at a subsequent meeting with Luhira Goliama, because of the more reasonable approach, the problem was amicably settled, with each village allocated half of the land in question.

It was understandable that the Litowa people should have been a little belligerent. No one believed that they could achieve

---

3   The British government picked traditional chiefs and gave them limited powers in order to prop up its colonial administration. This system was abolished with independence.

anything. They were laughed at by everyone in the neighbourhood, even by their own families. With this background, it needed considerable courage for people to carry on through the first
difficult years. Their perseverance slowly gained them respect,
and probably by the end of 1964 they were no longer the laugh-
ing stock of the area. In the middle of 1966, when Jim Brain of
the Syracuse University Village Settlement Project was to spend
a fortnight in the Liweta village after a short stay at Litowa, he
stopped off and set up camp for the night a few miles away from
Litowa to ascertain the surrounding people's feelings towards
those at Litowa. He reported favourably. The Luhira Goliama
people also eventually became part of Litowa.

It was in Dar es Salaam that I first met Ntimbanjayo Millinga while he was studying at Kivukoni College. We were on holiday from Rhodesia (now Zimbabwe) and Colin Leys had asked
me to talk one evening to the Kivukoni students on our experiences in co-operative rural working in Rhodesia. For a white
man from Rhodesia to talk to students in Tanganyika immediately before independence did not seem a very profitable enterprise, but it led to Ntimbanjayo approaching me afterwards for
advice on how to help those at Litowa. Some year or two later
he told me how all the other students thought him completely
mad to have invited a white man to go to Litowa to help, as he
would be sure to take the land from the people! He also said
that the reason he felt he could trust me was through listening
to the story of St Faith's and how at the end the bishop had given
me notice to quit – that this should happen in the situation I
described to him rang true. There was not much that I could
say to him at that stage other than that by my being at Litowa
it was possible to give advice only. We thus arranged that if, on
writing to explain to his friends at Litowa, they should agree
to invite me, we would meet that October of 1961, when there
was a break in the Kivukoni course. I was able to travel there in
October because my fares were paid by friends in Switzerland
who were later to form an organization which they called Fonds

für Entwicklung und Partnerschaft in Afrika [Fund for Development and Partnership in Africa] (FEPA) which was later to give much assistance to the RDA.

I was met at the Songea airport by Hinjuson and a number of TANU party officials, and I spent the remainder of the day in preliminary discussions with them and the agricultural officers, and in introducing myself to the district commissioner. That evening Ntimbanjayo arrived on the bus from Dar es Salaam and we made arrangements to be taken by the agricultural officers to Litowa the following day. It had been assumed that I would stay at the Ngoni Arms Hotel in Songea. I could neither afford this nor did I see how one could gather ideas for possibilities at Litowa other than by staying at Litowa. The idea of my staying in Litowa was thought rather strange, but when Ntimbanjayo arrived he immediately saw the necessity of this, showing again an ability to see needs and possibilities where others did not. However, although accepting entirely that I should stay in the bush, he did feel that I should have a bed rather than the earth to sleep on and an iron bedstead and mattress were produced from somewhere.

With a Department of Agriculture Land Rover and the car of one of the agricultural officers, we travelled from Songea to Peramiho, fourteen miles to the northwest, and then a further twelve miles northwards, stopping above the bank of the river Luhira where we had to cross the river on a slender footbridge of poles and bamboos. On the ridge between the Luhira valley and the Litowa valley a small shelter had been erected for us to sit under during the welcoming ceremony, otherwise all that existed in a small clearing was two grass huts, and in the valley beyond, three or four acres of land which had been cleared. The songs were written either for Litowa to express what they were attempting or specifically as a welcome for me. One of these latter, I remember, was to say how Ralph Ibbott had come to save them from their poverty. I made a mental note of the need at an appropriate time to disabuse them of such an idea. There were then speeches and a little unofficial talking after which the officials departed.

During the three weeks at Litowa we talked of many things. We walked extensively over the empty lands on that eastern side of the river. We walked up and down the valley of the river which had a good flow of water at that time although it was the end of the dry season. We noted the waterfalls, the places where the missionaries had dug out soapstone for the floor of the abbey at Peramiho and the stonework of the shrines. We heard how there used to be many large usable timber trees, *miwawa* (mahogany), *migwina*, *mtimbati* and others, but that most had been felled for building up the mission centres. Some of us walked to Peramiho to explore the services the mission there might be able to offer in the future. Also during these three weeks I sketched out something of the plans we discussed together.

During the welcoming ceremony I had sat next to one of the agricultural officers, an expatriate, who obviously felt that these young Litowa men could do nothing. He continually whispered in my ear that they could sing well and were able to drink but that was about all they could do. My impressions were very different. Here were people prepared for change and looking for a new way of life. Here also was adequate land. The people were prepared to start from where they were – the proper starting place. There was no land purchase price to be found, no legal fees for land transfers, no wages bill, no expensive building programme necessary before a start could be made. The main missing factors were the lack of experience of the people and because of this a lack of confidence.

It was not possible for me immediately to pack my bags at Nyafaru in Rhodesia and move to Litowa but it was necessary to ensure that this small group could carry on in the meantime. They had to get through the rains until the harvest the following April, and news of this reached Eglantyne Noel-Buxton in London who sent 1,000 shillings. The rains that year started very heavily, flooding the valley and washing the young plants away so that the crop was poor, none of the higher land having by then been cleared. A longer period of assistance with food was needed.

The work at Nyafaru was assisted by the African Development Trust in London. They were not in a position to extend their assistance to other territories, but on my suggesting that I move to Litowa they asked their field officer, Guy Clutton-Brock, to report his views on this. Guy, who was at that time in Bechuanaland, as it was then called,[4] suggested we meet him in Dar es Salaam. This meeting took place in March 1962 when we met various officials, Ntimbanjayo and his college tutors. Guy reported that he felt it a very worthwhile and genuine opportunity and suggested I be encouraged to make the move. My wife, Noreen, encouraged me to go. On the 2,000 acres at Nyafaru there was work which could be done but with the Land Apportionment Act[5] in operation little could spread beyond its boundaries. In a country just become independent we felt growth could be wider. The leaders of Litowa agreed and accepted the idea. During this visit I was again able to visit Songea and Litowa, this time for a week. The Litowa members had done a little more clearing in the valleys, and after the floods had some not very good maize growing and a little fire-cured tobacco. On the higher land beyond the Litowa valley another acre had been cleared on which they had planted experimentally a number of different varieties of ground nuts on traditional as well as newly-recommended methods. A small curing barn had been built for the tobacco.

Ntimbanjayo still had a month of studies at Kivukoni to finish, after which he travelled to Rhodesia to stay with my family at Nyafaru for a few weeks. During this stay we discussed the ideas of the people of Litowa and drafted a constitution which would provide a basis for discussion amongst them, helping to-

---

4   Now Republic of Botswana.
5   The Act (1930) formalized the separation of land owned by white Europeans, the most fertile, from land owned by "Native" people.

wards constructing an organization to realize their aims. Apart from this, the main advice that we gave in those early days was to concentrate on growing food and not on getting cash, and to work towards getting the members' wives into Litowa so that all would be fully committed. Ntimbanjayo was to return through Nyasaland, and the bus from Salisbury to Blantyre passed through Portuguese territory. After what he had seen of the Portuguese border officials on the journey to Rhodesia, he was worried about having the draft of the Litowa constitution in his possession, but the bus driver took this from him at Salisbury, placing it under his seat and returning it to Ntimbanjayo at Blantyre.

During 1962, others were becoming interested in Litowa. Grif Cunningham, a Canadian tutor at Kivukoni College, took an interest in Ntimbanjayo and came down to see what the Litowa people were doing. Donald Chesworth, who was connected with War on Want and was later for a time to be its chairman, also visited Litowa, became interested and so created a useful connection. Woodhead, the land planning officer for Nachingwea, also came, and arranged for his unit to do a survey of 2,000 acres for the Litowa people; this was done at the end of that year.

The reactions and behaviour of officials are an important part of the story of the RDA. Most were of course to be Tanzanians but a number in the early days were expatriates. I was not at Litowa for Woodhead's visit, but I heard of him in glowing terms when I next went – how he had spoken strongly to the staff of the Agricultural Department telling them not to belittle the efforts of the people who were only just starting, while there was little to show for the years that the department had existed. In the following year I was then surprised to hear of Woodhead's speaking against Litowa and working for the development of the people at nearby Liweta, seemingly in competition with Litowa. The first time I met him was at a meeting in the regional office in Songea, in the second half of 1963, when he had been called to advise on a site for the development of a government village settlement in the region. He advocated choosing a site near Magagura some twenty-five miles to the west of Songea, which became the Mlale settlement. This site was put forward by Woodhead as the only possible site in the whole region for such a settlement, and it seemed that he had no time for any other projects, Liweta now also having been forgotten in this new development.

I met him once more. There was always the accusation against the RDA that we took no notice of the authorities and officials. It was a strange accusation when Ntimbanjayo and I spent an amazing proportion of our time in meeting and discussing with officials, in an endeavour to ensure that there would be no misunderstandings. One afternoon while the Mlale settlement was in its preliminary development stages, we were in Songea when a small government plane circled the regional office to announce its arrival before heading to the airport. We were told that it was bringing the commissioner for village settlement, Fraser-Smith, and we decided that we would wait in Songea to meet and discuss with him. We met him that evening at the Angoni Arms Hotel; and with him was Woodhead. Proper conversation proved impossible, as throughout Woodhead whispered, loudly enough for anyone to hear, rude comments into Fraser-Smith's ear at everything we said. At the end of this impossible conversation Fraser-Smith suggested that we go back and pack up Litowa, telling the members that they should put down their names to join Mlale. The reason he gave was that the Village Settlement Commission had all the resources, finance and expertise to succeed, where we lacked all of those. Some considerable time later Woodhead visited Litowa while I happened to be away. It was shortly before he left Tanzania for good. We were told that he was impressed by what he saw. This is worth reporting as a story only to show the mind-set that is not likely to help the growth of rural communities, which is what rural development is about. This development needs a stability and steadiness not often shown by those with training and expert knowledge and in positions to guide.

We were ready to leave Nyafaru at the end of September 1962. We travelled up to Nyasaland, and in early October boarded the Nyasaland Railway's lake ship "Ilala" at Nkata Bay, and were later put ashore at Mbamba Bay in Tanganyika's Ruvuma Region, where Ntimbanjayo was waiting for us. It was evening when we arrived and we had to wait till morning for a bus to take us to Peramiho, where it was planned that a mission Land Rover would carry us to Litowa. Much to the joy of our children, we slept on the shore beside the lake.

The bus the following morning was a converted lorry, and with many passengers who had also arrived with their luggage the previous evening from across the lake, it was overloaded and unable to negotiate the steepest parts of the road up the escarpment from Lake Nyasa without the passengers disembarking and walking up these stretches. The journey was otherwise uneventful but the 110 miles took most of the day and it was approaching evening when we arrived at Litowa and found a grass hut built ready for us – or rather two grass huts, one with three rooms for sleeping and the other with two rooms, one a kitchen-cum-dining room and the other with a latrine pit next to the kitchen!

We had not arrived to stay long – about four weeks – but were on our way to England for leave and to look for support for this project and for ourselves as part of it. The Africa Development Trust was paying our fare back to London. On the way we stopped off at Lucerne in Switzerland to meet our friends and inform them more fully of our plans. In England we found the support we needed from War on Want, Donald Chesworth having put in a word for us. They provided a car – a Peugeot station wagon – a tractor, plough and harrow, and support for our family. We arrived back in Dar es Salaam in April 1963 and, after a short stay there to collect the car and make a few necessary purchases, we set off again for Litowa.

3

DEFINING *UJAMAA*

Ntimbanjayo had heard the call of Nyerere to the people to work together on farming, given it his own interpretation and, along with his fellow Youth League members, attempted to put it into practice. The headquarters of TANU was also responding to the call and had sent instructions to all party branches telling them to encourage the establishment of groups of people farming together. In almost all of the developments growing from these instructions, the interpretation of farming together was different from that of the Litowa people. It meant a number of people while living in scattered houses coming together for two or three days of every week to clear together a plot of land on which to grow cash crops. In some cases, after the communal clearing, the land was divided into plots and each member who had taken part in the clearing had a plot on which he grew and harvested the cash crop. In other cases, all worked together to grow and harvest the crop which was then sold and the proceeds distributed amongst the members. The advantage was that it was easier to get government staff to advise when people worked together. The block farm, where each farmer had his whole land in a block with others, was an extension of this. This was the general basis of the projects of the Village Settlement Commission. It was also the pattern much encouraged by the Agricultural Department for self-help settlements.

At Ligera, some fifty miles to the southeast of Songea, the branch organization of the party was unable to encourage people to work together. In consequence the branch committee members themselves, led by their secretary Rangimbaya Mhagama, started work on a communal plot a few miles from Ligera, at a place they named Njoomlole (come and see). Here the members worked together for a number of days in each week, while retaining their old scattered homes and lands. There was in fact in the starting of this project a considerable element of opposition to the methods and aims of Litowa, and a desire to point another way. This feeling also existed when during the same period a project was started at Liweta, about eight miles to the east of Litowa, around the end of the Lupagara mountains. The people of Liweta copied the Njoomlole pattern and not that of Litowa.

The fact that there were groups such as Njoomlole and Liweta and others starting to co-operate was of considerable interest to me. Working only with one village would have been difficult with my strongly-held belief that I should never take any responsibility or make a decision on behalf of the people. I believed that the very essence of development and the education of rural peoples could only happen if they themselves took full responsibility and made all decisions. Perhaps partly because of this, it was not easy to forecast how things would develop. So I recommended an organization to begin work with a very simple constitution to serve until such time as a clearer pattern of what was required could be formed. It was fortunate that the first area commissioner in Songea was Hinjuson; he was not only willing to discuss but encouraged Ntimbanjayo and myself to visit other groups. He wished to use us as an example to the others. In talks with Hinjuson in 1962, it was decided that we should form an association called the Songea Development Association, and we prepared a short draft constitution. In the following year there were administrative changes in the southern part of Tanganyika. The old Southern Province was divided into two, forming the Ruvuma Region out of the western part and the Mtwara Region out of the eastern part. In the Ruvuma Region the Songea District, a large one, was also divided into two, the eastern part keeping the original name and a new Mbinga District formed in the west. To the east the Tunduru District became part of Ruvuma. As there was a village group in what was now the Mbinga District wanting contact with us, it was necessary to change the name of the proposed association, and it was decided that it should be the Ruvuma Development Association, thus covering the extra Tunduru District.

At this stage, when the villages were only forming, the real need was for Ntimbanjayo and me to have an organization through which to work, which connected our efforts with party and government. The proposed constitution set down a committee of which the regional commissioner was chairman and which included other party officials and the heads of the appropriate government departments, such as Agriculture and Community Development, as well as village representatives. These discussions were held with A S Mtaki, the first regional commissioner, who became the first chairman of the RDA, but he stayed only a few months before being posted elsewhere. During his short time as chairman he was able to pay a visit to Litowa and made an encouraging speech to the people. His interest in Litowa was, I think, genuine, and he sensed opposition in certain government quarters to the Litowa people working as a community, told us of this, and backed us. All of the correspondence dealing with the application for the registration of the RDA as a society was done for us by the regional administrative secretary and the registration under the Societies Ordinance came into effect in September 1963. Ntimbanjayo became secretary of the Association and I the adviser.

A few weeks after this, Michael Haule became regional commissioner and so chairman of the Association. This is important to the story of the RDA, as later on there were many accusations that the Association would not co-operate with officialdom, when in fact we spent a very high proportion of our time trying precisely to produce proper co-operation. In newsletters and other correspondence, particularly in the earlier years, not a lot was written of any difficulties with officials. This was for obvious reasons. Much of what I write on this subject will therefore have to be from memory, whereas our attempts at co-operation are often recorded. However, it is an important subject and I shall write of it separately later, giving here only the events.

We began to make a number of visits outside Litowa, encouraged by Hinjuson. We fixed a day to visit Liweta when they would bring all their members to their communal plot. It is a visit I remember well as on the particular morning arranged for it, I awoke to find that a cut on my foot had gone septic, giving a lot of pain and the foot beginning to swell. Although Liweta was only eight miles across the mountains it was about fifty miles by road through Songea. In Songea I visited the medical officer who gave me pills of one of the sulfa drugs and recommended my going straight to bed. We decided to carry out our Liweta appointment first, as lack of communications made it difficult to let Liweta know we were not going. There was no bridge fit for cars over the Liweta river at that time and it meant a painful walk up the hill out of the valley to the few storage huts they had in the centre of their cleared plot.

Our main impression of Liweta was one of a very genuine effort to achieve something, but of the impossibility of managing the plot with the project members scattered over such a wide area and without the possibility of any enforceable discipline. There were many groups in existence; some, such as Liweta, where a leader from amongst the peasant people had brought them together; others where political leaders had more or less told people that they must go and work in a certain place; others where people were collecting young men from school to work as groups in an attempt to find an answer to the problems of the employment of school-leavers; others again, where missionaries were starting projects to try to help the people.

All of this led to discussion amongst ourselves of what projects we should try to assist, since it was obvious that in such a large area, if we answered all of the calls of groups starting in many places, we would spread our efforts too widely and achieve nothing. Our decision was that for a group to be assisted by the RDA they must first be working seriously towards living in a proper village, in order to be fully committed to their project, giving up any other allegiances, making possible the growth of the necessary organization and disciplines.

In addition they should have a considerable part of their agricultural work done communally, as addressing the basic necessities of life together would most rapidly produce the organization of people necessary for their development. At Liweta this seemed a possibility, so that we promised a token gift of a few hoes and axes and some second-hand clothing which was being sent to us from Europe. We pointed out the steps we felt were necessary for coming together in a village and for working together, and why they were important to achieve. We stressed strongly that the Association was not designed to be an instrument for providing things for people but rather that it was to be an organization through which people could work in order to develop themselves.

At this time also we were asked by Hinjuson to visit a group at Matimira which was working with one of the Peramiho mission brothers. On arrival we found that the brother was an old man with strange ideas who, all the way to the site where the group were building a pig-sty, was repeating that if people didn't do it his way he was not interested in helping them. It was quite obvious that there was no real community and that there was little that could be done to help. The "war" between this brother and the group of people he had collected together went on for a few years, during which time they built, under his direction, a marvellous pig house. We were brought in several times by one of the fathers at Peramiho to mediate in the troubles but there was never any real organization of the people, which was necessary if the project was to move towards becoming a member of the Association. Eventually the bishop had to remove the brother, after which the people split up. If the brother had been removed much earlier it might have been possible to form a group, but with the troubles going on for so long, divisions were formed amongst the people which made this impossible.

At Matimira our initial judgements seemed right, but this was not always so. At about the same time Hinjuson also asked us to visit the Matetereka group about a hundred miles out of Songea on the road going north to Njombe. This was on higher land in open hilly country out of the thicker bush, where the people grew coffee as a cash crop. The group seemed energetic and with great promise, but all of these men who came to work on the plot two or three days a week when the season required and were growing mostly maize and wheat to make a little extra cash, had established coffee plantations of their own in the surrounding districts. It was hard to see that they would give up these to establish a new village; and so it seemed likely that the communal plot would carry on as it was for a number of years with the members learning a little more on cultivation through working together, which would then benefit them on their own lands. In the light of this we encouraged them but told them of the Association working only with integrated villages which could be points of continuous growth. We were wrong. There were those amongst the membership who were looking for something more than that little bit of cash. We were approached again much later, when the Matetereka people had decided that they wanted to come together into a village, at which time they became members of the Association. From the time the families moved into their communal plot Matetereka became a fast-growing village.

In visiting Njoomlole we again felt that there were good prospects and that if the people came together things would move. Among the people there were those who seemed quick to see this, and the group very early on decided to move in together. However, this was to become a village that set itself against the others. I shall deal with it later since it even played a part in the politics which led later to the disbanding of the Association.

These first visits were very encouraging to us but they showed a great need for steady advice for these new groups, and in particular for them to come together to discuss their problems and what they wanted to do and how. We faced problems, however, in particular the feeling that there were officials who looked upon our ideas with suspicion because they themselves were working along different lines. We never felt ourselves in competition with other methods of working. I had a vague feeling, when talking with the commissioner for Village Settlement, that he felt that if there were competing villages his large settlement might not get enough recruits, but I may be wrong in this. Another high official in the Village Settlement Commission who had never met or discussed with me, travelling to Songea on the same plane as the regional commissioner, warned him against me as a person he suspected of communism.

Then there was the experience of Woodhead who had turned against us. These antagonisms and undermining gossip, which were to increase, made us feel that it was absolutely necessary that everyone knew what we were doing. It seemed impossible to get quietly on with the work. It was the beginning of the difficulty that we were to face constantly, of the struggle between the need to put the greatest possible effort into the growth of the villages and the need to enter into the political life of the region and the nation, in order to try and ensure the acceptance and protection of the ideas on which the villages were based. We felt that the best plan was for Ntimbanjayo to work in this political sphere, while the others got on with the job, but that he should live and do considerable work with the villagers, to ensure that his political work was based on the needs of the people and was practicable.

Another problem we faced was that of distance. It was not easy to get to distant villages often enough: travelling was time-consuming and expensive, and on top of this many roads became almost impassable during the rains. From the beginning we felt the necessity for the people of the villages to get together as often as possible, to learn and gain strength from each other. This was difficult over great distances. From the shores of Lake Nyasa, which form the western boundary of the Ruvuma Region, to the eastern boundary with the Mtwara Region, is well over three hundred miles. This led us to feel there was need for concentration in a limited geographical area, and we wrote of this in our newsletter of December 1963:

> There is a great need for an example in one area of what is possible, so that this one area may be an education for the spread of development to other areas. By first developing a communal farming scheme such as Litowa as a base, developments may be effectively carried out, after a time of preparation, in the surrounding Village Development Committee area (some 150 square miles in extent).

In 1962 the word *ujamaa*, often interpreted as "familyhood" or "brotherhood", began to be used by Nyerere in explaining his political philosophy to the nation. This became known as African socialism. As always with these things, the party took up the idea, and meetings and seminars were held to discuss it. Little resulted from this talk. However, the deputy regional secretary of TANU in Ruvuma – Kiluvia – invited us to a meeting of political and government officials in Songea to discuss the meaning and implications of *ujamaa*, and as a result, a committee was set up to look further into the question.[1] Ntimbanjayo and I were both on this committee with Kiluvia, Masumba, the district education officer, and Kapilima from the regional administration. This was a very interesting little committee. Masumba and Kapilima were both people of intelligence with a genuine interest in the development of their poorer brothers. It has always been my experience that in all situations, however great the lack of

---

1   The document of this committee, *Ujamaa* – an Outline of the Principles, is quoted in full at the end of this chapter.

understanding or interest generally seems to be, there are to be found those who can get things going. I remember feeling at the time how much could be achieved if a regional commissioner would accept a committee such as this, to meet and discuss with at a local level, to help him to decide what to work on. The official regional development committee meetings which I used to attend at this time were very disappointing and official affairs.

Several of us wrote papers for this committee. I wrote down the thoughts on development that we had discussed together at Litowa. Masumba wrote on co-operation in rural life in the days of his forefathers. These papers were put together and presented to the regional commissioner, and then distributed to those who had attended the initial meeting.

During the second quarter of 1964 there were to be elections for the Songea district council, for which Ntimbanjayo decided to stand. He was elected by the voters, and then elected by the councillors as chairman of the council. This position meant he had to travel throughout the district, giving him a chance to meet many people, to see conditions in all parts of the district, and to enter into discussion on development problems.

From this time, we began to feel the growth of opposition to our work but it was not easy to give the exact reasons for it as the people concerned would not talk. We had lost Hinjuson as area commissioner, and had instead a rather ineffective man who, when visiting Litowa, unintentionally said all the wrong things, but quite willingly, when we went to see him about it, sent his deputy to apologise for what he had said. It was not long before he also was posted away.

We wished for meetings of the Association's committee but found it increasingly difficult to meet Haule, the regional commissioner, to discuss matters or to get him as chairman to call a meeting. There was always some excuse. I feel it was in part a completely different approach to the people, and in part that Ntimbanjayo set himself against officials: government and party playing the time-honoured game of organizing things for their own benefit and misusing public funds. During his period of chairmanship of the council (nearly a year and a half), it was singularly free from troubles.

We then heard that Ntimbanjayo was to be appointed as area commissioner in the Tunduru District of Ruvuma and sensed from the situation that it was an attempt to divide Ntimbanjayo from the village people and take him away from the Association. To accept this post would have meant that he forfeited his freedom to be based with his friends in the village and to work with them and for their combined interest. Because of this he took steps to ensure that he could turn down the offer. The regional commissioner was the responsible officer for the district council and there was thus much contact between him and Ntimbanjayo, but the subject of the Association was not one on which he would accept discussion and we had to carry on quietly without meetings of the committee.

Towards the end of the year Haule was moved from his post to become for a time a junior minister and later a manager of one of the failing projects of the Village Settlement Commission and finally out of any position of authority. Just before this we had received a new area commissioner, Chilumba; Haule was followed by Peter Walwa who in turn became ex-officio chairman of the Association.

When the Ruvuma Region was first formed in 1963 we had an expatriate regional administrative secretary, John Arnold, efficient, sympathetic and progressive. With Africanization, he left in May of 1964 and there followed one or two people in this post who were not well trained for it. With the coming of Walwa we also had a new administrative secretary: Makinde, who had worked in government administration for twenty-seven years.

During this time the people of Litowa through their own efforts began to understand that there were benefits in working together. Although there were initial difficulties in working on a larger scale, they could see that in spite of the difficulties they could produce more. Together they felt a greater security and had more power over their lives, able for instance to discuss the problems of educating their children and to do something about it.

The Litowa school also started in these early years. It hardly took the form of a school but when work permitted, Ado Mgimba collected all the children together and began teaching them a little. Later, as people became more keen on the idea, he was helped by Kufabasi Mapunda, the secretary of Litowa, who had been educated at school to standard VIII.[2]

From outside there may have appeared little to be seen as yet, but those who lived in the conditions of the locality saw it, and it led to a growth in the work of the Association. It was encouraging that visiting groups started their own villages through what they saw at Litowa, and groups which had been in existence before came for advice. The first of these was Luhira Goliama just across the river from Litowa whose action committee, a small sub-division of the official village development committee, decided to start communal working in the early months of 1964. This was significant. As we described earlier, only nine months before this, the people of Luhira Goliama and those of Litowa had been in dispute over the use of the Kidigidigi valley. On top of this the elders of Luhira Goliama had also stated their fear of having a group over the river which included a number of unattached bachelors which they looked on as a potential danger to their daughters. As well as all of this, at such close range they knew all the details of the Litowa village, the difficulties as well as the achievements. At about the same time the village development committee, of which Litowa was part, decided that all leaders of the action committees within their area should visit Litowa, and having seen what was happening, should consider whether it was possible to start anywhere

---

2   Secondary school.

else within the area on similar lines. As a result, a small group of people led by Claudius Haule left their homes and founded a new village called Mhepai about twenty miles to the north of Litowa.

It was also in the second half of 1964 that we first heard of a group at Chimate by Lake Nyasa who were hoping for a visit from us, and the chairman of Litowa paid an initial visit to them. Many people expressed doubts as to whether the people by the lake would co-operate together as life was relatively easy on a diet consisting mainly of fish and cassava, both fairly easily come by. It was, however, an area becoming rapidly poorer with changes resulting from changing political situations. Much money came to the area through its young men travelling to work in the mines of South Africa. At independence this was stopped. What trade there was in crops was often with Mozambique to the southeast of Malawi across the lake, rather than with Tanganyika. With the freedom struggle developing in Mozambique gradually putting paid to the first, and national quarrels with Malawi to the second, very little in the way of new outlets were developed with Tanganyika. Haule had ideas of developing a fishing co-operative down there, called people together and spoke to them of it. They were asked to put their names forward. There was almost no response but that does not necessarily mean that the people would not co-operate. Such non-co-operation may have been a method the people were using to express their disappointment at what was happening in the area. The Chimate group was, however, very small and did not seem to have outstanding leaders, so we did not expect too much.

The first inter-village meeting took place when a group of Liweta members visited Litowa towards the end of 1963 to look around and discuss. In August of the following year leaders of eight village groups met for a simple conference at Litowa which the regional community development officer attended (for a short time), as well as members of staff of the Agricultural Department. The emphasis was on agriculture but the representatives discussed together all problems that they had come across and ways of overcoming these. We presented to them problems they were likely to meet in future. This meeting obviously supplied a great need and we were asked by these village representatives to repeat such meetings regularly. This feeling of the people played a large part in our proposals later for a new constitution for the RDA.

In the dry season of 1964 we received our first visit from Jimmy Betts, Oxfam's field director in Eastern Africa. It was directly as a result of this visit that we received a grant for the materials for a water supply for Litowa. As Donald Chesworth of War on Want had already been to Litowa, this meant that both War on Want and Oxfam were not only interested but had representatives who had been to Ruvuma and talked with the people.

Litowa village always had many visitors from many walks of life. During this early period the visitors included a number of government ministers. The first, in early 1963, was the minister for agriculture, Derek Bryceson. Rashidi Kawawa, the second vice-president, visited in 1964. At the same time Minister of State Makame came. The secretary-general of TANU, Oscar Kambona, came twice while he was minister for home affairs. Edward Barongo who was later to become regional commissioner in Ruvuma visited in 1963 while he was junior minister for agriculture, Vincent Mponji when junior minister for labour, and Lawi Sijaona when minister for lands, settlements and water development. It was originally the custom on such visits for all the village to greet the minister on arrival with waving tree branches and welcoming songs. Early in 1964, when Vincent Mponji was to visit Litowa, the members discussed giving up this custom as it occupied so much time which would be better spent working. They decided to do so and to explain why to Mponji. He understood and appreciated this; he said he had come to see the work and encourage people and not to hinder. This has a certain significance as this was not only always accepted, but readily agreed to, even with presidential visits, while certain people during the break-up process of the Association in 1969 implied that this showed a lack of courtesy.

The following is the paper produced by the committee on *ujamaa* mentioned above.

UJAMAA

An Outline of the Principles for a Plan for the Introduction of African Socialism into the Ruvuma Region of Tanganyika

NB: What is written here is from the experience gained in the Ruvuma Region. We realize that conditions differ in different parts of the Union and different approaches and methods may be necessary and possible. We do not put these ideas forward as a concrete answer to the problems of the introduction of *ujamaa*, but merely as something that from our thoughts we believe is worth attempting. We must always be prepared to alter our approach in the light of experience.

Some Basic Principles

When considering the introduction of African Socialism it is important to realize that it is not a state which can be achieved immediately. There may be many stages in its achievement. There would seem, however, to be certain basic principles to bear in mind. Consideration of these principles should lead to a knowledge of what the first steps might be.

a) To Involve People Widely

African Socialism (for convenience termed here Socialism) is for the whole of the people and not merely for one particular section. Any consideration of its details must consider the necessity of working in such a way as to involve people as widely as possible and eventually the whole community. Consideration must be taken of the slender resources existing with which to start and the fact that many of the older generation will be unable to take to the new ideas and methods involved.

b) To Gain People's Confidence: to Lead and not Drive

As whatever is introduced is for the benefit of the people it is necessary to ensure that the people understand what is being done. To obtain the confidence of the people is absolutely essential. Plans implemented for the benefit of people often fail because the confidence and understanding of those people was not first gained. It is not an easy thing to gain the confidence of people with a peasant background. Peasant peoples the world over are distrustful of governments. In the present situation, when many people are not yet fully conscious of the new Nationhood, it can hardly be expected that a government can easily have their trust. If the trust of the people can be obtained, producing a good spirit of widespread co-operation, then much can be achieved. There is a limit to the distance that people can be driven, but we believe that there is no limit to the distance people can be led.

c) Communal Work and Ownership

Communal ownership and working is the foundation of a socialist economy: to be rid of the master/servant relationship and have a society where people work together as equals.

From these principles the task is to have a leadership capable of introducing a system of communal ownership and working with the consent, trust and understanding of the people on a scale which will involve people as widely as possible and without requiring large financial resources.

Some Basic Facts Affecting Economic Development

As well as the basic principles, there are certain basic facts of life in the Ruvuma Region which must be taken into account if an approach is to be realistic.

The Ruvuma Region is a large area of land with plenty of fertile soils and adequate water. It is however an area with very poor communication, with many places cut off from road transport for at least half of the year, and others difficult of access or cut off for shorter periods. Transport for goods into and out of the area is a very expensive business.

Within this very large area there is only a population of some 300,000 persons. It must be recognized that this low population does not make possible the introduction of modern factories. The high productive capacity of modern factories requires a large population to consume the products manufactured in order that they should be economically feasible. Transport costs out of the area will also rule out much in the way of modern industry being possible through selling to other parts of the country.

Yet this Region does not want to be left out of industrialization and in the future the population will vastly increase. A realistic approach to the problem of industrialization must therefore be sought, taking the facts of the situation into account.

Communal Villages

We believe it is possible to establish a reasonable number of communal villages in the Region over the next few years. The economic life of these villages would be based on agriculture, and apart from small pieces of land for individual use around family houses, the whole of agriculture would be carried out on a communal basis making possible the use of agricultural machinery on the most economic basis. Increased production through the introduction of modern methods and machines would enable the villages to be fed by only a proportion of the members of the community. This leaves labour free for the building of better houses and village amenities. It would also leave labour free for engaging in the village industries such as would be possible without great investment, using largely local resources. Industries such as furniture manufacture, pottery, hand spinning and weaving of cotton and wool, leather tanning and manufacture of shoes and other leather goods, manufacture of carts and wagons, and vegetable oil extraction. Each communal village might have one or two such industries and trading with surplus produce could take place between villages.

This we believe possible because of the existence in the region of small self-started settlement schemes. These schemes have had considerable difficulty in holding together, a tendency to die out, and no idea of the real possibilities. However, this year with a certain amount of success at the TANU Youth League (TYL) Farmers' Scheme at Litowa, a new interest in these schemes has awakened and it would seem possible to start a considerable number of new ones. One great advantage of this type of start is that people come together before any money is spent and can work for the first year without any assistance while a plan is being made of how each one should develop. This is not possible when a project is started from the central government. Much spending goes on at an expensive level before a single tree is uprooted.

A greater advantage however is that the project is growing out of the people themselves and not being implanted from above. A certain spirit therefore exists to begin with and without this spirit little can be achieved. The members of the project themselves seek advice, building up a confidence between the group and the district and regional departmental officers. Starting here we believe it is possible to get the confidence of the people on a growing scale.

A start can be made immediately, on a fairly wide basis with little capital, working with the confidence of the people, and on a scale small enough for people to be able to begin to understand.

Village Life in Pre-Colonial Days

The idea of working communally and of responsibility to all one's fellow members in a village is not new but is part of the African culture.

Before the advent of the white man everybody lived in a village. Some villages had thirty or forty people while others had more than a hundred souls living in them. The way of living in these villages depended on the land at their disposal. The soil produced what was necessary for life. The head of a village had to see that every person, or every family, had a piece of land which they could cultivate to produce food. If a person had not enough land to enable him to produce sufficient food for his family, he could approach another person whom he knew had more than he needed. It was customary for this other person to be ready to spare his neighbour what land was available. It was thought inhuman to see somebody suffering while his neighbour next door had a surplus of something.

Normally, every family worked on their own land and produced what they could according to the effort they put into it. But it was also a common thing for individual families to work together in groups for they realized that in doing so they could do a lot in a very short time, and this, of course, meant that everybody would have something at all times. So working communally was typical of the African way of life in those days and still is in some places. As we said, some villages had at least fifty people living in them. It often happened that four or five of these went fishing or hunting as life also depended on these as well as on cultivation. The fish or the animals that were caught were shared among all the village dwellers. However, if a person was very lazy and did not take his fair part in these activities he was regarded as an undesirable soul in the society and was often neglected.

Food was, as a rule, taken together, except that men took it separately from women. If there were six families in the village they all expected to see six dishes of food brought to the *baraza*[3] every afternoon and evening as long as food was available. When one family could not prepare any food they knew they would not starve because they would be helped by the other families – there was always something to eat as long as there was peace.

When the white man came and introduced money and work for money, life in an African village began to change. Money became a factor in life as well as land. As a result, folk from the villages travelled to the newly established places in search of money. However, their stay in these places was not long. After working for a year or two in these places and collecting a little money, they bought such things as pieces of cloth, beads and articles likely to interest their families and fellow villagers. When doing this shopping they had to see that they were buying at least one article for every person in their village – they wanted everyone to be happy. Money was hardly ever brought home – in fact it had no value as there were no shops in the villages. For people in those days life had more meaning and there was therefore more real happiness. This was brought about by a real African socialism.

This ancient African socialism is part of the African cultural heritage which is in danger of being lost and for which there is a great need. Recently an African artist, Elimu Njau, speaking at the East African Women's Seminar at Nairobi, said ". . . without some definite form of cultural identity our political independence means nothing more than grabbing or requiring more and more material wealth." We see this happening around us today: people forgetting their background and responsibilities to their fellow beings and using independence for purely selfish ends. A return is needed to a basic socialistic background from which

---

3   School hall.

the country had grown, otherwise the present leadership in this "grabbing and acquiring of more and more material wealth" will not gain the confidence of the people and consequently not be able to maintain control.

This does not mean that we put the clock back. Many changes are necessary in the light of scientific knowledge which has come into the world, to suit the organization to the needs of modern methods (e.g. to make a tractor economic), and to take account of ideas that have entered the world which add to the total of human happiness, such as the equality of women.

Village Industries

We believe the introduction of village industries manufacturing the quantities of goods necessary for only local markets to have many beneficial effects.

a) It would assist in producing a spirit amongst the people. There is a satisfaction to be gained through creating things.

b) People are learning skills on a wide scale. These skills are often more basic than those learnt by people working in larger industries where they are often merely machine operators.

c) The local natural resources will be more rapidly made use of and perhaps new ones discovered.

d) A more diverse local economy will be developing, making possible many improvements.

e) As the population grows these industries can grow, thus assuring that in the future industry is more widely based than happens today in Africa, with more usual forms of introducing industry. In all African countries there is a great rush to introduce secondary industries set up through foreign capital producing consumer goods for a very limited local market. Many countries which have gone furthest in this development already rely heavily on exporting their goods to neighbouring countries. The scale of production through the size of the internal population usually makes it impossible to compete in larger world markets. As other countries introduce these consumer goods factories, existing ones tend to work below maximum. Many young people are attracted to the towns through these industries and after an initial rapid development a pause comes when more and more young people hang hopefully around the towns robbing the countryside of those who should be leaders in its development, which development is necessary for producing the larger internal markets so necessary for the health of Industry. We are not economists, but might it not be that the accent on secondary industries introduced through foreign capital is a wrong one, and that production of the goods these produce on a smaller scale widely spread through the country would be economically more realistic, help to keep youth and talent in the rural areas and lessen reliance on overseas countries. The accent might then be placed on primary industries on which eventually industrial independence rests. If the rural areas are more energetically developed might it not in fact be possible to have coal mining and iron and steelworks paid for, say, by increased production of groundnuts. These are the industries which make possible the tar for road building, steel for railway building, etc. We believe this to be worth considering.

With the technical knowledge available in the world today it should be possible to produce small-scale industries not relying to any great extent on expensive imports with a larger output and improved quality than those industries of a similar size which used to exist in Europe before the growth of large-scale industry.

These village industries would be introduced in the communal villages. Those who work in the industries would be fed by the village's agricultural workers. Incomes from industry and agriculture would be used for distribution on the same basis to all workers. At times of peak work on the land, such as at tobacco-curing time, all workers could join in with the farm work.

Finance

One of the difficulties in the early stages of this type of development is that there is a great danger of the results of local productive effort leaving the area through people spending their money on imported goods. This would delay the buildup of a local economy. This might be overcome by dispensing with the use of East African currency within the projects taking part in this development, and using instead some form of exchange vouchers only valid within these projects. Thus a local trade would be ensured.

Leadership

If people are to be led there must be the leadership with the understanding to be able to do the leading. Anything new to be introduced needs first the people of understanding to think and plan what is possible. It is then necessary for this leadership to spread the ideas at the same time as beginning to introduce them. It is advisable for the two to go together to ensure that ideas are practical and not merely theoretical.

There is much mention of socialism but very little idea of what it really implies. There are also very few people with the desire to find out or willing to do the hard thinking necessary. Government at present would seem to have nothing of socialism in it. The task of taking over responsibility on independence has not left room for the necessary changes to convert a conservative British colonial administration into an independent socialistic one. In fact the immediate task is probably not to do this but to produce socialists – no administration can be socialistic without the people in it having an understanding of its nature and fervent belief in it. At present, then, we have an administration which in the eyes of the people is almost identical to the colonial one, the difference being that the office-bearers are now African instead of European. They still lead a life far different from the ordinary people. The work of gaining people's confidence is not achieved automatically on independence but is still to be done.

This also applies to TANU which since independence is inevitably thought of more and more as being part of government. There is at present no dominating political philosophy in the TANU party. This lack of political philosophy makes possible a peaceful revolution to socialism if there are enough people prepared to think out the problems and make an honest attempt to live as socialists. They must also realize that to be effective it is not just necessary to have a feasible economic policy; people also look to the quality of a person's personal life if they are to accept him as a trusted leader. Leadership entails working hard and living in an upright and honest way. The present broken state of society in the country shows as much in the leaders and more educated people as it does in the peasants. The traditional acceptance of responsibility to one's neighbours has not been carried into the larger organization of people as a nation. So many are seduced by the glitter of the products of modern industry, using them for purely personal pleasure rather than working towards the time when these things can be produced in their own country. Thus making them available to all.

Adult Education

It is also a duty of leadership to disseminate ideas and plans as widely as possible. With examples of communal villages growing up it should be more possible to get ideas of what is necessary over to people. In Songea the Community Development Department are planning an adult education centre. This can be a vital part of the introduction of socialism. Two things are very necessary. First, that all things taught and discussed in this centre should fit in with a plan that is beginning to be put into practice. Second, that there are people able to do the lecturing and lead discussions and conferences.

With the lecturers and the plan there are then many opportunities with many different sections of people, courses for district councillors, executive and sub-executive officers; teachers; political leaders; agriculture assistants; community development assistants; leaders of communal villages.

It also becomes possible for teams of speakers to go out holding conferences at the various communal villages. All the time, all the speakers must be working to one plan carrying practical projects stage by stage towards the goal. Lack of a properly understood and carefully worked out plan will only lead to confusion in the minds of the people.

The task is difficult. It cannot be done rapidly but we believe that if attempted honestly and with integrity the rate of progress will steadily increase.

4

PETER WALWA VS THE RDA

Towards the end of 1964 Peter Walwa became regional commissioner and although he was in this post for only about a year (having been posted away shortly after the parliamentary elections of 1965), it was a period in which much happened in the RDA. We also had the new area commissioner, Chilumba, in the Songea District. Both Walwa and Chilumba seemed very willing to help in the early days of their appointments, and I think this desire was genuine, but they both soon moved into opposition. Chilumba collected some people together working a block farming project at Kakong'o, some twenty miles to the north of Songea, and built this up later as a showpiece for visitors, partly to take attention from the RDA villages. He was not during these times very willing to talk. Walwa was always willing to talk and kept a friendly atmosphere on the surface even when he was trying to destroy us. This certainly made life more pleasant but perhaps it was more difficult to know where one stood. During this year feelings against the villages and Litowa in government and political offices grew more marked. Previously it was as if certain individuals instinctively reacted against the villages, but as 1965 progressed it seemed as if there was gradually more realization of what was involved. Individual officers who felt themselves drawn towards the villages began to feel that they were the odd man out in Songea.

One of these was Edward Mwakabonga, at first district community development officer and later acting regional community development officer. He was I think the first government officer to sit down with the people and seriously discuss what they were trying to do and whether his department could help. He was responsible for one of the most important pieces of 'aid' given to the RDA: in May 1965 he sent a community development worker to help with the work amongst the women at Litowa. This was Grace Chips, as she was always known, although her full name was Chipungahelo, whom Mwakabonga considered his best woman worker. Grace was an exceptional woman, very capable and one of those quiet people who achieve so much without others realizing they have done it. She was through her work supporting her brothers with their education, one through to university – her father was separated from her mother – and at the same time Grace had three children of her own to support. She had been a teacher before transferring to community development. Educationally she had completed primary schooling and been through a two-year teachers' training course. She liked the village and quickly saw the possibilities of life there, so she approached the leaders of the Association with a view to transferring from the Community Development Department to the Education Department to be able to teach in the growing RDA school at Litowa and make a home there.

This was the year also that the school at Litowa became officially registered. The RDA was the agency for the school and Ntimbanjayo the manager. From January 1965 it had standards I, II and III. We were trying to develop the school on lines which would direct the children towards developing further the work in the villages which their parents had started. Since the days when Ado and Kufabasi had at times done a bit of teaching, we had had the addition of a man called Soko who was from Luhira Goliama. He was not qualified as a teacher but had been a catechist teacher with the mission at Peramiho and in that capacity had also taught subjects other than the catechism. He did not have much understanding of what we were trying to do with the school. But there was generally a shortage of teachers and most were drawn towards work in more developed and tradition-

ally structured schools. It was not easy to find those prepared
to start at the bottom, who would also be prepared to listen to
and discuss with the parents and their organization what was
needed. However, in November of 1964 we were approached by
Lighanga Mahundi, a teacher who was out of work after getting
into difficulties with the education authorities. Perhaps for this
reason Lighanga was more prepared to listen to what the RDA
had to say to him on their educational ideas than most teachers would have been. He found it difficult to accept new ideas
but tried hard and did much in the establishment of the Litowa
school. It was obvious that he would not be suitable for leading
it as it developed further. His wife was a trained midwife who
was also very useful to the village.

Also at the end of 1964 the work of the Association spread
into the Tunduru District to the east. In this district were two
or three groups which had been started at the instigation of the
area commissioner. This was always a difficult way of starting
as it meant that the man with the ideas was not himself directly
involved in the project. There is generally in these cases a lack of
genuine leadership. The difficulties are often accentuated by the
fact that young people have been directed to go to such groups
and therefore go unwillingly. With an unwilling membership,
constant pressure is necessary to keep people at it and if this
pressure is not constant, as it can hardly be in the case of an
area commissioner who has many other duties, then the group
is likely to give up. For these reasons these groups in the Tunduru District were slowly disintegrating. The area commissioner
invited Ntimbanjayo to visit the group at Ligoma, a few miles to
the east of Tunduru town, which was still hanging on. Ligoma
was over 200 miles from Litowa. It seemed difficult from such a
distance to be of much assistance to such a village, particularly
when it was in a state of crisis. Ligoma had been lent money by
the district council on a short-term basis, mostly for food to start
off with. This was all arranged between the area commissioner

and the district council. When the district council pressed for repayment, the money was not available and a large part of the membership left for their old homes.

It is perhaps hardly true to say that they were lent money, as the financial arrangements were done without any proper consultation with the members. It is hardly possible to expect people to repay money when they were not in on the borrowing. A very similar thing was done with the large government settlement schemes. At the Commission's settlement at Mlale in our region, attempts were made to get the settlers to repay money for things provided for them, by making it compulsory for them to sell their tobacco through the settlement organization. It then appeared that little tobacco had been grown. In fact much had gone out at night to the settlers' friends and relations, who had sold it on their behalf. Thus they avoided having money deducted that was due to the settlement scheme, as had been planned by the settlement authorities. One can hardly blame the settlers as they did not have things properly explained to them in the first place, and what explanations they did have were largely cancelled out by the way the idea was sold to the people when the authorities were asking people to join in. It reminded me of advertising where in the biggest possible letters is the word FREE: only if you read further do you find the catch. At the annual anniversary of the TANU party on 7th July – *saba saba*: seventh of the seventh – at the showground in Songea, the regional commissioner shouted out "Development – see what the government is doing for you. Put your name down to join Mlale", and so on. At this time the area secretary in Songea seriously told me that there would soon be many settlers at Mlale as after a year or two, when the first settlers began to buy their cars, many more would want to join too!

I have often wondered since how Ntimbanjayo and I managed to create an interest in the villagers we went to meet. Against the government talk they were used to, what we had to say must have sounded pretty dismal. We told them that development of their villages could come only from very hard work, that they were unlikely to see big remits quickly and that we would not be likely to give them much in the way of help other than advice. I think that this approach in fact sounds much more sensible to people who somehow survive year by year directly from their own efforts, generally with very little to spare. At any rate while we were proposing they tread this hard road, those who had joined Mlale appeared to be doing just what they were asked to do. They were seeing what the government was doing for them, and putting what they were given to good account, although not in the way intended. Being used to very little ready money, to receive pocket money was wonderful. Some took this, journeyed to the lake shore where they bought dried fish very cheaply from the people there. Returning with this to Songea, they were able to make a good profit, showing what is possible with a little capital. Returning to Mlale they might find a couple of bags of fertilizer on their doorsteps and not a word as to how it got there. This again was fortunate as the small farms round about were being encouraged to grow tobacco and were only too pleased to be able to buy cheap fertilizer. This all showed initiative even if it wasn't going into the channels that it was intended that it should go.

In the early part of February 1964, I had been in hospital for two weeks with malaria. It was at a time when I should have been at home caring for our children, while Noreen also came into hospital to have Christopher and we had to make other arrangements for the other three. In December of the same year I was invited by the Christian Council to give a paper at a conference they organized in Dar es Salaam called "Rapid Social Change Study". For a few days before this I had felt a little off-colour and then on the evening before I was due to fly to Dar es Salaam I began to vomit badly and thought that I might have a recurrence of malaria. Going on this assumption, I took the prescribed dose of chloroquine and the following morning, feeling somewhat better, decided to fly as arranged. On the last part of the flight I began vomiting badly again and instead of attending the conference I spent two weeks in hospital with infectious hepatitis, and a further week convalescing with friends at the university. This gave time for thought, particularly as the doctor had told me that it was possible to have periods of feeling weak for as much as twelve months after this illness. I had originally thought of working with four or five village groups. Already the number of villages was far above this, and some of these at considerable distances from Litowa. On top of that there were already many visitors coming to Litowa to see the village and this took up much time. Time meeting and talking with officials to try and get understanding of what the RDA was doing was also more than I had envisaged. And there were calls to attend conferences, write articles and papers and so on, as well as an increasing correspondence. This was all pulling away from what was the real work – assisting the growth of the villages.

Thinking these things over, it seemed to me that whereas I had always felt that the villages should build their own organizations in no way relying on me, now that the overall work, the work of the association of villages, was growing rapidly, there needed to be equal care to see that neither should any reliance on me develop at the RDA level. Just before Christmas 1964 when I returned from Dar es Salaam, I suggested to Ntimbanjayo that we needed to build a small group of the more capable people from amongst us into a body to do the sort of work which originally I had thought I would do. Over the next days, Ntimbanjayo discussed this suggestion with the individual people he thought would be suitable for the work, with the Litowa management, and with individual villagers.

Ntimbanjayo and I had found that, rather than to have official meetings of people who were not very interested, the most effective method was to discuss points as they arose, with the regional commissioner as chairman. Constitutionally the RDA was not functioning as it was supposed to. But there was among the villages a rapidly growing feeling of unity and a desire to work together.

After a few days Ntimbanjayo returned to say that all seemed to think the idea a good and useful one, and that in discussing they had felt the work to be done needed a group of people with considerable self-discipline. There was such talk in those days that development was a war against poverty, ignorance and disease, and consequently they felt that the discipline needed was like that of the army. They wished to be known as the Social and Economic Revolutionary Army, fighting this war and trying to bring about the social and economic revolution called for by the President. This group then met with Walwa who rather reluctantly accepted the idea and the name, and they became known as SERA.

One of the first works of SERA was to send Wayakile to stay for a few weeks at Ligoma to see if the group could be saved and start again with more understanding. As a result the village asked to join the Association. There were also other new villages joining in that year such as Njaramatata (hunger trouble) some thirty-five miles to the south-east of Songea. Here was a project with a communal plot where a number of the surrounding people worked a few days a week. They had achieved little and most had given up, leaving a small number who decided to carry on by moving into a new village to work full-time. Matetereka had also decided to work as a communal village and joined the Association. The people in a group at Kakong'o had also got into difficulties with which the area commissioner was unable to help, and as a result they had approached the Association and joined. (They were later to leave; this story is told later.) Also joining was another group which had started some thirty-five miles to the south-west of Songea and which called their new village Mtakanini (what do you want). This was the second village of that name; the other was only a mile from Chimate by Lake Nyasa. As this village and Chimate were both small, we suggested they think of working towards combining, and to help towards this, they together called themselves Mapinduzi Farmers' Scheme; *mapinduzi* means revolution.

With all this growth we had to face the constitutional issues of the RDA and talked much on this over a number of months. The fact that most government and political leaders showed little interest in what the people were doing was a fact to be much taken into consideration, as lack of interest was not likely to produce much help with development. On top of this was the fact that when government officers had come they had often given bad advice. A body of people in the Association could hardly do more harm. We had come to believe that the greatest results would be obtained if those whose lives were wholly dependent on these new villages were themselves the people responsible, not only for those villages but also for the Association, which would then become a co-operative of producer co-operatives.

In August of 1965, the President paid his first visit to Songea since independence. We had heard that when he came he would visit Litowa. This fact was known by both the area and regional commissioners, yet their dislike of the Association was such that when making out the itinerary for the President's visit, Litowa was not included. However, a couple of days before he was due to arrive, a government messenger was sent to say that the President was coming to Litowa. He had, it appeared, been sent the programme for his approval and seeing Litowa omitted he sent word that he was going there.

After his tour around the Litowa farm and village, a few of the leaders of the Association met with him in our kitchen cum dining room, together with the area and regional commissioners and one or two others. Over a cup of tea we discussed what we considered the most important questions facing us. One of these was the constitution, and we put forward our desire to have a new constitution which would make the villages responsible for the whole of their organization. This would mean the Association would be run entirely by the people in the villages, independent of the regional commissioner. He told us that we should go ahead along those lines.

After this meeting we went out and he spoke to the people of Litowa. In this talk he asked that the people should develop the *ujamaa* life at Litowa because many people came to him in Dar es Salaam and asked what *ujamaa* meant. He wanted Litowa to be a practical example where he could send such questioners to see for themselves *ujamaa* in practice. He asked three times whether the people would do this job for him and three times they said they would. The people looked upon this promise as a pledge and it was a promise that they certainly kept and nearly destroyed themselves to keep.

At this time, the leaders of all the villages began to come together every three months, having more and more of mutual interest, particularly in such things as the school which was an item of great interest to all the villages and which was growing rapidly. The new constitution was also a major mutual interest. When a draft was presented, it was discussed in detail with the SERA members and the village leaders who took the draft back to their villages and discussed it with all their village members. Each village was able to call any of the SERA members to visit them if required to assist in the explanation. As a result of this a number of alterations were suggested, discussed at the next meeting of village leaders and a number of them were accepted. This was then the constitution proposed for the Association.

We required that this should be legally sound as the Association was becoming a fairly large organization, and on approaching the President's office we were directed to take our draft to the attorney general's office where, we were told, they would redraft it for us, taking any legal requirements into consideration. The attorney general passed us to Rahim, the man in charge of the drafting of parliamentary bills, with whom we had discussions. Rahim warned us that it might take some time as he was very short of capable people. He would, he said, do it himself, but it would have to wait as he was always very pressed with parliamentary work and having to do too much overtime. As a result of this we introduced the question at the end of one of the Regional Development Committee meetings in Songea, where all regional officers and political officials were present, and therefore more than the RDA Committee. We had found this the easiest way in rather difficult circumstances to get things discussed. Makinda, the regional administrative secretary, was in the chair on behalf of Walwa who was out of the region. This meeting ruled that from that date the RDA should operate as if the new constitution were registered.

We never got any further with the attorney general's office but not for want of trying. At one time Rahim told us that he had a new member on the staff, a man just arrived after receiving his degree at Makerere University in Uganda. In due course we received a copy of his proposals – a constitution which had no resemblance to anything whatsoever in the RDA. We took this back to Rahim who apologized and said we would have to leave it to him. On another occasion when calling on him he told us that he had not been well. His doctor had said he suspected the beginnings of a peptic ulcer and that he should give up smoking and overtime. Rahim said he could give up the overtime but not the smoking.

During 1965 also there was much discussion on the possibility of buying the grain and timber milling business in Songea, owned by an expatriate. If my memory serves me correctly the idea of some organization of villages purchasing this business was first suggested to us during one of my visits to Songea in 1962. The suggestion came from the co-operative officer in Songea at that time – Slaymaker. At that early stage it was obviously impossible, but by 1965 it was much discussed in the Association and in particular in relation to marketing.

Officialdom had put nearly all of their effort into the expansion of cash crops, while in the Association we had suggested to the villagers that their first effort should be put into food crops grown for a surplus which could either be sold or would enable the village to take on new members. This was one of the differences which caused friction. The Songea District cash crop was fire-cured tobacco and Litowa began to grow this crop in the rainy season which began at the end of 1961. They found that the crop was not very profitable, a lot of work and little return for it all. Tobacco realized only about a third of the price realized by farmers in areas where flue-cured tobacco was grown. Reasonable returns could be made in some areas where there was virgin land or particularly fertile soil, and this had apparently been the case around the Peramiho area in the 1920s when the crop was first introduced. As the population grew in the area and the initial fertility of the soil was used up, tobacco as a crop was dropped by the people. In the 1963/4 rains Litowa grew eight beautiful acres of tobacco by using an area of highly fertile valley soil, but these areas are particularly damp during the harvesting time, which produces a very high incidence of leaf spot diseases, very much reducing the price. On the higher lands fertilizer was essential and this was extremely expensive. Sulphate of ammonia – the one required – was a shilling a kilo.

On the other hand, the farmer was also getting very low prices for maize, the main food crop. The co-operatives had been given a monopoly in marketing the maize crop which, although it may have helped the farmer in that he avoided being cheated by the traders (undoubtedly often the case), it lowered the price which he actually received. The co-operatives in Songea were able to pay around 18 shillings per 200 lb bag of first-grade maize. On top of this they did not have the capital to be able to buy all of the maize, or the organization to collect from the primary societies all that they had bought. In some areas, therefore, people's surplus maize was never bought, and in others (because it was never collected one year and was left in the primary society storage depots) the following year's maize could not be purchased as there was no further storage space for it. On the other hand the price of maize flour to the consumer was high, being about 60 shillings for a 200 lb bag.

In the Association we felt that since a good part of our income would be put back into development, it was reasonable to ask that we might be exempted from having to market through the co-operatives and instead be allowed to build an organization where we could sell direct to the consumer. This was another of the questions which were put to the President on his visit and to which he agreed. Shortly after, we had word that he would like to help the Association. We were requested to prepare details of costs and amounts that we could raise from other sources showing what was still required. This of course we did.

In this period also there was introduced a new Interim Constitution for Tanzania. This meant new elections for the National Assembly. Ntimbanjayo felt he should put himself up for election as this would give us an entry into national affairs at a time when the meaning of *ujamaa* was being much discussed. We were not expecting elections so soon, but the change in the constitution had suddenly brought them about and, barring other such changes or unforeseen events, there were not to be other elections until 1970. The feeling in the villages was that Ntimbanjayo should go ahead. In such situations, while knowing that there was a need to be involved in the development discussion at national level, I always took the opportunity to express my view that it was absolutely essential to be firmly based where the people were with their down-to-earth struggles. Ntimbanjayo strongly agreed with this and felt that it was too soon for him to be completely involved at a national level and move away from the Association, but that his work as a member of parliament would allow him to remain with the people. He planned to remain living at Litowa. As a result of this he handed in his nomination papers for the Songea South constituency and was selected by the district TANU Committee as one of the two candidates to contest the election. At the last minute Mhagama, the leader of the Njoomlole village who had at the end of the previous year returned from the Kivukoni College course, announced that he would like to contest the Songea North constituency and hurriedly prepared and presented his nomination papers. He likewise was chosen as the other of the two candidates for that constituency and both were elected by the people.

There were during this time also a number of other events.

Ntimbanjayo had been a member of the President's party to China in February 1965.

The Association felt the need to train a few young men from the villages as mechanics to deal with repairs and maintenance. As a result we approached Voluntary Service Overseas (UK) who sent a mechanic volunteer to start the development of a workshop and the training of a small group.

The auxiliary bishop at Peramiho, James Komba, visited Litowa to say that they wished to help where possible as they saw that at Litowa there had developed a "higher morality" than elsewhere. He arranged for a priest to visit the village regularly and this was Stefan Mbunga, one of the priests teaching at the Senior Seminary and later to be the rector there.

The number of people visiting was on the increase. Our friends in Switzerland, through their new fund-raising organization, sent Hans Meyer, who stayed several weeks and saw a number of the member villages of the Association, taking back first-hand information. Donald Chesworth of War on Want paid a second visit. War on Want was also assisting through the bishop of Masasi, Trevor Huddleston, the Mahiwa Agricultural Training Centre and Donald pressed us to assist there when possible to give them the benefit of some of our experience.

To remind us that it was Africa, early one morning a woman was killed by a lion on the far side of Luhira Goliama across the river, and the Litowa men led a lion hunt, eventually tracking down and killing the offender.

To remind us that some things are the same the world over, our children had the measles, mumps and chicken pox in rather quick succession.

At about the same time as the elections, Walwa organized a regional conference which was supposedly to decide what type of settlement the region required. We were asked to participate but were tipped off by one of the regional departmental heads that it was planned to use this conference to say that the RDA type of settlement was not wanted. (This is reported more fully later.) Very soon after this Walwa was posted away to Bukoba.

5

EDWARD BARONGO VS THE RDA

Edward Barongo's arrival as regional commissioner in Ruvuma towards the end of 1965 was to begin the longest period we had with any one person in that post. He was not to leave until April 1968 when he was posted to the Morogoro Region for a short while, after which he was dismissed from the service. He was to become a bitter enemy of the Association. By the time he arrived in Songea, opposition to the Association villages was considerable and we discussed very seriously our approach to the new commissioner. It was not possible in the situation then existing in Tanzania to retire into the village and go quietly on. This meant that an attempt to explain fully the Association to the regional leadership was essential, with if anything more determination rather than less. We decided that I should not take part in this; it would be done primarily by Ntimbanjayo but where necessary also by other leaders of the Association. Quite apart from the political reasons for this, it was practical as there was increasing work to do, particularly in view of the growing interest in the Association which brought an increasing number of visitors, increased correspondence and such unsought-for jobs as preparing papers for meetings and conferences.

I met Barongo and asked if he would accept my not attending Regional Development Committee meetings and resigning as treasurer of the Regional Development Fund. I had also been a co-opted member of the Songea district council since just after the 1964 council elections, but with a change in the working of the council, new elections were to be held, so that my council membership automatically ceased with that of the oth-

ers. I explained the increasing workload and Barongo said that
he would accept this if I felt it was a correct move. Although
the Regional Development Fund had not been operating a full
year, I undertook to produce an income and expenditure account before resigning. This was relatively simple as the executive officer of the council had recorded items rather well, which
was fortunate as he had at that time been moved from Songea
and was not available to answer queries. There was, however,
one large irregularity. The previous regional commissioner had
sent 10,000 shillings of the fund to the TANU party headquarters in Dar es Salaam in payment of fees due to be collected, no
doubt creating an impression in Dar es Salaam of efficiency in
his post as regional secretary of the party. I cannot imagine that
this money was ever made up to the fund. However, everything
was handed over quite amicably.

In Ntimbanjayo's relations with Barongo also, things went
well in the initial stages. Barongo at one meeting told him that
others had reported that he should beware of Ntimbanjayo but
that he had studied the question, looked at the files and saw
nothing to justify what people had told him. This amicable beginning was not to last and Barongo came to be at loggerheads
both with the Association and with Ntimbanjayo. The details of
this are described later.

In the first part of 1964, Songea district council had passed
a regulation making the growing of fire-cured tobacco compulsory for all farmers with the exception of those in the higher
northern parts where the climate put it out of the question. In
the beginning of the sixties this tobacco production had been
dropping rapidly. There were probably several reasons for this.
It was not a very profitable crop requiring much labour, and
many farmers who had taken up its production in the early
years of the co-operatives when a month's work with traders or
missionaries only brought in a few shillings, were now getting
too old to farm, while the rising generation felt it an unreward-

ing crop. In many areas the soil was being worked out; tobacco produced on such soil was generally in the fourth grade which only brought in a few pence a kilo. With rising costs of sorting, grading and preparing for shipment in the co-operative factory, by the end there was very little payment and sometimes nothing at all. With the compulsion of regional regulation, the yields began to rise and were to reach record proportions. Barongo put as one of his major tasks the enforcement of this compulsory regulation. Quite apart from the friction it caused in our case in particular, this was at a time when the RDA villages were beginning to question whether it was a crop worth growing, and since they were organized communities, they gave a voice to this questioning. It also seemed to me that it made a much greater rift between government and people generally. For us it was a time when very few new groups of people were coming together. This was in no way worrying to us as we had plenty to do with the existing villages but it meant that individual farmers were not willing to join existing villages. We would have welcomed additional people in many of the villages to enable growth to be faster.

The finance committee of the Songea district council had been in the habit of allocating funds every year in the budget to be used in grants to self-help projects. This was generally never used but in 1961 Litowa had had a small loan which by this time had been paid back. Matetereka had received a grant of corrugated iron sheet for a store hut. The people always hoped for development money from their own government, district council and party, but what came was negligible. Towards the end of his time as chairman of the district council, Ntimbanjayo tried to rectify this a little, believing that it would increase confidence all round. The council agreed to a sum of 10,000 shillings being given for various projects in a number of the Association's villages. This never came. Walwa's extravagance with his fund had increased the difficulties of the council so that the money was just not available.

Offers of assistance, however, were coming from other sources at this time. War on Want's financial aid went on steadily, mostly in the continued support of myself and family but also with other items. Oxfam showed not only a continuing, but an increased interest. Jimmy Betts again visited in December 1965 and was at Litowa on the day that the first water came through the pipes; this was the installation for which Oxfam had provided the money for materials. He also accepted, and recommended to Oxfam, the idea of a mobile workshop for the Association; we would begin to train four sons of the village who were standard VIII leavers to be able to care for and repair the machines of the Association and the villages. The arrival of a volunteer mechanic through Voluntary Service Overseas has already been mentioned; and when the grant from Oxfam arrived early in 1966, he was able to start this work, putting plans into effect with a minimum of delay. Our friends in Switzerland, through their organization FEPA were also providing help, at this time towards the purchase of the Songea milling business. They were in consultation with War on Want over this.

The Volunteer Teachers for Africa (VTA), an organization of students of Harvard University in the United States, approached the Association asking if they could send volunteers, particularly girls, to work with and assist the women in the villages. We arranged that one of their volunteers who was teaching at the Kurasini secondary school for refugee children in Dar es Salaam, should spend the last half of her year at Litowa to see how things went. If successful, on returning to Harvard she would be able to help arrange what support their organization could provide in the future. Shortly after this we were also approached by the American Friends Service Committee (AFSC) who had a volunteer service in Tanzania. We agreed to investigate whether they could be useful when their next group of volunteers arrived, which would not be until toward the end of 1966.

Peter Wiesmann, a member of the Swiss government Department for Technical Co-operation, also visited us at Litowa during a study tour of projects with which his department was involved and of projects which they might be able to assist in the future. Shortly after he returned to Switzerland he wrote suggesting that they might provide an agricultural extension expert. This was agreed to by the Ministry of Agriculture in Dar es Salaam and the plan went forward.

In the middle of January 1966, Barongo paid his first visit to Litowa as regional commissioner. He came to present a cheque for 90,000 shillings to the Association from President Nyerere. This was what we still needed for the purchase of the flour milling business, the amount he had asked for during his visit which we had shown him on our account. The regional commissioner did not take this opportunity to see the village and the village farm, merely coming in, giving a short speech and handing over the cheque. The people were disappointed but at that time we did not know whether it was done deliberately or whether he really felt he had to leave before a gathering storm broke. He had come in his Mercedes, not a government Land Rover, and the steep road out of the Luhira valley could be difficult after heavy rain. Whatever there was of disappointment over this was as nothing compared to the feeling given to the people by the President's personal gift: it was no small thing and showed that his interest in what the people were doing was real. We had during our discussion with the attorney general's office already made arrangements for this purchase and carried out all that we were told was necessary on the legal side. There were thus three trustees appointed by the Association to sign all legal documents on its behalf. These were the Secretary of the Ngoni-Natongo Co-operative Union in Songea, the secretary of the Credit Union at Peramiho, and Ntimbanjayo. The Association was then able to complete the mill takeover almost immediately.

The provision of education meant so much to the villagers. Their interest in this sphere grew as they began very early to see that their first efforts in trying to make the school integral to the work and ideas of the villagers appeared to be having a good effect on the children, giving them a tangible feeling of being part of the whole enterprise. The emphasis in the country generally was at that time on secondary education. The district councils, which were responsible for primary education, were enormously hard-up for money, and it seemed that it might be difficult to obtain authority to carry the children's education beyond the lower primary. Standard IV, the last of the lower primary classes, was started in January of 1966. It shows something of the interest in education that with people not accustomed to thinking much beyond the immediate future, the Association was already discussing the problem of opening standard V which was then a whole year away. As a result Ntimbanjayo, when in Dar es Salaam, met Minister for Education Eliufoo, from whom he found out that there would be no difficulty in going on; the President had already spoken to the minister about it. It was the President's wish, and although there were cases of attempts to sabotage, or perhaps to just neglect, in our dealings on these matters with the Ministry of Education in Dar es Salaam, the President's wishes were respected and finally influenced the education office in Songea. It was at this time that Grace Chips, who originally came as a community development assistant, started teaching in the school.

There were also a number of calls on us for assistance or to take part in seminars and so forth.

Bishop Trevor Huddleston at Masasi was pressing that we should visit the Agricultural and Co-operative Training Centre that he had been instrumental in getting going at Mahiwa. This request was backed by War on Want which had provided the funds for the centre. We made a visit towards the end of 1965 and were to make a number of other visits, but it was not possible in these short visits to do or say anything that can be of much effect. A new trend in the teaching in such a college depends on the attitude and ideas of the staff, and introducing new attitudes and ideas needs a principal with such ideas who can patiently get them over to his or her staff.

Near Peramiho, one of the elder Tanzanian priests was trying to get a group of standard VIII leavers engaged in agriculture. He came to us for advice. Although our advice was that this type of project can hardly succeed – made up as it was of young men at a most unstable time in their lives – a number of our people much wanted to help him. There seemed very few cases where there was a genuine respect for any of their priests over and above a respect for their position, but the people said that in his case their interest was real. After his first rather difficult year with this group his bishop moved him to another parish.

Ntimbanjayo and I were invited to a four-day seminar at the University College of Dar es Salaam organized jointly by the university and a group from Syracuse University, New York, who were doing research into the large, high capital settlements of the Village Settlement Commission. All expenses being paid, we went. The opening speech was given by Second Vice-President Kawawa who used the opportunity to announce that the government was giving up its present settlement policy – it was clearly failing – and was to rethink the line of action. However, it was not only these which were failing; we also learnt while at the seminar that the Rural Settlement Agency had a list of over 400 self-help settlements which had failed. This 400 was probably only part of a total of failures.

Jimmy Betts, the Oxfam representative, wrote suggesting that we write on our possible future developments to discuss in Dar es Salaam in June with both him and Michael Harris, Oxfam's Secretary for Africa, coming out from their headquarters in Oxford. He particularly asked if we thought we could do any training with a view to spreading the RDA methods to other parts, with Oxfam paying costs.

Some of these happenings were useful – for instance, the small leadership training project we were enabled to carry out with Oxfam money.

It was also valuable experience for Ntimbanjayo to meet the academics at the university and, seeing it all from the light of his practical experience, to lose any improper respect that he may have had for the circles of high learning in relation to what they might be able to do for the peasant poor. In my view, the most telling remark of the whole seminar was made by Ntimbanjayo when talking to them of the RDA: "One of the things we have learnt in the RDA", he said, "is patience."

At this time we were in fact just able to cope with the number of villages, the growing organization of the Association and its developing business side, but outside activities were quite an extra strain. Although we generally went into them under protest, I feel now in the light of experience that we would have often done better to have stayed in the villages, as outside calls on our time were later to increase and to cause a very definite holding back of development. It was not only the time taken to attend such conferences and so on, but also that as a result of them many people began to visit Ruvuma to see the Association, particularly in the second half of 1966. I resigned myself to spending much time acting as a shield for the people, taking the burden of visitors. It was a pleasant burden; nevertheless I might have been better occupied doing other things as far as the villagers' interests were concerned.

This takes us to the middle of 1966 when work in the villages was going very well. Litowa, the oldest of the villages, felt able to start work on more permanent houses for its members. The first plots on the permanent site of the village were marked out and building began. Before the end of the year the first one or two families moved into larger and better houses of entirely local materials. Ntimbanjayo approached the village authorities for permission to build his own house in the new village site.

This being given, he and his family built with their own labour a pole-and-mud-walled, thatched house. There were those in Songea (not in the villages) who criticized him strongly for this, suggesting that now that he was a member of parliament the sensible thing was to build a good permanent town house in Songea.

At the same time, in the discussions of the Association, it was decided that it was time to start planning permanent buildings for the school. All the villages sent one or two members to Litowa where together they moulded and burnt bricks under the guidance of one of the Liweta members who had had experience of this work. This was so that in the following dry season they would be able to start building the first classrooms.

Also in the middle of this year a few expatriates arrived to help the villagers. The arrangements with the Swiss Technical Co-operation produced Roger Pasquier who, with a background of small farming in a Swiss village before his university training, was able to do a very useful job in agricultural education through the work of the villagers. The Harvard group produced Jill Weisell who worked very effectively with the women and children at Matetereka; and Kate Wenner who did the same at Litowa with great energy and wrote an interesting account of her experiences in her book *Shamba Letu*.[1] A few months later four members of the American Friends Service Committee arrived, two of whom stayed for two years to do useful work: Ann Mullin who did similar work to the Harvard volunteers at the Liweta and Nalunya villages, and Keith Stickford. Keith worked for a time in the villages by Lake Nyasa close to the border with Mozambique, until the frontier situation made it politically necessary for him to be called away.

The development of what we were to call the leadership training centre at Litowa was perhaps the point of most discussion at that time. We had talked a little around this question sev-

---

1   See Further Reading.

eral times in the past, partly because we felt there would be a greater security for these villages if there were others like them in other parts of Tanzania, and also because quite a number of visitors asked whether the methods of the RDA could be used elsewhere or whether perhaps there were special conditions which made their application possible only in Ruvuma.

As there were considerable differences in climate, crops and tribal backgrounds in such RDA villages as Chimate, Litowa, Matetereka and Ligoma, it seemed to us that, although these methods may not be applicable everywhere, they would certainly be possible in many places. The suggestion by Jimmy Betts that we might think more about this, led to further discussion at the Association's quarterly meeting. Again, despite realizing that we were short of human resources to deal with this, the meeting felt that an attempt should be made. There was considerable worry in certain quarters about the Association engaging in such a project, but as always moves were only made after Ntimbanjayo had ascertained that it would be acceptable in high places. The Association, in this training, was really acting on behalf of the TANU Youth League which accepted the idea and carried out the necessary work of recruiting the trainees and directing them to Litowa.

We planned to get away from classroom teaching as with such methods it would have been difficult to convey what we felt was necessary, that is, a vision of what it is possible for a group of peasant farmers to build up from very little if they had learned to co-operate, and the spirit needed to help them achieve this vision. Trainees were to be selected from self-help settlements around Tanzania which were struggling to exist. Only a grass hut and latrine pits would be provided before they arrived, so that discussions with them would then take place in the same sort of conditions in which their own settlements had started and from which they had had to struggle. Much of their time would be spent working in different villages of the Association, to see and feel the village organizations, the various problems of the people and the methods they used to overcome them. The Association gave the work of organizing the trainees to Ngairo and Bwanaliko. The latter had also been appointed to work with the Swiss agriculturalist Pasquier. He was to concentrate particularly on agriculture so that the Association would in future have its own expert. There would, however, be a certain number of lectures organized for the trainees with a great emphasis on agriculture.

There was discussion at this time in government and party circles about their future policy on rural settlements after the abandonment of the previous policy. We were invited to take part in a conference in September that Kivukoni College was organizing and which Oxfam financed. The purpose of the conference was that we should discuss our experience of settlements in Ruvuma with others while certain members of government and party were sitting in so that it could be part of the process of their rethinking a policy. I don't think much of this happened. The party sent a number of members who participated, but government – represented by the Settlement Commission and the Ministry of Settlements – sent only expatriates on their staff, which was hardly a sign of taking things seriously. Shortly after this the Research and Documentation Department of TANU wrote asking for copies of any writings we had on RDA; in our reply we suggested they send one of their staff to gather information for the party, but this suggestion did not produce a response.

Towards the end of 1966 the regional commissioner visited together with the minister for settlements and we felt strongly that both had agreed that they did not like the RDA type of village. Opposition became stronger and more public.

Shortly after this, just before Christmas, President Nyerere again visited. He had stated again that he wished to visit Litowa and again it was left off the programme, leaving it to him to insist that he was going there. Before he reached Litowa he was "told about it" by officials. One of the stories was apparently that the Litowa people did not follow the instructions of the agricultural office. On arrival in the tobacco field, where the seedlings had been recently planted out, he asked the regional agricultural officer what the correct spacing was between plants and between rows, and when told, checked the measurements himself. With this and other things, he drew from the officer the reluctant admission that everything was correctly done. Ntimbanjayo, who was in the same Land Rover as the President, told us that while driving back across the Litowa valley which was planted with maize, at that time about knee-high, Nyerere had said that he didn't know if the maize was planted properly but it looked good to him. We later learned that he had had a meeting with the government officers in Songea and heard all their complaints. It had always been a sore point that our villages would not put enough emphasis on tobacco and we felt that it was good that he said to these officers that Litowa had built a stable community because they thought first of feeding the people, while at the Mlale government settlement this was forgotten. None of this appeared to have any effect on officialdom. Opposition from this time was very strong and quite open.

There was in this last part of the year a crescendo of visitors. Different people see different things. The Israeli ambassador and his first secretary seemed impressed by what they saw on their first day at Litowa, and yet it was not until they visited Liweta on the second day and were also impressed that they realized that the achievements were those of the people themselves.[2] There was no expatriate at Liweta. Without visiting Li-

2   In the 1960s Israel was known internationally for the *kibbutz*, a form of rural commune. Tanzania had recognized the State of Israel but after its 1967 war against Egypt, Jordan and Syria, President Nyerere condemned Israel: *"The establishment of the state of Israel was an act of aggression against the Arab people . . . the United Nations which sanctioned her birth is, must be, unalterably opposed to territorial agrandissement by force or threat of force . . . We cannot condone aggression on any pretext, nor accept victory in war as a justification for the exploitation of other lands, or govern-*

weta they might never have realized that the people of Litowa completely managed their own affairs, assuming that I managed things. It was for this reason that we always preferred those visitors who were prepared to stay a while and walk around and talk with the people. The report on Liweta in Chapter 1 by Jim Brain was written after such a stay.

Again, Harold Miller, the secretary for relief and service of the Christian Council, could feel that people were ready to talk, that they had a good knowledge of what they were doing and that what individuals said showed that they discussed much together. On the other hand there were those who saw nothing: the US ambassador who had a cup of tea in the kitchen but could not be bothered to walk around the village, and whose biggest impression seemed to be one of shock that an American volunteer (Kate Wenner) wore no shoes and had dirty feet.

The early part of 1967 saw the Arusha Declaration followed by the nationalization of the banks and of a number of major industries. The TANU party stated its policy of socialism and in the following year in the Ruvuma Region, a group of villages trying to express the party's policy of socialism in practice met steadily increasing opposition from the local party leaders. Nevertheless work went steadily on.

January 1967 saw the beginning of the upper primary section in the Litowa school but also the arrival of Suleiman Toroka, to teach in the new standard V. In Dar es Salaam, Ntimbanjayo had found Toroka – or perhaps Toroka had found Ntimbanjayo. Whichever way it was, Toroka, who was a student in the Changombe Teacher Training College in Dar es Salaam, was one of those people looking for something a little more adventurous than a teacher's routine existence. During the last college vacation in 1966 he came to see what the Litowa school was like.

---

ment over other peoples." Policy on Foreign Affairs, *Freedom and Socialism*, pp 371-2.

By 1973, many African governments had broken relations with Israel, including Tanzania. It expelled its ambassador, cancelled all Israeli development programmes, and allowed the Palestine Liberation Organization to open an embassy in Dar es Salaam.

Very quickly he understood what the people wanted with their school and the possibilities it created. He wanted to come; the RDA wanted him. Ntimbanjayo approached the Ministry of Education which agreed that he should come to Litowa. We then heard after the teacher training course finished in December that he had been posted to the coastal region. Again Ntimbanjayo went to the ministry, and we got Toroka. He did much for the RDA school.

The President on his visits had singled out the school as of special interest in Litowa, and in the middle of January 1967 he sent his personal assistant to study the ideas and practices of the school to help provide material for his policy paper, Education for Self-Reliance,[3] which was published in March. This publication started much discussion in the educational world in Tanzania and inspired many innovations in many primary schools, particularly in introducing agricultural work – rather sadly, generally by teachers with little understanding of their implications, so that they would not have had their full possible effect on the children.

The work of mechanical training went on with the arrival of a first-class mechanic from Switzerland who went to live at Liweta, where the Association workshop was now based, with his wife who was to work with the women there. Our previous VSO mechanic had completed his term and returned to England. The new people, Armin and Krista Schriber, were on a two-year contract.

At this time also Ntimbanjayo went on a tour of Israel at the invitation of the Israeli government. Our Area Commissioner Chilumba was moved from Songea to the Mbinga District, still within the Ruvuma Region. In Songea we were given Mhagama whom we already knew as he had been area commissioner in Mbinga. To remind us of the ever present vagaries of life, in April unusually heavy rains for so late in the rainy season lifted

3   *Freedom and Socialism*, p 267.

the top off the Litowa bridge and floated it downstream, causing a little inconvenience until the river's water level fell enough to make repair work possible.

With the coming of the dry season in May, the first group of trainees, who had arrived in November, came to the end of their course and went back to their own settlements.

Also towards the end of the rains, our family left our grass hut in the original village, which then became the village dispensary and sick room, and moved into our new house in the new village. The new building had no doors as yet and there were many items to be completed, but we were to go on leave to England and wished to move everything before we went. The last months had been rather difficult for me as a series of illnesses had caused what I was told when I got to England was peripheral neuritis. We had planned on three months away but it was four months before the UK National Health Service pronounced me fit to return.

One of the last things before we left was to prepare the plans for the first brick classrooms. The school children had cleared the site. I set out the foundations with Ado Mgimba and the children dug them. When we returned in the first week of October they were beginning the roofing. We had no really expert bricklayers but they collected from the villages those with some experience, and employed one competent builder to organize these and teach them a little further. This produced a very satisfactory result.

We had now raised overseas nearly enough money to purchase the sawmill, and in preparation for the takeover the Association started felling trees and carting them to Songea to have a supply with which to start operations. Arrangements were also started to purchase on an instalment basis, a Fordson tractor and six-ton trailer for the log-carrying work. We considered this would be less expensive to run on this rough type of work and easier for our mechanics to maintain.

While this work was proceeding two other important things were happening. Ntimbanjayo had been asked to accept the post of assistant secretary in the TANU Youth League headquarters in Dar es Salaam, with a view to spreading the *ujamaa* settlements in Tanzania. There was increasing discussion on village *ujamaa* and he felt both that it was necessary for him to accept and that the Association was strong enough for him to move away. His post would automatically keep him in touch with the Association and the villages, as would the fact that he was a member of the legislative assembly representing part of the area. At the same time, Regional Commissioner Barongo's campaign against Ntimbanjayo and the Association was building up and in September, while we were still in England, he made a strong move to destroy Ntimbanjayo and the Association. This was extremely important as it showed the strength of the villagers. Barongo called all the RDA village managers to a regional party meeting in Songea, and in front of them tried to discredit Ntimbanjayo by suggesting to the leaders that he was using the villages for his own benefit.

I don't think any of the political and government leaders ever understood the relationship of Ntimbanjayo with the villagers as his methods were so different from theirs. He stayed with them, worked with them, attended their meetings, explained to them his visions, encouraged them, explained what a hard path they had to tread, pointed out their errors. Barongo's methods were bound to fail; to the villagers Ntimbanjayo was not an outsider, he was one of them. Faced with this attack, the managers one after the other with varying degrees of directness told Barongo to mind his own business.

A couple of days after this meeting, another policy paper of President Nyerere was published – Socialism and Rural Development.[4] This called for the establishment of *ujamaa* communities, and stated towards the end that "the experience of existing *ujamaa* villages, such as those now operating within the Ruvuma

---

4   *Freedom and Socialism*, p 337.

Development Association, could be helpful and the Ministry of Local Government and Rural Development should try to make this experience available to people from different parts." In his official position, Barongo had publicly to explain this paper to the people.

Ntimbanjayo, because of his Dar es Salaam appointment, planned to hand in his resignation as chairman of the RDA at the next general meeting for which he would come back to Songea. During these preceding months Ngairo had been very active in the work of the Association and to very good effect, but I felt a short while after coming back from leave that he had a tendency to take too much onto himself. There are situations when this is a good thing in order to get things done. In a developing situation as in the Association I did not feel that this was the right course, as what would be possible in the future depended so much on the number of people prepared to take responsibility, and how much they had learnt about life through taking responsibility. What produced the quickest immediate material results was not always the correct course. This was in fact one of the points of the Arusha Declaration, that it is easy enough to get particular things done if you have the money, but in a poor country to follow this way limits what is possible in the long run. As adviser I felt it necessary to point this out and as we had built up a "tradition" of frankly discussing problems this was quite easy, although I felt for some little time after that Ngairo thought I was rather hard on him in these judgements.

When the quarterly meeting of the Association came, Ngairo was elected as the new chairman of the RDA and Wayakile as the vice-chairman. This surprised me a little as I would have expected it to be the other way round. Ngairo had to a degree come in by the back door; all the other leaders, bar one, had come through the villages and the villagers tended to hold a great store by people coming in the right way. This was not altogether Ngairo's fault. He had attempted to found a village which they called Furaha with some of the men from his home area but two things prevented it succeeding: criticism and pressure from his family stopped him from moving in with the group, and he was not in fact very strong physically. The experience was useful and when he did eventually take the decision to leave his home area it was to Litowa that he came with his wife and children but not as a village member, as he was asked by the Association to look after the leadership training centre. He was used to operating in the political sphere and was unafraid, and it was mainly for this reason I think that the villagers elected him. Faced with a political struggle they chose a political type. I think Ngairo was genuinely surprised at his election and in the first stages as chairman made a very great attempt to operate in the traditional way of the Association of handing on responsibility. The fact that later he again took too much onto himself was partly that it was in his character to do this, but again I do not think it was entirely his fault – it was at a time that much of what happened was no longer in the hands of the people of the Association and was happening through decisions from above. As a result he as chairman was under considerable stress.

The other member of the Association who had come in through the back door was Aidan Mapunda who was at the same meeting elected as secretary. He had spent much time in town and had learnt many of the undisciplined ways of the town but he had a very quick and true understanding of the Association's objects and methods. He was also quite fearless and very tough. A person to whom you could always talk straight.

It seemed to us at that time that with the publication of "Socialism and Rural Development", opposition to the Association increased rather than decreased. We were then in the last months of 1967 and the first few months of 1968, the end of the time with Barongo. The battle went on to the very end of his time in Ruvuma, in April. The district schools inspector was asked to visit and make a bad report on the Litowa school. It was along the lines that we were not following what the official handbook said we should be following. We had support from the education officer for primary schools, JEF Mhina, at one time headmaster of the secondary school in Songea. Because of this I was asked to write to him and find out if he could pay an official visit to Songea to try and put the education office there on the right lines. This he did very successfully in November.

In December the Region was declared a restricted area as it bordered onto Portuguese East Africa. In the first weeks after this declaration we had visitors arriving at the RDA without the necessary permits, notice of the change not having been very well advertised. The airways in Dar es Salaam for instance seemed not to know, and consequently did not inform passengers on this route of the necessity for a permit before issuing them with tickets. The regional commissioner used this to prevent visits to us. In the case of two of such visitors at any rate, he should have used his special powers to allow them to carry out the purpose of their visits. Freddie Wood of the Commonwealth Secretariat was in a sense a Tanzanian official. His visit to us was arranged before he left the UK and agreed to by the Tanzanian government. Salvi of the Swiss Technical Co-operation was visiting the work of Roger Pasquier, seconded to us by the Ministry of Agriculture. Both were refused permission to visit and had to stay, one in Songea and the other in Peramiho, until the next plane out.

However, there appeared to be a break in the opposition early in 1968 when, quite unexpectedly, we began to receive peaceful overtures from the Area and Regional Offices. The area commissioner asked me to discuss with him our ideas on development and after the discussions asked that I should write these ideas down for him. There had been another reorganization of government ministries and out of this had come the new Ministry of Regional Administration and Rural Development. The President held this portfolio but a new man, Peter Kisumo, as minister of state, did the work of minister for him. The President had been pressing more and more for an emphasis on rural development, and we learned that Kisumo had been told to go and visit the RDA. This impending visit had been the reason it seemed for the friendly overtures but in the Association we were happy to be able to talk and express our views. Kisumo was to visit Litowa and Liweta, and the chairman of the Association asked if the minister would meet the leaders of the Association for discussions, and this he did. It was felt better that I should not attend this meeting but I saw Kisumo separately for a two-hour discussion as it was also felt that, because of my existence within the Association, he should be given the chance to meet me. There were a number of other officials with the minister including Makame, the new regional rural development officer – the title for what used to be the community development officer.

Official visitors at this time began to say that they had come to see the RDA villages to learn from the people. There seemed to us in the case of Kisumo a difference between his saying this and the way he conducted himself. In spite of a very critical approach all the way through his visits and meetings, he did say that he had seen something new and this he described as "pure socialism". He also in our presence instructed Makame to give the Association every assistance. Nothing came of this and soon after opposition seemed stronger than ever. While official emphasis was on people working together, two of the villages reported officials visiting them and telling them that they should not cultivate together. No regional funds became available to help the villages.

There were things happening behind the scenes helpful to the Association. We received a letter from the Ministry of Agriculture notifying us that they had been appointed by government to act on our behalf through assistance in the provision of technical help from overseas. It was an extremely good letter stressing that their role was only to assist and in no way to take the initiative from the people. Unfortunately this very promising move came to nothing. After the first very encouraging exchange of letters there were staff changes in the relevant department of the ministry, after which we never received answers to our correspondence.

Another item on the sidelines which encouraged our people was the dismissal by the party headquarters of our district TANU chairman. If the local hierarchy continued to keep such a dishonest person in his position, it was good to see that at the headquarters another view was taken. This gentleman, Mustafa, had been ordered to Dar es Salaam to be told the news. On his way back to Songea whilst in Lindi he was arrested on a charge of obtaining money on false pretences and was subsequently tried and convicted, thus ending in jail where he would have been many times before but for his position.

The rainy season that year was a difficult one. The first maize plantings at Litowa were made as usual in the valleys where there was exceedingly fertile soil. In most seasons these later became very wet but by that time and because of early planting, the maize had its roots well down and, apart from a greater task in weed control on these soils, the crop was good. This season, instead of the rain starting with the usual isolated showers and dry spells in between up to the end of December, from the first the rain continued almost every day, flooding the valleys and washing away the maize seedlings. Higher land earmarked for other crops had then to be planted to maize, but having been planted later it did not produce comparable yields. The years of very heavy and continuous early rains are always difficult ones, giving poorer crops. Throughout the season there were heavy rains in many parts of the country so that often the airfields were too wet for planes to land and take off, considerably delaying the mail. This was made worse for a time when one of the bank seats of the bridge on the Great Ruhaha river between Iringa and Nikumi was washed away, cutting out the only wet season road from Dar es Salaam to the Ruvuma Region.

A number of the villages in discussion with the Association and Pasquier, the Swiss agriculturalist, were starting to keep livestock, wholly or partly financed to begin with by Swiss Technical Co-operation. Matetereka started a small flock of wool sheep and a small herd of general purpose cattle. Liweta started a herd of beef cattle, and Litowa dairy cattle.

The Association had also agreed to try and help with the education of the students in the Mahiwa Agricultural and Co-operative Training College, and all their second year students came to our villages for six weeks, accompanied by a number of their staff members.

Before the rains ended soon after the start of April we heard that Barongo was to leave.

6

THE PARTY DESTROYS THE RDA

From the time Barongo left as regional commissioner in April 1968 until the disbanding of the Association in September 1969, there were two different regional commissioners. In the first place Kapilima and then for the last few months Mwakaia, who is still in the position at the time of writing. As far as the Association was concerned, they were of lesser importance than the previous holders of this post, as Nyerere was more and more pushing *ujamaa* as a national issue and was using the villages of the Association as a training ground for people from other parts of Tanzania. Thus national politicians and officials became involved, rather than only regional and district ones.

Throughout this last eighteen months, as in the times before, the villagers were primarily concerned with getting on with their work. The results of this steady continuing development were beginning to be quite impressive, and even those with little time for the ideas of the villagers and their Association had sometimes to admit that they were getting somewhere. Such a one was Kapilima, the next regional commissioner, a man with more formal education than any of our previous commissioners and one whom we never saw smile. He was engaged in a number of works against the Association and had been in office for eight months before he ever visited Litowa. After touring the village and farm he told the people that he was impressed, that he had that day seen things which had been done by peasants which he had assumed before could only be done by experts. This was of course what the Association was about: the rural population themselves organizing and carrying out their own plans is rural development. There was no noticeable change in Kapilima's attitude after this.

As well as Litowa, the other older villages, Matetereka and Liweta, were making a beginning on more permanent buildings. Both of these began brick-making in the dry season of 1968 and both went in first for storage buildings for the village. Matetereka was assisted by the regional development fund but at Liweta the effort in all aspects of the building – design, construction, financing – was very much a village enterprise. Assistance was needed but the initiative for getting this was from the village. Both of these villages also started to install piped water supplies and more permanent housing. The development of agriculture was progressing well with a steady learning on the part of management. All had a feeling of stability so that minor upsets no longer worried people – they were events of the day rather than threats to the life and future of a village.

There were stable villages following some way behind such as Nalunya, Njaramatata, Chimate and Mtakanini in Unyanja, about which one was not worried. In regular contact from year to year, one was not always conscious of their progress but in fact even Chimate – made up of lakeside fishermen who, with their fish and cassava to keep life going, traditionally took things fairly easily – had come a long way. Because of their position by the lake, with troubles on the Mozambique border, and frictions with President Hastings Banda of Malawi over the water, it was not politic for me as an expatriate to be in those parts. When towards the end of 1968 I did go again, I was impressed and found much more a sense and look of stability than I had expected.

There were two classes of village at this time which needed a lot of attention. First, Ligoma (this was the other Mtakanini) and Mhepai were suffering from internal personal worries. Second, a number of new villages which were starting and had applied for membership of the Association. Neither of these things was in itself a worry as it was all in the course of the work of the

Association, but a number of events put a great strain on the Association's resources in this last period, causing it to be unable adequately to help these villages. It was important that with all the worries, strains and excitements of the time, the need to help these villages and the awareness that it was basically the most important work, was always strongly in evidence and never contested. While many of these difficulties were sorted out, in the last few months of the Association's life when all the political junketing was taking place, the leadership was working hard again in the villages where they were needed. The Association judged in terms of its main purpose was a live and very vital organization at the time of its demise.

The difficulties that began in the middle of 1968 were many. To begin with, the Association had chosen the wrong chairman. Ngairo had many good points, was committed to the ideas of the villages and did much good work, particularly on the material side, in organising the most rapid development of the school buildings, and was politically unafraid. His tendency to want to control everything came, I think, from a certain unsureness in him which made it difficult for him to deal with the stronger and more useful leaders of the Association – people like Toroka in the school and Wayakile, the vice-chairman of the Association. In July the executive committee decided to help the Mahiwa Agricultural and Co-operative Training College by sending a man to care for their second year students who were to start a more practical training at Chipite. This was a few miles from Mahiwa in simple living conditions, with the students themselves organizing their work and managing it. At the time, many people connected with Mahiwa were pressing us to help; and in particular Bill Thomas, the principal, had asked for help when he had stayed a while at Litowa while his students were with us early in the year. Nevertheless, the decision to send Wayakile for a year worried me as he was one of the few who might be available at the time for travelling around to help villages. Against this, I remember feeling that for him to work for a year in a situation outside the Association and with agricultural officers, who were the staff of the school, would be a useful experience that might be of help in the long run. We were not to have a long run, but rural development is a long-term business, and at all times should be faced as such, even when people are making generalized statements about the world only having ten years to deal with the problems of world poverty before we are overtaken by catastrophe. I think there is a possibility that the sending of Wayakile to Chipite was pushed a little by Ngairo as he probably felt happier working without Wayakile around. Wayakile had had much practical experience in the villages, and although a quiet serious person, had great strength and determination when he took up an issue.

At the same time Toroka had to be doing his five months National Service. This put a great stain on the school. Not only was he acting headmaster but he was more than any other among the staff, with exception perhaps of Grace Chips whom he had now married, the one who had the understanding of what the villages of the Association were trying to achieve for their children and how they were trying to achieve it. At the same time I discussed with the leaders of the Association the possibility of trying to get him excused from his National Service but all assured me that it would not be a good thing even to try; it would have seemed like blasphemy. When he did return, authority would not let him alone to carry on with his work. The Ministry of Education placed him on a panel to discuss the primary curriculum. This was good in that a ministry was prepared to use an exceptional young man who was less than two years out of training college, but again it took him away from working out new patterns of primary education in practice. This was not the only thing to take him away. He was later called to political seminars to take part in the education of the party leadership for which the President was pushing.

Amon Mapunda, another young grade A teacher we had from the Changombe Training College, also had to do his five months National Service when Toroka returned. It was hard to see that Toroka had gained anything from his National Service experience except perhaps to increase his enthusiasm for his work with the schoolchildren, helping them to grow up as thinking and responsible members of a community. His main impression of National Service seemed to me summed up in what he once told me, that the officers and NCOs looked upon those coming through for training as so many stones.

We also lost for a considerable amount of time the work of Bwanaliko, the man who worked primarily on the agricultural side and with our Swiss agriculturalists, gaining knowledge on livestock in particular. He went down with TB and had not fully recovered when the Association was banned.

Even with our family we had extra strains. Living a simple life in simple conditions in a tropical village is very pleasant but continuous work, and Noreen in particular had to be constantly active keeping the household going as well as giving an English education to three of our four children, dealing with many visitors, teaching spinning and weaving and so on. As a consequence of this workload, we had to send her away for a holiday at the end of September, and even on her return she became easily tired. This was no wonder; rather it was a wonder that it hadn't happened earlier.

Officialdom then began to attack the business enterprises of the Association. First it was the grain-milling business, taking away government contracts for maize flour to such places as the prison, hospital and secondary school; and much later, in June 1969, the timber milling business, by taking away the timber contracts of the Ministry of Works and Communications.

Towards the end of 1968 the President created a section in the TANU party headquarters, the Department for *Ujamaa Vijijini* (*ujamaa* in the villages) and put Ntinbanjayo as secretary in charge of it, moving him from the Youth League to the party headquarters. At about the same time another of the President's booklets was published called Freedom and Development.[1] The people in the Association were in wholehearted agreement with this writing. In the following year (1968-9) the President, working through this new party department, proposed to use the villages of the Association in a process of education of political leaders, government officials and people from settlements throughout Tanzania. The people of the Association were very ready to give their time towards helping, in spite of the great strain on their resources which it caused. Association and village leaders had to give their time attending a number of long seminars in far places – Dar es Salaam, Handeni, Sumbawanga – as well as talking to the many people who came to the villages to learn.

It may have seemed to many at that time that things were moving very much in our favour. I believed in the possibility of self-governing farming communities developing in other parts of Tanzania. We had seen the successful growth of the communities of Mbambara in the north and Ndivu in the Njombe District, when Bernardo Kilonzo and Ludovic Mgimba had gone back to these villages after a very simple course in the Ruvuma villages. In October 1968, in Freedom and Development, Nyerere wrote:

> *Ujamaa* villages are intended to be socialist organizations created by the people, and governed by those who live and work in them. They cannot be created from outside, nor governed from outside. No one can be forced into an *ujamaa* village, and no official – at any level – can go and tell the members of an *ujamaa* village what they should do together, and what they should continue to do as individual farmers. No official of the government or party can go to an *ujamaa* village

1   In *Freedom and Development*, OUP, Dar es Salaam, 1973, p 58.

and tell the members what they must grow. No non-member of the village can go and tell the members to use a tractor, or not to use a tractor. For if these things happen – that is, if an outsider gives such instructions and enforces them – then it will no longer be an *ujamaa* village!

An *ujamaa* village is a voluntary association of people who decide of their own free will to live together and work together for their common good. They, and no one else, will decide how much of their land they will cultivate together from the beginning, and how much they will cultivate individually. They, and no one else, will decide how to use the money they earn jointly – whether to buy an ox-plough, install water, or do something else. They, and no one else, will make all the decisions about their working and living arrangements.

It is important that these things should be thoroughly understood.[2]

I felt at the time that this was just the thing that would not be understood either by government officials or party leaders. The setting up of a department such as Ntimbanjayo headed was a reasonable move, but to be successful I felt it would have to be used to protect the villages from departmental bureaucracy and party enthusiasm, whilst supplying the necessary services for getting done what was needed. When, for instance, we had run our first leadership training project, we had to rely on the Youth League headquarters to provide the potential leaders. They were neither very interested nor did they have any idea how to go about it. The real necessity was for some knowledgeable person to go around the country staying with existing farming groups and selecting suitable candidates. The RDA did not

---

2   *Ibid*, p 67.

have the resources to do this; neither would it have been politic for them to try. By the beginning of 1969 it seemed to me that things were not moving towards making this possible, but rather towards a national movement run by government and party. I remember the time of these thoughts, as in January we were visited by Leonard and Bill Elmhirst, Peter Sutcliffe and Michael Young, Dartington Hall[3] trustees, and I used them as visitors to express my feelings of the danger of the situation. Again in the next month, at the time of the seminar when a number of us were asked to be with the central committee of the party for a week, I wrote to friends in Switzerland: "The last weeks I have been becoming increasingly depressed at the overall situation in the country and have felt that we are moving towards the end."[4]

I considered at this time that one of my main tasks, despite the political excitement, was to ensure that the realities were not lost sight of, and in my letter to Switzerland in February, I wrote ". . . engaging in this sort of work (i.e. political education) tends to take the energies of our leading people away from practical development and in the long run it is on succeeding in the agricultural revolution that all the other things depend."

The political excitement, I believe, helped to bring to a head the leadership crisis in the Association. This was a most interesting struggle. It was a much easier thing to fight the enemy outside, as in the Barongo episode, than to deal with the problems within, which required changes in important posts. Ngairo as chairman was called to take a big part in the seminars arranged in different parts of the country and in the training of people in the villages, and it was an exciting thing to a politically conscious person who believed in what the RDA villages were doing. It was also for him a great strain flying back from an exciting time in Dar es Salaam to chair meetings of Association committees dealing with business or with the school, or dealing

---

3   Charity based in South Devon, specializing in the arts, social justice and sustainability.
4   Private correspondence.

with all that was required of him in his position as manager of the school. In these spheres it was too much, and his tendency to run things came to the fore again. People such as Nsuya on the business accounting and Toroka in the school, felt that authority was being taken out of their hands, that they were not consulted properly nor were they given a chance to have the real problems they were facing dealt with. He saw the needs and the difficulties, but more and more it seemed as if he felt he had personally to do all the things that the various strains made impossible for him to do. This sort of situation soon deteriorates. Behind the scenes, criticisms begin to be voiced and these invariably get back to those who are criticized, and a division into camps begins. There was an added complication which in the end made it easier for action to be taken. Association leaders were expected to live simply and as much with the villages as possible, although for such things as trips to Dar es Salaam on Association business it was recognized that something better in the way of clothing was necessary and that the expense of living was higher. Perhaps it went with the tendency to control, but while in Dar es Salaam, without consulting anyone, Ngaire spent Association money on personal items and failed to show proper accounts although asked to do so a number of times by Nsuya who could not complete his books without them. He handed in a few cash sales slips which did not account for everything. A number of the executive members approached me with what they knew and after giving me all available details asked me to prepare an account of what appeared to be missing – a little over 1,000 shillings (about £50) had been unaccounted for. As a result, a meeting of the executive was called which suspended Ngairo after he had admitted that he owed this sum to the Association. The meeting appointed Ado Mgimba as a temporary chairman until such time as a general meeting could be called. I was asked to go to Chipite where Wayakile, the vice-chairman, was working with the Mahiwa College, to fetch him back for this general meeting. Ado was chosen as temporary chairman because it was known that he was not prepared to accept the post as chairman. His temporary appointment did not therefore seem to pre-empt the choice of chair by the general meeting which might have created a difficult situation.

The subsequent general meeting approved the action of the executive and elected Wayakile as chairman, the people having taken a serious view of the matter. Ado Mgimba became vice-chairman. At this time there was only a week or two left until the second year students at Chipite finished. Wayakile returned there until their course ended and then came back permanently to Ruvuma.

From this time, July 1969, within the Association the position became much better. Wayakile was back, Bwanaliko's health was much improved and not only were both Toroka and Amon Mapunda back from National Service and in the school, but we also had a new and very useful member of the staff, Martin Lindi.

Kivukoni Adult Education College in Dar es Salaam had been holding a course in political education for teachers and during the course had sent four likely members to the RDA so that we might choose the one we thought most satisfactory as teacher for the Litowa school. Lindi was the one chosen. He was a local person and older than the rest of the staff. The school committee felt that an older man, if suitable by other standards, would be good for the school.

This last year was a very interesting, in fact fascinating one. The speeches of Nyerere on *ujamaa* appeared to be having a fairly wide effect, together with the activity of officials who, through instructions received from higher up, were telling the people that they should come together to farm. All over Tanzania, as in the time just before and after independence, people began to come together to work in groups and Ruvuma had its share of new people. One or two came to ask to join Litowa, amongst them a trained rural medical aide with seven years' experience working with the Tunduru district council. After proper enquiries he was eagerly accepted. More interesting perhaps was that the teaching staff, who were all paid by the district council, began to discuss becoming village members and what were the implications of this in terms of their salary and sharing it with the village. Before the end Lindi had in fact asked for membership and been accepted. This was a great achievement and was helped by the general climate of discussion of *ujamaa*, but it was I think mainly due to the general feeling of stability in the villages and by the increasing diversity of village activities which brought more variety and interest into rural life.

There was one aspect where it appeared that we might obtain a little more stability. In his position as secretary for *Ujamaa Vijijini*, Ntimbanjayo had put to Nyerere his feeling that the development of the policy required a stable base in Ruvuma to work from and that this was hardly possible without regional and area commissioners who understood the policy and with whom the communal farmers could work. As a result Ntimbanjayo began to look for likely people to suggest to the President. The first of these was Mahekula, who was our divisional executive officer with the Songea district council; he was appointed area commissioner in Tunduru, the easterly district of the Ruvuma Region. This was as far as things went. The next name Ntimbanjayo thought of putting forward was of one of the security police in Songea, a man he had been impressed with for some time. He held back a while on suggesting him, feeling that the man in his present position was very useful to the Association, but he did eventually give his name to Nyerere. It was unfortunate that it was at a time when the President had to dismiss the area commissioner in Handeni who had been using force to get people into what he called *ujamaa* villages and who had, it seems, put on a show of an *ujamaa* village for a presidential visit, by staffing it with convicts! With this post vacant he

immediately filled it with the name that Ntimbanjayo had con-
veniently produced just then. Similarly, when visiting the Rufiji
Resettlement Project, Ntimbanjayo had been impressed by the
area commissioner there but he never came to Ruvuma, Nyerere
appointing him as regional commissioner in Bukoba when he
had had to dismiss Walwa.

In fact in his position as secretary for *Ujamaa Vijijini*, Ntimbanjayo was never able to work out a policy for the development
and spread of the ideas of *ujamaa* villages as he became merely
the agent of the President. The work of his department which so
greatly affected the RDA was dictated by Nyerere. There were
several aspects of the programme, any one of which was a major
task. And yet all had to be tackled at once; and at the same time
as this was being done, Ntimbanjayo had to build up a staff in
his department. This was not easy and it is probably not a bad
result that of the four selected – not counting the two drivers –
two were suitable. We were unfortunate in Ruvuma in receiving
Binamu from amongst these, to organize and teach those sent to
the RDA villages. He was an outstanding failure.

To my mind, potentially the most exciting work of the department was the bringing of people from settlements about the
country to the Ruvuma villages and to Mbambara in Handeni
for them to see how to organize themselves, understand some
of the possibilities and gain confidence. This was very different
from the time when the Association ran the course as its organization was not in the hands of the RDA. The thinking behind
it had been very different. Where we had assumed that a considerable time was necessary to achieve training of leaders able
to establish strong villages, the thinking of the President was
on a much wider basis. This thinking was based in reality, very
much recognizing the difficulties. He told us that when the people began to come together around the time of independence
the country failed to be able to help them. The people had, he
said, very little understanding and if by sending them to Litowa

we could give them a little wider horizon then we would have achieved something. Now, he said, the people are coming together again, and that this time we should not fail again. In my view, with the number of groups that were springing up around the country and with the little knowledge that existed as to how to work with them, there would again be a large proportion of failures. A little wider horizon was not enough and, hard as it was to face, I felt that such a movement had to build up in a much smaller way. In fact only two of these courses for people from settlements took place: the first of people from a number of different areas, the second of people from the Rufiji Resettlement Project. There was a third group made up of individuals from the police force and the army. I'm not sure quite how this third group came to pass or what the thinking was behind it, but I think it must have been the result of some idea of the President at breakfast one morning, and passed on to Ntimbanjayo for implementation. There were plans for more such courses but other work in the *Ujamaa Vijijini* department made it impossible to organize these further courses.

The item in the work of the department which I would put second in importance was the training of party cadres. For this, about a couple of dozen names were put forward by the Teacher Training College at Morogoro as suitable candidates from amongst those completing their course at that time. Thirteen of these, three of them women, eventually trained as party cadres. They first spent a week or two in the RDA villages and had a limited number of lectures and discussions at Litowa. From there they travelled to Mbambara for a further short stay, after which they attended a week-long seminar at the Changombe Teacher Training College in Dar es Salaam. After this training they were sent to selected areas of Tanzania to help, wherever they could, in directing the development of *ujamaa*. These young people were likeable enough but the difficulties facing them were immense. They had years before, as children, left their peasant home backgrounds and since then lived in a formal educational world, and even in this world they had not begun to build up the confidence which is gained through experience whilst taking responsibility. The development of *ujamaa* villages was dealing with the whole of people's lives and thus called for much experience, as also does agricultural development which was another large part of their work. There are no shortcut courses that can take the place of experience for this type of work. On top of all of this, their work was starting amidst a fierce political battle.

Apart from these problems there was a great danger of these people becoming just another part of the administration. For some of them at any rate their real education soon began as, after a few weeks in the field, those in the northern part of the country attended the seminar at Handeni held for the members of the central committee and seeing there the opposition from the politicians to the people's organizations, they felt themselves involved with the people. A hopeful sign of what could be possible.

The greatest part of the effort of the *Ujamaa Vijijini* department the President had set up was an attempt to educate the political and government high-ups. Any movement that may be called revolutionary, in that it seeks to cause a radical change in emphasis on the organization of the country as did Nyerere's policy of *ujamaa* in rural development, is bound to cause great opposition from the establishment. But there are bound to be a number (not many) within the establishment who will understand and go along with the revolution. In my view, seminars and what-not create a very minimum of change in a situation where the balance of power is against radical change. The speeches and writings on *ujamaa* of the President reach many more of those who are capable of understanding, and the greatest effort should then be in developing the work with the people. The growth of this if successful will in itself be the further education. The reaction will come, but so will those who go along with revolution. Formal educational methods attempting to achieve such things tend to be superfluous and take away from the essential tasks resources in very short supply.

The President, however, put great store on trying to educate TANU and government leaders. In 1968, before the founding of the *Ujamaa Vijijini* Department, he had begun to send people to Ruvuma. We heard that he had told the minister for rural development, amongst others, to go and stay in the Ruvuma villages, but the order was ignored and none of them ever came. Even in cases where the people did come, the visits tended to be farcical. Such a case was that of the principals from all nine of Tanzania's teacher training colleges. This visit was in the November of 1968 and had considerable repercussions, but was, I feel, an example of the difficulties of trying to educate those members of the establishment whose minds are already made up. The plan was, so we understood, that they should spend four or five days in the villages. There was never at any time any approach to anyone in the Association as to planning the visit. They did in fact spend five days in Ruvuma, arriving by plane on a Sunday and leaving by plane the next Friday. They stayed at Peramiho Mission which is one of the training colleges, the principal of which, Fr Martin Changula, was also the TANU party regional representative for Ruvuma to the national executive. On the Monday morning they motored in two cars to Liweta village where they had a quick look around, completing their tour in two hours. They then motored to Litowa where on arrival they went directly to the school classrooms. From there they took a leisurely walk down to the river where a new bridge was being built, walking from the bridge site back through part of the village to our house, outside which, in the shade of a tree, they met a member of the Association and village leaders who answered some of their questions on the school. In just two hours after their arrival, they climbed back into their car and returned to Peramiho. This was the total extent of their study of the Association villages. They did occupy themselves in other ways, travelling for example some 300 miles in Land Rovers to and along the shores of Lake Nyasa and being shown around the mission at Peramiho.

Mention is made of this visit in a later chapter, as I believe it has a great importance, since it shows the attitudes of people in responsible positions helping to produce the next generation of teachers. The principal of the teacher training college in Dar es Salaam, Muwowo, wrote a report on the visit to which the people of the Association took great exception, and asked Toroka to write an official reply on their behalf. This reply led to the Association losing the access to the Peramiho mission workshop facilities as it contained a rather rude remark about the missionaries called forth by a passage in the report where Muwowo says that "Ruvuma Region is Peramiho." Toroka's rude remark was, I think, in the circumstances fair as this constant ignoring of the people is a great insult: the people are the region. In this instance Muwowo's remark came as a result of his having been told of a statement that Nyerere made when speaking at Peramiho – *Peramiho ina kila kitu isipokuwa Jela ya kufungia watu*. (Peramiho has everything except a jail to freeze people out.) However, I feel this may have been said with a little sarcasm and Muwowo's interpretation may not be a correct one.

Much later, after the end of the RDA, I think the President was also responsible for ignoring the people. A university student in Dar es Salaam, one of the few knowledgeable about the Association, asked the President at a meeting about the disbanding. The President ignored the people altogether and answered by discussing me personally. At that time it might have been politically convenient to use this method. Nevertheless it was a great insult to all who had made the RDA. Subsequent happenings would seem to suggest that if he did not wholly see things that way at the time, this is more as he came to see them.

The end of 1968 was a time of innumerable visits taking up much time of the villagers and particularly of their management, mostly to little purpose, although a number amongst the officials did show an interest. In February the major work of attempting to educate the top politicians started with a week's seminar at the end of the month for the central committee of the party at Kivukoni College. I was asked to attend together with Ngairo and Toroka. One of the earliest questions in the minds of the committee was "Do we want the RDA?" In my view the dangerous step had already been taken in making the RDA villages a national issue.

In such situations I generally feel that my work is to keep quiet and let others talk. On this occasion as the seminar was opened by the President and he was to stay for the first session, I felt it was an opportunity to attempt to say certain things to him by way of addressing the seminar, and Ntimbanjayo agreed. I tried to show, without saying it too directly, how difficult it was to carry out a village development programme with attitudes of officials as they so often were. I quoted such examples as the Training College principal's visit to question whether, with people at the head having these attitudes, changes in education to suit the needs of the people could really be brought about; and the fact that when the second vice-president was to visit Liweta, a long-established and a very successful *ujamaa* village only twenty miles from Songea, the Rural Development Department in Songea had to send an official to the RDA office at the sawmill to ask how to get there.

Shortly after this seminar, the set-up in the party was changed. Up to this time the central committee was predominantly appointed by the President, which gave him considerable power. There was also a national executive of the elected party representatives from the seventeen regions of the country. The power lay with the central committee, the national executive being as it were the talking shop. Now the two were combined and the seventeen elected members from the regions became the basis of the twenty-four strong central committee. This seemed a strange change at a time when the President was trying to put over a policy of village democracy. One could not by any stretch of the imagination see these elected members assisting the growth of peasant communities which could really manage their own affairs. The regional party cliques were very much people in self-perpetuating groups in the towns of the regional headquarters, having little real contact with the party out in the branches. An elected representative to the central committee was one of this regional clique. Once such limited groups as these gain considerable power, it is hard to see how there can be a growth of real democracy amongst a population of individual peasant farmers.

With this change in the central committee, the President set Millinga on a further educational venture with the new group, this time with a seminar lasting a whole month at Handeni. This started in July and following this it was arranged that the central committee members should spend about five weeks living in *ujamaa* villages. One group went to Mbambara, three groups to villages of the Association – Litowa, Liweta and Matetereka, and one group to Njoomlole in Ruvuma. Ngairo and Toroka went to assist at the Handeni seminar. When this was over Ntimbanjayo had to move to another seminar of administrative officials held at Sumbawanga at which Ngairo and Ntotera – the Litowa manager – attended and from that to a further seminar for officials at Kasulu.

While all of this was going on, one of the main points of discussion in the Association was the preparation for the post-primary training of the village children in the practical work necessary for the development of the villages. The first village children were finishing primary in September and would be due to start on a three-year technical training course in November. This was a project of very great interest both to the children and to their parents. On the agricultural side, we already had the staff with our Swiss agriculturalists and Bwanaliko, and they were already preparing buildings and collecting livestock, etc., for the course. Kisumo, minister for rural development, had said that he would arrange for the salaries of a builder and carpenter of our own choice to be paid by government but was using his position to prevent the Association having the services of volunteers, which they wanted. Three proven past volunteers wished to return and the people wished to use them in this educational programme for their children. Ntimbanjayo had seen Kisumo on this question as had Ngairo, and following this I also saw him. After my interview with him, I checked up on the people's wishes at Ruvuma on volunteers and wrote him on the subject. In reply he gave an answer which ignored most of what I said and accused me of going against the President's policy. He sent a copy of this to the party headquarters. We were also discussing these plans directly with the Ministry of Education through the principal secretary, Mwingera. It was he who told us that in the present discussions on the next five-year plan, they had talked much of the possibilities of technical training for primary leavers on a very wide scale at the request of the President, to fit the children for rural life, but had not been able to take up the idea as at that time it was economically impossible. However, money was to be put aside for assisting with two or three experimental efforts in this field and the ministry was to assist the Litowa effort under this heading.

August saw the arrival of the central committee members. The three villages in the Association who were to receive them had the message that they were coming to stay in the villages and work with the people under the village management. The villagers also knew that at the Handeni seminar these committee members, far from learning about the villages and their problems, had decided that they did not like the villages or, in particular, their Association, and were coming looking for trouble. They would not accept the accommodation provided by the villages which was carefully selected and quite adequate, but insisted on staying separately in tents. At Litowa they immediately claimed that they were not met properly, seeming to expect the type of meeting that was given up at Litowa, with the full approval of visiting dignitaries some five years before; and with no previous notice of what time they would be coming, they arrived while the villagers were all out working in the fields. The most outspoken of those staying at Litowa was Bisekwa. When they arrived I was working with Ado at Matetereka on the installation of the tower for the windmill to pump water for the village supply. When returning to Litowa I first met Bisekwa while he was working with the people on some alterations to the dam on the Luhira river for fitting a larger hydraulic ram. I was introduced to him by Ado who had asked me to come to advise on a point of the construction. The introduction and our short conversation before attending to business were perfectly natural. That evening I visited their tent and sat explaining my position and a few points on the Association. There was little that could have appeared more friendly; yet I was told the next day that they were saying that I treated them with disrespect. It was part of what we soon saw was to happen throughout their visit. Their reports had already been written in their minds; they now had to imagine those reports as happening.

Soon after these committee members left Ruvuma, I was asked to go to Dar es Salaam with Ado to push on the conversations with the Ministry of Education on the children's technical training and also to see Kisumo again on volunteers. In Dar es Salaam Ntimbanjayo told us that since the central committee members had returned, none of them as much as noticed him if he passed them in the streets or in the corridors of the party headquarters offices, with the exception of one member, an old man who had stayed for his time in Liweta, got on well with the people and thoroughly enjoyed his time there. Likewise, all other officials also ignored him, again with, as always, the odd exception. We had interesting talks with the Ministry of Education at a civil service level but Kisumo made it quite clear that he did not want to meet us.

The central committee after their rural visits met on the 24th of September under the chairmanship of the President. Only two stood with the President for the Association: the old man who had stayed at Liweta and Joseph Nyerere, the President's half-brother and secretary general of the Youth League. No formal vote was taken but with twenty-one out of the twenty-four crying for an end to the RDA, it was decided that it should be disbanded. It appears that there was no discussion on how this was to be done. On the following day Kisumo flew with others of the central committee by government plane to Songea to see that this decision was put into immediate effect. There was no legal machinery involved; the action taken in the name of the committee was entirely despotic. The assets of the Association which belonged to the villages were considerable; the grain mill, the sawmill, mechanical workshop equipment, tractor and trailer, lorry, Land Rover, school buildings and equipment, these were simply taken away. Kisumo on arrival in Songea had a short meeting with the regional TANU committee and then went straight to Litowa where he informed the people that their Association was finished. He told the villagers that the Association was plotting against the party, that the party was to put a secretary in the village, that the party was to control all village development, and that the development in the Association's villages was too slow. There was no possibility of the people questioning this action, no official or magistrate would have contemplated sticking his neck out. Questions by the villagers received intimidating answers and showed that, apart from deciding that there was to be absolute party control, other details concerning the future of activities carried out by the Association had not begun to be thought out. As a result of the meeting being told that all the starting and control of village groups was to be by the party, one new member of the school staff at Litowa asked what an individual should do if he lived where the branch of the party was weak, and people wished to come together to work as a community village. Should he help as an individual? The answer showed that discussion was not wanted and would have been useless: "The party is strong everywhere!"

Kisumo returned to Dar es Salaam the same day but the others remained to tell the party decision to other Association villages. At Matetereka after telling the people of the committee's accusations against their Association, the village manager stood up and told the committee members that they had better go away as the people didn't understand what they were talking about. There was then set up a TANU committee in Songea to decide on what action to take. The grain and timber mills were closed; the police were sent to take the keys, and to take over any Association property in the villages. The villagers quietly got on with their work. It was quite obvious that we as a family had to get out as quickly and quietly as possible to help prevent any nastiness. Ado told us that from talking to people in Songea it was obvious that some of the political leaders expected physical resistance from the villages and in fact hoped for it so that they could act tough, and were upset because there was never an opportunity for this. Instead they were landed with decisions to take and operations to organize. The children had just finished their term and the lorry was to take them back to their various villages. Now it was shut in the mill and there was consequently no food planned for the children in the school and no organization to cater for this. The women in Songea town were asking for the mill to grind their corn.

Ntimbanjayo came down from Dar es Salaam but stayed with his in-laws in Peramiho, as he felt it might be dangerous for the village people if he visited any of them. Although he was a member of parliament and a party official, he tried in vain to see the regional commissioner. I also had difficulty in seeing him but after an exchange of notes through a messenger from me in the corridor to him in his office, I did finally speak to him for a few seconds in the corridor. Everyone was worried at putting a foot wrong and it seemed to me that the RDA people were the calmest of all. Ntimbanjayo did visit Litowa very briefly to attend a farewell party that the villagers so kindly put on for us in the midst of their troubles.

After a few days a group of civil servants, Mwingera from education and the others from rural development, arrived to talk to the Litowa people. The villagers told them that there was no point in discussing with them as they were only one member village and could not by themselves say anything on behalf of what had been the whole Association. There had always been this difficulty in getting officials to understand that Litowa was not the RDA and still at this time this group did not at first wish to accept this. However, after having had their say they decided to return to Dar es Salaam and leave one of their number behind to meet the old committee of the Association at a date fixed for a few days later, when those people could be gathered from the villages, as some had to come from a considerable distance. Before this, we left for Dar es Salaam where we stayed for four or five days awaiting a plane for London. It was interesting that the official left in Songea was one who was much taken with the RDA. There were a number of these in high positions in the Ministry of Rural Development, but it appeared that many in authority were not previously aware of how members of their staff stood on these matters. It seemed that some soon began to find out and the man in Songea was rapidly recalled before he had a chance to meet the old Association committee.

Shortly after we left Tanzania we heard that the teaching staff in the school had been dispersed throughout the country to Mara, Kigoma, Mbeya, Dodoma and Singida. Considerably more than half a year afterwards we heard that the regional commissioner in Ruvuma had made moves to try to have Ntimbanjayo, Ndonde – a university graduate who chose to ally himself with the people of the Association villages in the last months – and other ex-leaders of the Association "detained". It appears that this did not come off as the second vice-president was not prepared to confront the President with the issue, since his approval was necessary for any detention orders. Those whom they wished to detain were people who for a number of years, with the approval of authority at all stages, sought to help find patterns whereby peasant peoples co-operating together could begin to build up societies through which they could move out of their poverty. Their methods in villages and education became the same as those put forward by the President which became official national policy. They tried hard to explain themselves to officialdom and showed remarkable patience in their dealings with officials who were only very seldom ever able to help them, and yet after all this time they felt the need to try and detain them. I believe this is because government and party have no proper contact with the people; the people are more and more told what to do and not allowed to question; and in these situations officials always fear for their future and tend to look for scapegoats. Even if people cannot say much very openly, officialdom often knows what the people feel. In Songea there must have been a wide feeling amongst the inhabitants that the party had stolen the possessions of the people in the Association, as at one time the area commissioner felt it necessary to try and explain at a public meeting that the party had not stolen from them.

7

ADVISING LITOWA IN THE EARLY DAYS

I was invited by the people of Litowa to advise them and my position in Ruvuma was always one of advisor.

Before our arrival at Litowa at the end of the rains of 1963, I had visited Litowa three times during which I had given very little actual advice. I felt that it would be a mistake to advise unless we could be there full-time. I had, however, let the people know that I strongly agreed with their stated plan of building a more modern type of farm by working communally to achieve this development. It had been possible to get a little aid from Europe to buy maize and beans to ensure the continuance of the village. While Ntimbanjayo had stayed with us at Nyafaru in Rhodesia, we had together drafted a proposed constitution for Litowa village and had sat doing this over a period of two or three weeks. Most of the result was arrived at by asking Ntimbanjayo the views of the villagers on specific points and incorporating these. It was obvious that the people had discussed much amongst themselves and thought about the various aspects of what they were trying to do in some detail – more in fact than any other of the groups we met later. This was not because Litowa was in any way a special group: later some of the other villages were able to organize more strongly and perhaps develop a little more rapidly. Apart from the fact that Ntimbanjayo was in the group with a perceptive and inquiring mind, it seemed to me it was because when the idea which they were developing was presented to them and accepted by them, it was no more than an idea: they had to work out for themselves what it meant in practice. Its aim was simply that the people should not go to the towns but stay in the countryside and develop the rural areas by working together in groups. The other groups, however, had generally started as a result of hearing from officials who told them that they should work on a communal plot for two or three days a week to grow cash crops to get more money. This latter could not leave much room for development of and by the people.

There was, however, one aspect when drafting the constitution, on which I did feel advice from me was necessary, and that was on management. The people's experience of organizations was with political groups with their "democratic" structures. I stressed to Ntimbanjayo that I felt that as there was the need for steady and continuous work, there should be strong management with considerable continuity. The system eventually adopted at Litowa was that the main governing body should be an elected management committee of a dozen people with elections to be held annually, one third of its members resigning every year. From these members a manager, a chairman, secretary and treasurer were elected. This body was responsible finally for all aspects of village life and work, answerable to the meeting of the whole village membership. The management committee had to meet quarterly to discuss the work of the village and at one of these meetings would produce the work plan for the following year. The carrying out of this plan, after the approval of the village meeting, then became the responsibility of the manager. He was the one who selected those to be in charge of the various aspects of the work – field work, gardens, dairy, building, carpentry (other areas, such as cattle-raising and mechanical repairs came later). These heads of department formed a manager's committee which met as often as necessary to plan the day-to-day work, generally two or three times a week.

Here again the original membership had had a certain amount of foresight as they had recognized the need for strong management. Some time after we had come to Litowa, walking with Ntimbanjayo across a part of the Litowa valley where there was a small hill rising from the level floor of the valley like an island in the sea, he told me that before I came, when they had first discussed their plans, they looked upon that hill as a possible site for a manager's house, imagining him as someone separate from the other members of the village. It was at Liweta where the first leader of the village who was also the first manager had his house built larger than and separate from the other villagers. It resulted after a time in his removal from the position; no-one occupied this larger house, which slowly decayed. The new manager lived at the same level as the other villagers. This was, I think, a very important aspect of the RDA villages: the manager was given very considerable authority but had no material advantages over the others, no special benefits.

In the first instance it was necessary to get the managing principles and routines going. Our final arrival in Litowa was at the beginning of the dry season, when normally work was taken rather easily and there was time for talk and beer drinking. The members had only recently brought their wives and families to Litowa, so that it was also a time when the women were unsettled, having little idea what things were about. The men would normally look towards a number of easygoing months. On top of this there was generally only one job, the uprooting of trees to have a reasonable acreage during the next season in order to provide for the present village membership and for additional members so that the village could grow. The work was hard, the ground in the dry season tending to be like rock. It was also monotonous.

There were three main tasks: to help the management to get going; to increase the people's understanding of what they were aiming for; to explain to officialdom what was happening and why. The last of these, discussed earlier, was never very successful, unless one assumes that there were only going to be limited numbers of people in this section of the community who would be sympathetic enough to understand anyhow.

With the management, the suggested constitution had first to be accepted by the people. Most of this work of discussing with the people had been done before we arrived, by Ntimbanjayo when he took back the draft we wrote together at Nyafaru. There were one or two small alterations but otherwise it seemed generally accepted. Ntimbanjayo's visit to Nyafaru had been well worthwhile as, apart from our discussions, it had enabled him to see something of common working in agriculture and what it could achieve in people's attitudes, even in the difficult racial situation of Rhodesia. For instance, there were two people working at Nyafaru when Shem Marunda and a small number of us moved up there from St Faith's, who stayed on to work with us: Joe, a driver, and Matsera. In Rhodesia, the Europeans, having the power, made what they could out of the African people, and to even things up, wherever possible African people looked for what they could get out of the Europeans. As a result, in the areas around Nyafaru it was common for Europeans to "lose" some of their livestock. Joe had been one of those helping in this loss! Shortly after we arrived one of the corriedale sheep disappeared. It became obvious that Joe was involved and as a result he left to take a job in town. Some time later, when in the district, he admitted to Shem that he had taken the sheep but said that at the time he had not understood and thought that it was "just another European farm".

Matsera was one of those people who soon understood. It was not long before he not only worked reliably without any supervision but when told by local passersby, seeing him work so, that he was a fool to do this for any white man, he could explain to them what Nyafaru was about.

Although Ntimbanjayo had by this time a much wider understanding of possible directions, these had to be put into operation at Litowa by people who had no experience and no example of how it could work. The Litowa people had to produce the first example for the area. There was no difficulty in arranging the necessary elections, and together we were able to have the first meetings and begin planning the village and the work, and to get the manager and his team going, as this was the basis of the day-in, day-out hard grind in the work necessary for the development.

At the first manager's committee meetings we all sat together and made a list of the work that needed attending to, to create a farm and a village. Even at such an early stage and for so small a village this list was considerable. For a week or two we met regularly to see that the various jobs were begun. With things going reasonably well, I then moved away from attending the meetings, reiterating what I had said many times, that it was their village and that all the work, organization, decisions and responsibility had to be theirs. They were to save themselves from poverty. At this point the manager's meeting gradually met less and less and the effort put into the work also became less, with members finding excuses for being away.

After this had been going on for a while, I asked the village chairman if I could speak to a meeting of the village which he then called. At this meeting I told the people that I had been invited to come to Litowa by them as an adviser and I had given a bit of advice. As the work done was getting less and manager's meetings were not being held when necessary, I could only assume that the advice I was giving did not suit them, and in this event it would seem that I would have to go and take my family back to England. After some discussion the manager stood up and apologized and asked me to please forgive them as they had not understood well, the missionaries not having educated them properly. There was a spurt in work. But the dry season is long and it is not easy to do much harder work than one is used to when you have nothing by which to judge whether or not you will benefit from it. Thus these first months were a rather up-and-down business as were the first months of the rains which that year started early in November.

Through these efforts there was some good maize coming along by the end of January and also some very good tobacco.

There came quite suddenly a very big change and it came, I am sure, from the people seeing crops which to them looked impressive and which they had produced in quite large areas through their own work and their own organization. From then on I never attended another meeting of the manager's committee. Not only did the organization of the village carry on regularly year after year under its own steam, but other villages growing up adopted a similar form of organization generally with differences only in details. They were adopting something which they had seen and the results of which they had also seen, however small these were in that first year. Those with the right leadership started with a steadiness of organization which it had taken some little time for the Litowa people to achieve.

Meanwhile, there had been a lot of informal talk. During the months of June, July and August the nights in Songea can be quite cold but generally very clear. A log fire makes a good village centre after supper and much talk took place round the fire of a semi-informal nature. The understanding of people differs very much from individual to individual. Ntimbanjayo felt that at any one time one should only deal with a very limited subject matter and for a limited time, but within those limits that one should not talk down to the people. From these discussions there were one or two who understood things very well. A number gained a fair bit and others very little; but even those with only a faint understanding, by being part of the discussions had their confidence increased and they developed a trust in the leadership.

One of the main items in these talks was to dethrone money and attempt to get an understanding of the fact that all that was needed for development came from mother earth and people's labour. This was not a terribly difficult thing to put forward as these peasant farmers had by then only come to the edge of the money economy. They were starting together from where people were used to starting. The peasant family often moved to new land when the soil was worked out. The Litowa people started with nothing but their labour. It was possible to point out that this regular moving was not good as it was never possible to build anything permanent which would be an asset for many years into the future. It was quite easy for the people to see that by establishing a permanent village, not only was it possible every year to put a little more effort into making more permanent and better houses for the people, but also to put effort into more permanent village amenities: workshops, cattle houses, grain stores, trading store, children's nurseries, schools, etc. New members could only be taken on if there was enough food; having enough food meant clearing enough land; better food meant better work. It was not difficult for the people to see that to produce much of what they wished for in their village meant prioritizing growing food rather than cash crops.

This may seem an elementary fact but at that time no one was saying it and all the pressure on the peasant farmers was to get them to grow cash crops – crops which are sold mostly to overseas buyers: coffee, sisal, tobacco . . . There was soon a genuine agreement at Litowa that the group would not look for money but would concentrate on their labour producing the necessary assets for development: well cleared land, buildings, roads, bridges, water supplies, and so on. There were one or two worries. "We cannot go naked," someone observed; that is, there was a minimum of clothing required. To help here we requested and obtained bales of second-hand clothing from organizations in Europe. We also undertook to find a small amount of money to be able to pay for any essential medical treatment, and in the case of the one or two members who had children in school, we paid the fees.

Another thing that I felt needed saying in these winter evening village talks, was that such a village development as we spoke of was very long-term and that it was by no means easy, requiring much hard work and sweat. It may be that this knowledge of the task as long and difficult plays a considerable part in creating the spirit necessary for progress. People perhaps prefer something with a real challenge rather than the promise of something for nothing. However this may be, the point was certainly well understood because, as is pointed out in the chapter on the children's education, it was during these talks that the villagers raised the question of how their children should be educated. They knew that if the education was conducted by the existing schools, the children would be led away from the village and the land, towards salaried posts in the towns. The villagers argued that if this happened they themselves would have been wasting their time in beginning this new development: what would be the use of it if their children were not there to carry on where the parents left off?

Recognizing the long-term nature of the development process is also important when considering what the final aims are. In these early discussions I pointed out that the Ruvuma region was far larger than Switzerland and yet in the whole region there was perhaps only one place which could be called a town – Songea – and this had a population of only about 5,000; whereas in Switzerland there would be many towns. The region would not want to copy Switzerland or any other of the economically more developed countries, but whatever the form of growth, it was hard to see anything but a certain balance between town and countryside. At present it was nearly all countryside. I thought it was unlikely that any of the existing centres would grow into small towns (that had local government offices and missions), as the distribution of the population did not seem to exist there yet. It seemed reasonable to look upon the development of some communal villages in the region into centres; in future a few might slowly grow into country towns.

It was only for a comparatively short period that this particular phase of advising went on. By early 1964 Litowa was well-established and a good number of people had a fair idea of where they were going. With the number of villages in the Association increasing, there was more needed in the way of visits to other places and at the end of that year the formation of the Social and Economic Revolutionary Army (SERA) was being talked about. With its formation, most advising direct to the villages from me ceased and then I discussed primarily with the members of SERA and other leaders of the Association.

These early discussions were very important as they very much set the course the villages and their Association took.

8

THE SOCIAL AND ECONOMIC
REVOLUTIONARY ARMY

The Social and Economic Revolutionary Army (SERA) started in order to do the sort of work that originally I thought I would be doing, but which became impossible for one person because of the speed at which the Association and work in it had grown. Apart from this, it was obviously better in so many ways that any advice I might have to offer be given to some such local body instead of directly to large numbers of villagers.

The members of SERA did not come from a wide area of Tanzania. They were merely a handful chosen from amongst those who had joined the villages. In the beginning all happened to be people who had given up regular paid employment in order to join in with those who had almost no chance of such employment, to find ways of developing the life of the whole community. For example: Wayakile had been trained as a shoemaker. In the economic situation at that time there was not much work for shoemakers, and he was employed in the Peramiho mission bookshop. Ado had worked in the police and before joining Litowa was employed also by the mission as an assistant in their trading store. Bwanaliko was a clerk in a large trading business, and so on. Thus they were not people with any special training for the type of work expected of them by SERA, and in some cases perhaps found it at times difficult since it was not necessarily what was best suited to their characters. Ado, for instance, through his upbringing, was somewhat unsure of himself, it was particularly upsetting for him to face criticism. Aiden Mapunda, on the other hand, had no fear of criticism and in fact great courage in difficult situations, but he had a background which had rather tied him to his beer and his fellow members had to give him constant reminders that his beer was not always his best friend.

People with an education and paid employment needed the courage to fight fairly difficult battles before they could ever get to join the RDA villages. They were great assets to their families; their earnings were by no means their own or belong just to their immediate family. Anyone in this position contemplating putting his knowledge to any other use than making money would face very strong family opposition. These people had gone through this struggle.

The work of SERA remained much the same through its short history. The members could be called by any village to assist with problems they might be facing of whatever nature – social, economic, technical. When there were volunteers or experts from outside they introduced them to the people or acted as go-betweens between them and the people. In some instances a SERA member would be specially attached to an expert bringing in knowledge from outside, so that whilst working with him he might himself gain this knowledge and later be able himself to act in an advisory capacity. A number of them also had specific posts within the Association, such as business manager or school manager or lorry driver. They also very often acted as liaison between the government and the people.

There were a number of changes in thinking about the position of SERA members as time went on. This was not so much because the original decisions were wrong but rather that the changing patterns brought about a developing situation necessitating changes. When it was first conceived, there was a very strong feeling that the SERA members must not be attached to any particular village. Although the idea in the Association was not that it should be an instrument for channelling aid from outside to the villages, looking towards such aid was still in

people's thinking. If the officers of the Association came mainly
from one village there would obviously be the fear, which could
hold back development, that that village would get more than
its share of whatever aid was going. It was also fairly generally accepted that the few people with more education would
be those holding such posts in the Association as secretary and
treasurer. These would also be obvious choices for SERA, and
they happened also to be members of one village, Litowa. As
a result of all these considerations the suggestion was that if a
person became a member of SERA he would give up his village
membership. At this early stage in the development of the Association and the villages, there was no way of financially com-
pensating them for this. It was understood that they received
second-hand clothing from the Association in the same way as
other villagers, that they would be fed by any village in which
they were working, and that their wives would remain living in
their original village, working in the normal way with the other
villagers, thus receiving the food for their families in exchange
for their work.

As time went on the conditions in the villages considerably
improved and it was obvious that the work of the SERA members had contributed to this improvement just as much as had
everybody else's work. It was only fair that they should also benefit from this improvement. This situation came at a time when
the developing businesses of the Association made it possible to
pay the SERA members for their services. However, there was
a very strong feeling both amongst the villagers and the SERA
members themselves that no members of the Association should
become paid employees. But it was agreed that when travelling
on business they should receive a small allowance to enable
them to purchase food and accommodation when they could
not be in any of the member villages.

Also as time went on, it was no longer only the SERA members who were officers in the Association. Nungu, the Liweta
treasurer also became treasurer of the Association. This showed

that many of the old fears of favouritism had disappeared and that there was an increasing degree of trust among the villages. Other changes were that there were members of SERA who had little formal education, and also that they were no longer only from Litowa. Because of all these changes and the constantly improving conditions in the villages, there was in the last year of the Association renewed talk on the position of SERA members which ended in an Association decision quite opposite to the original one. It was now decided that all SERA members had to be members of one of the Association villages. They were not bound necessarily to choose the village of which they first became members.

The decision that SERA people should never receive a wage was a very important one. I am certain that one of the rewards was that the teaching staff in the school, who were not members of the Association and were employees paid in the main by the district council, were deciding at the end almost unanimously to become members of the villages, which meant their salaries went to their villages.

It was always recognized right from the beginning that it was essential for the villages to be the controlling force within the Association. It was for this reason that the constitution laid down a restriction on the total number of members that SERA could have – the number allowed to equal the number of representatives from the villages to the Association. In practice the numbers never reached anywhere near this, and with the later change that brought SERA members back to being village members, any possible danger of control was further reduced. The villagers did in fact very carefully guard their relations with SERA people; any difficulties in relationships with SERA were very quickly discussed. This readiness to discuss such problems also existed to a very high degree within the SERA body itself. The SERA membership was considerably self-critical and jealous to maintain the principles by which they operated. The fact that they were completely dependent on the villages was a great assistance towards maintaining basic principles.

How successful was SERA? In my view some such body was an essential part of the development, and SERA contributed very highly to the growth of everything that was the Association. There was a time, however, towards the end when SERA did not seem to be coping with the needs. Many calls were made on the Association to assist the spread of village socialism and quite naturally those most affected were the SERA members. This was recognized very much, and at all quarterly meetings in this period the question of the need for more effort in assisting the slower villages would be raised. Even one person can make a tremendous difference, and in the last few months this was very noticeable when Wayakile returned from Mahiwa and immediately began to get out into the villages. He was always a highly effective person in that type of work, his whole mind based in and focussed on the villages.

It would be very difficult to create such a body artificially, and I feel that in the villages an organization of villagers must come first. The SERA type body can grow out of this when the time is ripe.

9

THE WOMEN

Life for the women in the bush of Africa is very hard and they
seldom have any direct say in the affairs of their family. In the
days before colonialism when a village unit was close, the wom-
en probably did many things together and so would have had
some hierarchy of their own, but with the breakup of tribal life
and the spreading out into small individual peasant holdings,
the women became little more than servants for their husbands.

As a result, the villages of the Ruvuma Development Association were started by men. The wives had to come to these
new villages with them. Litowa was somewhat different: in the
group which came to restart in 1961, there were two unattached
women members of the Youth League who came of their own
accord. Both these women married men outside the village and
eventually left. In the first instance at Litowa only the men had
gone to the village, leaving their wives at their previous homes,
but during 1962 they built small family houses and before the
rains started towards the end of that year, they brought their
wives to their new homes. That they were "brought" was only
too obvious. They had no interest in the village, no knowledge
of why their men had gone to such a place – probably because
they had never been told – and were certainly determined to do
as little work as possible in a system they did not understand,
and had never had explained to them.

The idea existed that women should take part in the life of
the country; in the constitutional discussion for independence
the TANU party accepted that all have one vote, women as well
as men. In the minds of the first members of Litowa, there was

the assumption that women should in some way share the responsibilities but it was no more than a vague idea and was not immediately given any practical expression. The women's reaction to having been brought to this new situation and how they were to fit in, had to be discussed. The women were not in a mood to work well. But the village needed their willing co-operation, not their half-hearted efforts. Millinga at this time pressed very much that the women should take part in the committees of the village while the manager, Hambisa Komba, though appearing to agree, took a very "practical" line: however this was to be in the future, at present the work had to be done, and if they did not do it willingly, traditional methods would have to be used – the women would have to be forced.

First attempts at new ideas are often not very successful. The women were encouraged to get together to form their own section and elect leaders, including one to attend village committees and represent them. The first woman chosen was Millinga's wife, Bernadetta. Meetings of the whole village were always attended by women who sat separately and at the back. None had attended committee meetings. At the first such meeting that Bernadetta attended she sat at a back corner and took no part in the discussion until right at the end when she stood up to say that she wished to resign from her position! But the step had been taken. From then there were two women's representatives and it very soon became usual for them to have their say in meetings.

The reason for this rapid change was easy to understand. The women saw that they were benefiting from being in a village where all were working together. These events happened in the months after we came to stay permanently at Litowa at the end of April 1963. The first word from the women themselves on appreciating the advantages came at the anniversary celebrations in Litowa in November of that year, but not from the women at Litowa. The people from the neighbouring village of Luhira Goliama were invited to the celebrations and it was the womenfolk who said how fortunate those at Litowa were. This probably made it much easier for the men of Luhira Goliama to take the decision in the following year to copy Litowa and to change their village into one where the people worked communally rather than each on his own peasant holding. Most of the other villages started in different ways, generally after visiting Litowa, so that the women knew from the start there were benefits for them.

One of the greatest of these benefits was that of the health of their children (dealt with in some detail in the chapter on healthcare). When the women wished to express what they thought of Litowa they often pointed to the health of their children. Such a one was Mama Pilipili whose husband wished to leave the village because, after persistent aches in his back, an African doctor told him that they would not disappear while he was at Litowa. When Noreen asked Mama if she wanted to go, her answer was, "I am not foolish, Mama Noreen. Look how well my children are." She also mentioned that because of the Association her children all had schooling. But perhaps more important, she felt these things were hers because of her work. She had helped cut the grass which roofed the school, she had helped dig the trench for the village water piping, helped grow the food, taken her turn cooking and caring for the children in the nursery.

There were, however, many other advantages which became obvious if you consider just how hard life is for the mother in a peasant family living by subsistence farming where she is the chief labour force. A baby born at the time of the year when farm work is at its greatest is not much more for the mother than an extra job for a few hours. At Litowa in the month or two before and after a birth, the mother would do useful light work – such as shelling peanuts – sharing it with the one or two old women, mothers of village members who were also usefully occupying their time without strain.

On two or three occasions, we were called to take women from neighbouring villages to the mission hospital at Peramiho who had been in labour for a day or two with no result. In these cases these unfortunate young women had been beaten by the old women. In the first of these cases, when a young woman was being put into the back seat of the car, I asked how it happened that she had a swollen eye and a bruised and bleeding face. I was told that the old women believe that if a baby cannot be born it is a sign that the father is not the husband. Only an admission as to who the father is will enable the child to come. The girl is hit by the old women when she refuses to admit to being unfaithful and often I'm told will desperately mention the name of every man in the village to try and avoid the beating. A village organization such as at Litowa prevented these happenings. All village women when pregnant attended the ante-natal clinic at the mission hospital once a month, and cases likely to have difficulties as well as any other cases where the women desired it, were sent to hospital for the confinement. The old women can often be very hard on the young ones, as in this case. I have often felt it is largely because of the hard time they themselves have had in their position as servants of the men, that they require their own turn at taking it out on someone.

However this may be, women suffering beatings at the hands of their husbands was common, and in a society of scattered peasant holdings there is not much such women can do about it. No doubt some of this comes from inevitable attempts of the women to assert their individuality and much comes during drunkenness, but perhaps also it is helped by the tribal customs of population control where husband and wife do not have sexual relations for about two years after the birth of a child. This custom was more likely developed in times past as one to ensure an adequate population rather than to limit it, so each child would have a long period of breastfeeding and so was more likely to survive.

The people who came to Litowa were quite ordinary people from the region and similar happenings inevitably occurred, but they were far less and were generally regretted. Hearing new ideas does not mean that they are immediately understood, but people learn from their struggles and it is easier to learn if there is a freer atmosphere.

On one occasion the women had been discussing some of these problems while working with Noreen, who tried to explain something of what she felt relationships between man and wife could be. Some time after this, Mr Pilipili had a friend helping him to thatch a new building on his plot next door to ours. His friend during the work came down from the roof and asked for – perhaps demanded – a drink of water. Mama Pilipili did the unheard-of – telling him to fetch his own. It appears that this created much heated discussion next door and Mama must have been rather upset by her bold action for, while her husband had gone to see the doctor at Peramiho – a nine-mile walk – she packed a few belongings, took up the baby and went off to her sister – some thirty miles away. The husband returned the next morning to be told the news which we had not yet heard. During the previous heated discussions, things must have been brought up which Mama Noreen was supposed to have said. However, without saying anything of the matter, Mr Pilipili came to our house and asked Noreen for a drink of water which she immediately gave him. When hearing that he had just arrived after walking from Peramiho she also gave him a large slice of pawpaw. The water and the pawpaw convinced him that whatever Noreen had said to the women, his wife had misunderstood it and he then told us what had happened. Noreen asked if he had hit his wife to which he answered "No. It is not the custom here at Litowa to beat our wives."

Some have suggested that relationships are made more difficult between men and women by the sudden rejection by their mothers that men received when they were two or three years old. Whether this is so or not I cannot say, but it was this amongst other things that made us keen to have a village nursery. From the day a baby is born he is carried by the mother everywhere she goes, he is attended to as soon as he cries and must feel very loved. When the next baby arrives it is not possible, with the mother's workload, to continue to carry the first around and his life completely changes. He has to learn very suddenly that his turn is now finished.

Noreen's idea of a children's nursery was strange to the women and they did not immediately take to it. It was the men who first saw its purpose but there is no doubt that after it was established it was seen by the women as a great benefit to themselves.

Other things were more directly demanded by the women, such as sewing classes. Kate Wenner, one of our young American volunteers (mentioned earlier) spent her year in Litowa working with the women with much of her effort going into the nursery and sewing.

It would have been extremely enlightening to see how the village girls in the school learning the same things as the boys on the growth and development of their villages, would have turned out, and how much relationships would have changed because of this. During the last month or so before the disbanding, it was a point of great discussion amongst the older children at the school that much of the effort of the Association would be lost if the girls married men from outside the villages, and if the village young men had to marry wives who did not understand *ujamaa*. The vast majority felt that some sort of arrangement should be made whereby later on marriages could be arranged between the boys and girls of the villages. The boys pictured the girls in their school with the same level of education as themselves as their future wives.

There were other advantages for the women such as the peace of mind of knowing that their children were cared for while they were at work or away for a while. It is fairly common for children to wander off into the bush playing and to lose their way, often not found before being taken by wild animals. In our last year in Tanzania in a neighbouring area, seven children died from poisoning after collecting, cooking and eating mushrooms while their parents were away attending a funeral. Women had the security of being part of a community rather than on their own facing the vagaries of the weather, and of life generally.

With the women it is again a case of things succeeding which they themselves want. New ideas may seem strange at first but if they have a real benefit for the women, this will rapidly been seen and the strangeness will go. Other things may be tried or thought over but never really take hold. For instance because of much talk in government circles of literacy and the organization of classes designed to give a greater knowledge of Kiswahili, suggestions for such classes came up in the village, and although tried, never really caught on. Similarly there was very little general demand for knowledge of any more sophisticated methods of cooking. Similarly in sewing: the demand was for very practical things: babies' and children's shirts and dresses, boys' shorts, women's panties, and very little for fancy stitching or embroidery. It is strange, thinking back, that the things the women did not consider so important are by and large those most generally dealt with in courses for women run by missions and government. One of our women teachers could not teach the girls the sewing of ordinary articles of clothing because she had never done it herself, but she could make embroidered cushion covers and table mats with fancy stitches. Not many people have cushions – or tables.

There were of course individuals interested in these things. For example, to be able occasionally to cook a batch of bread or make a cake. Grace, another of our teachers, was one of these. She had previously been a community development worker, but I remember her saying to Noreen, "I like the way you make a cake, crack the eggs and empty them in and mix it up quickly. When we were given courses in cooking at Peramiho as development workers, the whites and yolks of the eggs had to be carefully separated and mixed in separately. With teaching as well as looking after my husband and four children, how can I possibly do this?"

At the farewell party given for our family a day or so before we left, an older woman stood up to make a speech. After recounting some of the beginning, the hard work clearing the land, the planting and cultivating together, the good crops, she went on to say how she remembered that when they first came the women complained there was not enough food – soon there was more than enough, and there was no money for clothing and soon they had plenty of clothes. Going on in this vein she broke down and cried. It was a joy too, to see how changed some of the women were after a year or two in the village. Two especially whose husbands had spent a great deal of time drinking before joining the village, looked tired and unhappy at first. That their husbands now enjoyed their work and had a healthy sense of achievement was reflected very much in the marriage and the wives' happiness. People shared in an uninhibited atmosphere. For instance, several of the young married men worked with and learned from the carpenter in their spare time making furniture for their homes. The women got together to make pots and at one time the expert potters were relieved of work on the land for a few weeks to make water pots for the whole village. It seemed that the freedom of the spirit was in no way curtailed through living in a self-organized community; on the contrary, it led to a creativity that gained momentum with each achievement.

10

DEALING WITH HEALTHCARE

Questions of health were very high on the list of priorities in the RDA villages. We may think that the desire to have pills and lotions for every little complaint has grown with so many of these things available in the chemist shops and hospitals of our modern cities, but Africa was quite equal in providing medicines to give people the comfort of feeling they're doing something while nature effected its cures. In Dar es Salaam local doctoring is said to be one of the largest businesses, and researchers claim that more is paid to unofficial doctors than is spent on the modern health services there.

During our stay in Ruvuma there was an increase in the medical facilities provided by the missions but little increase in the facilities provided by government. Tanzania is far too poor to cope with its medical problems in terms that we in the economically developed countries would call adequate. In such a situation, however, it is possible to do a fair amount for little expense.

At Litowa the results of this little had a very great effect on the spirit of the people, because they experienced the results. Many remarks by villagers appreciative of life in their Litowa have referred to health.

Such a simple village organization cannot of course cope with major illness, but I believe that what the village was able to do was of more educational value to the people than receiving treatment at a hospital because they themselves as a community were involved in providing it.

In the richer countries parents worry about their children who attend school crossing the roads and passing exams. In Tanzania they worry about whether they will survive into adulthood or die of disease. No exact figures are available but it is thought that little more than half of all children born live survive to the age of sixteen. Some authorities claim that the number of deaths in this group is far higher (but this may be because they work in particularly bad areas). When we first went to Litowa we were told that one of the objectives of the group was to say to death: "Stay away from our children and keep to the old folk." The people at any rate did not fatalistically accept that many of their children would die.

At the end of 1962 when we passed through Litowa and stayed for a month before going on to England (for a break and to look for support for our venture), the wives and children of the early members had just recently moved in. It was obvious that one of the children was dying and there was then little we could do about it. By the time we returned a few months later, three children had died. To the people this was nothing unusual, just one of the tragic problems they sought to overcome. With very little in the way of additional resources, it was possible almost immediately to transform this reality. From this time in 1963 until the destruction of the RDA six and a half years later, there were only seven child deaths at Litowa. This in spite of the fact that the children of school age from all the other *ujamaa* villages lived there for most of the year, giving a child population at the end of this time of about 300. Two of these seven who died were twins born rather weak who then went with the mother to the mission hospital where both died within three days. One was a small child who died after scalding with boiling water. Another was an older girl who died after an internal injury caused by colliding with another child on the sports field and before we were able to get her to hospital. Another was an older girl we sent to the government hospital as she was not well after having been treated for hookworm, and we had good reason to suspect that her death was due to negligence in that hospital. A baby girl a few months old became very weak owing to the ignorance of the mother who didn't breastfeed her properly, and who – after Noreen brought the child back to strength again through a great struggle – insisted on taking her, according to custom but against the advice of most of the village parents, to show to the grandparents over forty miles away. We suspect that the real desire was to ensure the future health of the child by obtaining some bush medicine from a local doctor: perhaps this together with the mother's lack of understanding about feeding the child may have caused her death. The seventh was another young child who died from convulsions – probably with the high temperature of malaria after the father (reinforced by the advice from one old member of the village) had refused to take the child to hospital in spite of hard pleading by many of the leading villagers. We feel that for a village at that time in Africa this is a very good record.

In the case of the child with convulsions, it was striking how hard so many villagers pleaded with the father to send the child to the mission hospital, despite a local belief that convulsions were a rather special disease not understood by "European medicine". It is fairly clear where this belief came from. A large number of cases of convulsions came with malaria which has a recurring fever. With the first fever comes the convulsions and the parents generally turn to local bush medicines before going to the hospitals. The fever subsides in the course of the malaria, the convulsions disappear with it, and the medicine is held responsible for the cure. The following day the fever and the convulsions return and the same procedure is repeated. If the child is strong, it might come through but is left very weak. When the fever and convulsions return the next time, the parents in desperation rush the child to the hospital where the staff are faced with a hopeless case. There is little they can do but they must try, so an injection is given. But in most such cases the child dies and the parents may blame the injection for the death.

The village at Litowa had learnt in this particular case that this was not so by an experience in the community which involved the youngest of the Ibbott children. Christopher quite suddenly ran a high temperature some days after being vaccinated and had convulsions. Any parents who have had this experience with their children will know how frightening it is. I have never driven the twelve miles to the mission hospital so fast. There was great anxiety at Litowa over us taking Christopher to the hospital, many believing that because of this he would die, but he came back the next day, walking out of the car. In the situation of the village community the reasons for the cure and the erroneous reasoning of local beliefs was not conveyed in a lecture; they came up quite naturally as the daily village gossip and had much greater force than any lecture would have.

There were many examples of this, always with the risk that cases would be brought too late, placing blame for deaths on the hospital. One such case was that of Lazarus in the Litowa school, a boy from Liweta village eight miles away by foot but a journey of about fifty miles by road. Shortly after recovering from measles, Lazarus contracted dysentery and there was no response to the drugs provided by the Litowa dispensary from the district council. He rapidly became very weak and it was necessary to send him to hospital. A message was sent to Liweta for his father to come and give permission for his son to go to hospital. The father decided to take him back to Liweta where he was sure he could get the right bush medicine. The Litowa dispenser, school headmaster and many others pleaded with the father to go with him to hospital. The father eventually broke into tears and equally strongly pleaded with us to accept his decision to take the child home to Liweta. We were forced to give up the battle. Two days later a messenger arrived from Liweta bringing a few shillings and a message to say that Lazarus was dying, if we were going to Songea would we buy a length of cloth ready to wrap the body in for burial. We immediately sent one of our volunteers with one of the Litowa members to Liweta asking that if he was dying would they at this last minute allow us to take him to hospital. Five hours later he was carried into the village on a homemade stretcher, our volunteer not really believing that there could still be life in a body with so little weight. The only transport available was the Litowa tractor and trailer which pumped its way with him over the twelve miles to Peramiho. The last thing we could do was to plead with the mission doctor, amongst his almost impossible duties of outpatients, student nurse teaching, operating, hospital rounds, etc., that Lazarus be treated as a special case because of the value of his recovery to the understanding of the villages. Three weeks later Lazarus returned to the village although still alarmingly thin. His father had been a blood donor for him, to his everlasting joy, I think. It was in fact very many weeks before he regained his normal weight. I remember some two years later when talking over this event, as such events become village history to be talked over, our eldest son Howard said, "Lazarus tells us that he has no recollection at all of being carried to Litowa, travelling in the tractor and trailer or arriving at Peramiho hospital." While writing this it has just occurred to me that he had a very appropriate name.

So often visiting officials ask the same old questions: "How many acres of tobacco will you be planting this year? How many of maize?" Looking at things in purely economic terms is not just a disease of the West. How unlikely that any official would ever ask how many lives have been saved. Yet this was one of the people's aims from the beginning. This was one of the reasons they grew the acres, and the improving health of the children as well as of the adult members was one of the things that maintained their commitment to the community. It is so easy for visitors to fail to see this.

A great improvement in the children's health came about very quickly in 1963 when the village had little land cleared and

consequently hardly adequate food supplies. This first improvement was brought about by better management of the children's
feeding. Noreen soon noticed after settling at Litowa that every
evening there was a lot of crying amongst the village children
and much shouting at them by their mothers.

An African mother is a very busy person: cooking for her
family, collecting firewood, carrying water from the river, doing
the family washing, bathing the children, all on top of the biggest job – working in the fields. When she returns to the house
at night she is understandably tired and thus easily irritated by
her children. The youngsters are also tired at that time of the
day and hungry, making them miserable. The food has to be
cooked during which time it grows dark and the children, sitting around the kitchen fire, after a few bites tend to drop off
to sleep when they are picked up and laid down for the night,
not having eaten properly. Noreen suggested that one or two of
the women should come in early from fieldwork and prepare
food for all the children – explaining the reason. The idea was
strange to the women and not easily accepted. It was in fact the
men who first saw the value of it and asked for it to be put into
operation, coming to Noreen with a request for her to start it off.
New departures generally need a time of helping whilst people
sort out the inevitable problems. In this case the feeling amongst
the women that everything had to be fair meant that the women
had to do the children's cooking in turn, it not being "fair" that
one pair of women always do it while the rest are still out in
the fields. This meant that every week started with having to
explain everything to mothers who were new to the job. It was
possible in quite a short time to see the benefit of this and later it
was extended almost automatically to the midday meal.

This sort of development is obviously not possible through
officials and experts visiting a village, talking and then going
off again. Neither can the real needs be seen and solutions proposed and put into effect.

It was obvious that the village had to have its own medical staff. Since these village groups were officially encouraged, they were also helped with medical supplies by the district council – when the council had them! With no trained medical person, what they offered was severely limited. What was given was first aid equipment – bandages, sticking plaster, gentian violet and seriflavine. It was unlikely that a trained rural medical aid would become a village member at that time when there was a shortage of them, making employment easy to find.

The Litowa management, therefore, approached the regional medical officer (RMO) who agreed to take a suitable member of the village into the hospital at Songea for three months. They would put him through the various departments, but as the RMO pointed out, this was not a course and what was learnt was very much up to the trainee; fundamentally he had to teach himself. The village chose Ngomaty, one of the members who came to Litowa in 1961, part of the second attempt at starting a village. Ngomaty only had four years schooling but since then he had worked for many years in the printing press at the Peramiho mission and without further classes had taught himself English to a standard where he could hold intelligent conversations in that language. After his training, though short and limited, much more could be achieved in the village.

It also increased the work, however. People in the surrounding countryside came to the new Litowa dispensary, started in a room in Ngomaty's house with the veranda as a waiting room. Not only the surrounding people came but also other member villages of the Association began to send cases they were worried about to Litowa, while the numbers of children in the school increased. As a result, more accommodation was required and in 1967 one of the houses in the original village which was vacated by a family moving to the new village site, was turned into a dispensary. The following year the village started to erect a more permanent building in the new village.

The village carpenters had over the years made several items of furniture for the dispensary out of local timber. With the new building under way, they sent two carpenters to the Association sawmill in Songea where the greater facilities enabled them to produce more quickly the remaining furniture required for the new building – an important factor when a few carpenters were doing so much work on the school, which was for all the villages (not just Litowa), as was to a lesser degree the dispensary.

It was with the medical side that the Association had one of its plans fail rather badly. We thought that it would be possible to extend Ngomaty's knowledge considerably by having a trained nurse volunteer to work with him for a year or two. This coincided with an offer from Switzerland – they suggested a pair of nurses. We accepted; we thought one of them would be able to travel around the other villages helping with their health problems, particularly as one by one other villages were also sending a member for a short "training" at the Songea hospital and building their own small dispensaries. The two nurses who came, through the Swiss government volunteer organisation, who we understood had had rigorous tests in suitability and had been through a special orientation course in the Swiss mountains, proved quite unable to adjust to the conditions of the bush. In my view the failure was entirely due to their inadequacies. Although older than most of our volunteers, they were emotionally rather young.

Towards the middle of 1969, quite out of the blue, a rural medical aide of considerable experience approached one of the leaders of the Association with a view to working in it. When the nature of the villages was explained and that it was not a question of paid employment but becoming a village member and being one of the villagers, he seemed unperturbed. Experience had taught us to be wary, but enquiries seemed to suggest him to be suitable and he was at school with Mgimba who told us that he was at that time a particular friend of his and a person who always took life seriously. He moved to Litowa only two months before the disbanding of the Association. In work and discussion he appeared to understand, to be one of those people who had taken genuine note of the teaching of the President. There were, however, difficulties with his wife and it transpired that whereas he had worked out his ideas and plans, he had not the courage to tell his wife about them, leaving her with the impression that this was to be another job similar to that which they had left. As soon as this was understood the matter was discussed at the village manager's committee which set out to help him bring understanding to his wife.

Judged by what modern hospitals can give, the development of the medical facilities has been slow, but for the villagers it had been very great. It was very much an aspect in which they had been involved in every decision and at every step forward. It was very much a case of the people bringing about their own development and in this way increasing community spirit. In some instances where large expenditure was concerned, a particular case might be discussed by the whole village.

Such a case was that of Namahara, a quiet and steady member of the village who was brought in one day from the fields to be rushed to hospital after having vomited up large quantities of blood. At Peramiho hospital they diagnosed a burst stomach ulcer and recommended rest and special food. In an individual peasant family such a health crisis can make life very hard, particularly if it happens during the rains when the year's food is being grown. When slightly recovered, Namahara did light work in the children's nursery, playing the guitar and singing with the children, taking them for walks and so on, and it was relatively easy to ensure that he had suitable food. However, later on the health trouble recurred, the village dispenser was told at the hospital that they could repeat the same treatment but it would be better to operate and this would cost 240 shillings which would have to be paid beforehand. To the people this was a large sum and the question was discussed by the whole village which approved this sum of money from their funds to be used for the operation. Namahara went to hospital and had to have special treatment to build up the blood and his strength before the operation. During this period every time one arrived back at Litowa after having passed through Peramiho, one was asked "Has he had the operation yet?" "When will he have the operation?" And afterwards one was always asked how he was getting on. At Litowa the credit for Namahara's cure was not given to the hospital but to the Litowa village. It was their achievement, and there is considerable justification for this feeling in the situation of the region. This became one of the historical landmarks of Litowa, an accomplishment to be proud of.

From top:
the villages of
Litowa (1961),
Liweta and
Matetereka

Ralph Ibbott and Ntimbanjayo
Millinga, founder of
Litowa village

Wayakile Sangu, chairman of the
RDA in 1969

Ado Mgimba, RDA vice-chairman
in 1969, Millinga and Ibbott

Litowa male voice choir, 1962. From left, third standing Kufabasi
Mapunda, Litowa's secretary; second crouching Millinga
Below: headteachers Grace Chips and Suleiman Toroka

Litowa valley, weeding the maize crop
Below: President Nyerere (in white) visits Litowa, 1965

Weeding the
groundnuts
crop

Bridge over
Luhira river
in Litowa

Headteacher
Toroka and
pupil planting
fruit trees

Clockwise from top: the first Litowa school; building the new school; the new classrooms; the school pupils committee meets

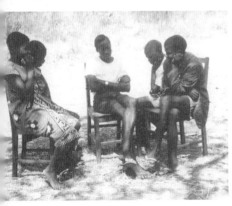

Learning
to spin:
Noreen
Ibbott
and two
students

Children's
nursery

Installing water pipes

Odo from Matetereka weaving

Litowa 1969: farewell party for the Ibbott family following the banning of the RDA

11

EDUCATING THE CHILDREN FOR *UJAMAA*

Part I – Building a School

Most of the first members of Litowa were young men with young wives and consequently there were generally only one or two children in each family, usually hardly of school age yet. There were one or two older members who had children already in upper primary boarding schools. Very often the payment of school fees for children who went on to upper primary was covered by a number of people within the extended family, as only relatively few reached that stage. When a man chose to go into one of these communal villages, often other members of his family refused to co-operate in the assistance of the fees for his children. With almost no money available in the early days of the development of the communal village, a member with such a child could not keep him at school. These one or two older members were in fact very much required in a village such as Litowa which was made up predominantly of young men, to provide a more balanced community. Rather than run the risk of losing these older members, and as there were very few, it was decided in the first instance to find money through the Association to pay these fees.

In 1963 before the Association was registered, these decisions had to be taken largely by Ntimbanjayo and myself. Before taking such a decision we discussed the questions in our evening village talks around the camp fire at Litowa. It was necessary to make it quite clear that this practice could not be

a continuing thing, but it was a subject on which there was tremendous interest as all the members knew that it would not be
long before their own children reached school age. In the discussions it was quite clear that people thought much further than
just the schooling of their children. Very early on the question
came up: what was the purpose of sending children to school
when experience showed that if one did so they left the villages
and went to the towns? The members felt that they would be
wasting their time starting on village development, which was a
very long-term business, if because of schooling, their children
then left the work that their parents had started. In fact it was
very obvious that much success in the long term depended on
the people's skill in bringing up their children to follow on after
them. My contribution to the discussion at that stage was not
much more than to say that I believed it was possible to develop
an education that led towards the children following on with
the work of their parents rather than going to the towns.

From the very beginning it was almost assumed that the
people would have to arrange for their children's education
themselves. Quite obviously with the few people involved
at that time and the urgency of other much more basic tasks,
the starting of an educational project had to be put off. Early
in 1964 a small but inevitably haphazard start was made with
Ado and a little later Kufabasi giving a few elementary lessons
in reading, writing and numbers to the older children at Litowa.
Even if it was haphazard, it was a start and things grew from
this start fairly rapidly. If it was to grow there obviously had
to be a person who could give his full time to it and it was here
that the village was fortunate in finding Lighanga who, being
out of favour with the educational authorities, was prepared to
come to Litowa and work in exchange for being fed. There was
also in the group across the river at Luhira Goliama a young
man named Soko who had been a mission catechist. These two
became the first permanent teachers in the unofficial school at

Litowa, which was rapidly becoming the Association school. We were able then to begin to work towards having the school registered. Fairly soon after this, Grace Chips gave up her community development work to teach in the school and we were also able to get a newly trained teacher, Anthony Luena, who was the brother of Ntimbanjayo's wife Bernadetta.

With the school registered and having a staff, it was then possible to think more about where the emphasis should be put in the children's education. Much of the initial work in ensuring that the emphasis was put firmly on the practical village work, and the teaching of the ideas of *ujamaa* which were growing within the Association, was done by Ntimbanjayo, who was the school manager on behalf of the Association. By this time the Association was a firmly established and growing body.

It became obvious that the stage had been reached when a really good headmaster was necessary, and one of the tasks that Ntimbanjayo set himself was to find one. He managed to do this by talking to some of the students at the Changombe Teachers Training College in Dar es Salaam where Suleiman Toroka immediately appreciated the ideas and felt they answered his desire to do more than just enter a routine profession.

Changes in staff in a community present certain difficulties as people do not like to cause hurt to those with whom they have been co-operating. They appreciated that Lighanga had been of great service in establishing the school on a firm basis; yet he could not be accepted by the department as a teacher; and at the same time he did not have the understanding or the qualities that were needed to develop a type of education different from that for which he was trained. In fact, the change was done quite amicably. The Association was able to put up a good and successful case to the Education Department for Lighanga's reinstatement as a teacher on his record at Litowa, and also to arrange for him to go on a special six-month course to Israel which would widen his experience. On his return from Israel he was able to get another teaching job. During this time Toroka came to Litowa. At first, on Lighanga's leaving, Grace became headmistress; and then later Toroka took over.

As the Association developed its confidence and understanding, it knew more precisely the kind of school it wanted. The conflict with the education department grew. This is a very common experience in anything which moves out of line with the patterns imposed by authority. One of the particular difficulties was the Schools Inspectorate. Toroka after a time nicknamed them the "Handbooks" because of the impossibility of discussing educational problems with them; on any question they seemed unable to do more than quote what the official handbook said should be done. Although it had always been difficult to have new ideas accepted through the educational authorities in Songea, quite a lot had been done through the Ministry of Education in Dar es Salaam. This was because the President had instructed Mwingira, the principal secretary in the ministry, to give Litowa the necessary assistance. But at the end of 1967 the atmosphere in the Songea education office changed completely after Mhina, the assistant chief education officer for primary schools, paid a visit to the Region and to Litowa, the purpose of which was "to find ways and means of helping Litowa primary school to convert to *ujamaa* primary school as outlined in [the] President's book – Education for Self-Reliance." This was a very successful visit when Mhina tactfully, yet through honest talking, made it possible to ensure that there was proper understanding on all sides and that it was the wish of the President that the educational authorities assisted the Association in their experiments with the education of the children from the RDA villages.

The first classes held by Ado were generally with the children sitting round in a semicircle in the open air. There were no special buildings and no equipment. Our first "equipment" was a blackboard, donated by the doctor in charge of the hospital at Peramiho mission, which had been used in the nurses' training school, recently rehoused in modern buildings with built-in blackboards. As this first stage was passed, the members in Litowa, helped by those from Luhira and Liweta (the two nearest villages), built a two-classroom block of pole-and-mud construction. Children from other member villages stayed in Litowa, housed with Litowa families. Later, additional buildings were constructed of the same type for further classrooms and for dormitories. The greatest burden of the early buildings and maintenance work and even of the feeding of children from other villages fell on the Litowa village. This was at such an early stage a considerable sacrifice; nevertheless it was about the only way at that time to get such things done, as the other villages involved had started so much later that they were hardly in a position to assist and there was never a question of Litowa excluding them. It was agreed that as villages became able to help they should do so, and the last of the early buildings were built with assistance from a number of other villages.

Some of these efforts began to show that village organisations were becoming strong. At one time a team of people with their manager were over from Liweta to help with the dormitory building when, because of particular weather conditions, a very great effort was needed in the fields in Liweta. For a week those remaining at Liweta worked extremely long hours to cope with the work, deciding to do this in the absence of their manager, rather than calling the others back from Litowa to cope with the rush.

In the dry season of 1966 the general meeting of the Association decided that it was now time to begin planning for permanent school buildings. As a first step each village sent a small team to Litowa to begin making bricks which could be fired and used for permanent buildings in the following year. This was a very successful operation and was followed up in the next year by the building of the first permanent classrooms, a two-classroom block. It was not so easy for all the villages to contribute equally to this work; very few had people with the necessary skill. There were a fair number of reasonable carpenters amongst the people in the villages but very few builders, and none with much experience. Because of this, it was arranged that the Association should employ a qualified builder who would do all the more skilled tasks and work with and organize those less skilled builders who were available from the villages. The villages with no builders provided the builders' labourers. The building that resulted was quite impressive.

With the school growing rapidly, there was a very great need for new dormitories, and it was obvious that it would be some time before these could be of burnt brick. Very good buildings could be constructed with solid mud walls about ten inches thick and a number of dormitories were built in this fashion, again with teams coming from the different villages, generally one village taking responsibility for building one dormitory. In the case of some of the smaller villages the work on one building was shared between two villages.

Part II – The Meaning and Purpose of Education

Within the school a considerable organization had grown up where the children took a great part in the running of their own affairs. To enable this, the school organization was modelled on the type of organization which had been developed to run the villages. This was well established by the early part of 1968, when Toroka wrote a fairly detailed account of the school which was published in the Kivukoni College magazine *Mbioni*.[1] It would be difficult to give a better description than this so that I am quoting it here in full.

---

1   Vol IV, No XI, May 1968.

Education for Self-Reliance –
the Litowa Experiment

By S Toroka

The Interpretation

On hearing Education for Self-Reliance sung about over the radio, written about in the newspapers and talked about in many speeches, it is easy to feel that we are hearing and reading everything there is to know about it. This important document is surely more than we have yet heard or understood. It calls for changes in the attitudes and thinking of the people towards the meaning and purpose of education for this generation and after. It requires a complete overhaul of the attitudes of the people towards education, remoulding the thinking in order to develop a socialist education which will serve a socialist people of a socialist society. The first essential is that those concerned with developing an education of this ideal type, must be dedicated socialist people of a socialist society. As well as being dedicated, the people concerned must also have a good understanding of the society we require to be built and of the practical needs of the economy underlying it. The President in Education for Self-Reliance says that the children must be brought up to realize those things and therefore should be put "to work together". He suggests that it might be done by setting up a school *shamba* or workshop in which they can be taught with practical work that our society is going to be a socialist one with people "living together and working together for the benefit of all", and that it will be one relying on an agricultural and rural economy. It is therefore necessary first to read and understand Socialism and Rural Development before one can fully understand Education for Self-Reliance, for the one cannot go without the other. It is necessary for those ideas to have practical expression and there must therefore be projects but the successful interpretation cannot be measured in projects.

Projects

There are several points which need attention when deciding on what sort of projects would be suitable for a school to work on. There must be economic gain. It is our experience that the pupils will understand, learn and be happy doing even the dirtiest hard work if it proves practically to be a paying one. It must also be related to the life the pupil is going to live. It is no use spending time planning something like a "project for training good party-goers". In the first place this is unrelated to the life of any Tanzanian and secondly, what the country needs is farmers and workers. Above all, the projects should not be done as clubs and societies, for such things have in the past been treated as optional. Projects have to be real and sizeable. Experimental school plots do not fulfil this condition. They are looked upon as a nuisance and thus prove to be failure. They had to be because they were only show pieces which in no way enhanced the real learning situation.

It is important to take into account the ability of the children, particularly the ability to be able to cope with the amount of work involved in projects, for it is easy when making plans to be tempted to make grandiose ones which may never be completed. These lack what one might call a practical vision like some parts of the Five Year Development Plan. Projects need to be planned carefully taking these things into account and not hastily just to be able to show something quickly. There is no rush in development neither are there necessarily quick results. The work has to be done gradually and maintained at a high degree of consistency.

It must at this time be considered whether the projects fit into the present syllabus and curricula, because the new policy is being grafted onto the old established and rigid policy of education. There will need to be big changes before any completely reasonable planning for a school can be fully effective in conjunction with Education for Self-Reliance.

Projects in Operation in Litowa School

We have 245 children in the school at this time but as a great number are very small, the amount of work they can do is limited. The first projects were farm work. Other projects have been and will be taken on as previous ones are established and other work appears possible. All the work is done by the school as a community. All property is communally owned.

1. Farm Work: We have a main school *shamba* with fifteen acres planted already with beans, ground-nuts and soya beans. There are various other small plots which total eight acres and have been planted with fruit trees, forest trees, cassava, *choroko* and cowpeas.

2. The Wool Industry: The work includes the spinning on the wheels of the wool into threads, washing, dyeing, weighing and preparing for marketing. The work was started and begun by the Ruvuma Development Association to introduce the idea. It has since been given as a responsibility to the school to train the children so that they can be efficient future operators of this industry. There are seven girls and one boy who work in two teams in this. They are drawn from the two top classes. The boy is also being trained in simple carpentry so that he could carry out minor repairs on the wheels. He is also being slowly trained as a future manager of the industry. At the head of this team of volunteers are one member of one of our villages and the wife of our Association's advisor.[2] She is the one with the technical knowledge and at this stage does the more intricate work such as dyeing and the weighing of the thread. She is also doing research in producing dyes from local materials, which we hope to use in the future in the production of higher class goods for export to countries where natural dyes are much sought after. When this research is completed and catalogued with necessary qualities and mixtures, it will be taught to children. These

---

2   Noreen Ibbott.

children are taught knitting and later when the equipment is ready they will also be taught weaving. It is a long-term project in which much care and thought are necessary.

3. Nursing and Nursery Work: Among the problems now facing our village communities is the lack of people with medical knowledge and of people trained for nursery work. The Association decided to start by training the children in the school. We have already two pupils who are working in the village dispensary and it is hoped that these children will learn as they work. It is our intention to add to this number so as to make a reasonable team which would be mining a knowledge of the basics of village nursing and also be trained as nursery nurses. We intend to do the initial training locally as soon as we have found the right people to do it. From within the team one or two of the most able children might be selected for further training in nursing at proper nursing schools outside the village.

On the nursery side, we have a group of six girls who work in three teams in the two villages of Litowa and Luhira with the preschool children in these villages. These go out regularly in twos. The work in the nurseries includes cooking and feeding the young children, washing and cleaning them and their clothes, making and repairing suitable clothes, taking them for walks and play, etc. As soon as these girls are old enough and have gained enough experience, and a proper organization in the nurseries has been made, they would introduce the children to numbers and letters, and teach and tell them revolutionary songs and stories so as to slowly build in them the spirit required by their parents.

Possible Future Projects

1. Poultry. A part of this project has already been covered as it was one of the few projects planned for last year. The children erected a wire run and built a house ready to bring in the hens. This was an example of a project not well planned. The farm was not going last year so that there was not the food to feed the birds. To start on modern poultry farming would be at first expensive. We had planned to start by cross-breeding with good cocks and using local birds. The children's parents had promised to send birds as part of their contribution to their school but it was not possible at that time to arrange the collection of these birds from such widely scattered villages.

2. Rabbits. Also in connection with the poultry we are thinking of keeping rabbits for these have been found to do well with poultry. Timber for building the hutches has already been found and we hope soon to start on this.

3. Fish Ponds. The children have been considering building a small fish pond near the school for two purposes – learning and food. On discussing it with the parents it was seen that it was of not much purpose to build a small one, but a relatively large one should be planned which would provide food for a large number of people and be economically paying. This was agreed but as there would be certain small expenses in buying a few materials for building it was decided that the village of Litowa should join with the school in the project. Discussion took place between the school and the village on the details of the work. Work started by clearing the site and we hope soon to start digging the furrow to supply the water and building the bank. On this same site we hope to build in the future a series of fish ponds. The fish for these ponds will be those recommended and provided by the fishery department.

4. Pig Raising. Near the fish ponds we are intending also to keep pigs as their droppings provide excellent food for fish. This will also be a combined project for the school and the village.

The School and the Community

Since the day this school was founded five years ago it belonged
to the community and has been part of the community.

There is one and only one reason why it has since maintained its originality. When these communities began, they
were setting out on a new way of life both in economics and
thought. They were building a tradition. A tradition which was
to be handed on from one generation to another. If they sent
their children to the ordinary schools in the country they would
be divorcing them from the life in the communities and the tradition they were building. Therefore this school was founded
in order "to educate the children to stay in these communities
and carry on the work their parents have begun." It follows that
for a long time it has not been the intention of the parents to
prepare their children for secondary school. If some want [to
go] into secondary schools or any other form of higher education it would be as a result of the geography and the maths they
learnt in school and not a result of the "preparation". This did
not mean that the aim was to deny the children an education as
given in other schools. They were to be educated as anyone else
in the country but with a different aim. This aim, to serve the
community.

The school is thus fully integrated with the community. The
children live and go to school within the community. They regularly work on the community lands. The parents also come to
help with the school lands. Children and parents together build
roads and bridges, repair and build houses. An example is the
school block which the parents and the children had worked
on hand in hand from the beginning to end. The children help
clean the village surrounding, to put fertilizer on the communal crops, to plant and harvest the tobacco, they assist the cooks
in the kitchen, grind maize for the school and the community,
take the village cattle to pasture; parents, as a voluntary duty,
come to cook food for the schoolchildren and so on. In fact the

children are part of the community, and they are growing up to serve it in future as full members. Their spirit no doubt is a communal one and their parents have great hopes in them and respect for them.

Furthermore, during two of the year's school holidays the children are sent in groups to live and work in any one of the twelve villages forming the Association. They are not sent there either as a study tour or to enjoy the comforts of being on holiday. The purpose is to show them the village communities of which they will one day become members and workers, and to allow them to see and learn for themselves the differences in progress and organization from village to village. From these visits we believe that a pupil can learn from experience. They can see that often the best leaders do not come from the educated elite. They will therefore grow to respect all useful persons. This is the opposite of the general trend of today when many children are brought up to respect people not because of their practical abilities, but because of their position or education. While in these villages the children are under the village authority and stay there as any other person, living with the village family. From this again the children learn to respect any parent, not only their own, which is one of the essentials of any *ujamaa* society. There is much that these children can learn in these times of living in the other villages.

On these points the school differs from other schools. In any school in town today, it is true that it is in the community but what is the relationship of the community to the school besides the mere fact that the children come from it? Does any parent other than the government schools inspector know or take any interest in what is taught in school? And he only does because it is his duty! Are the teachers in these schools aware in their teaching that they should be helping to bring up children to serve the community they are in? Or are they teaching them only so that they can pass exams and disappear from the community to the secondary schools? Do the children feel any obligation to this community they are in? Does the school spend even a few hours on Saturdays doing simple services to this community which is devoting so much of its meagre resources to educate its children? The fact is that many schools have been and still remain as the President says – "enclaves" – and the communities around them have been too ignorant or too reluctant to pay any attention to them.

Patterns of Working Together

We accept the truth that the practice of *ujamaa* existed in many of the African societies in the past. History shows that it has been the way of life in practice in those days. It has been there within people but affected by the changes brought about by the impact of alien cultures. It may be true to say that a number of the old understanding people of the country would feel no surprise to hear the practice of *ujamaa* talked about today. They would feel surprised because it is something that they have themselves experienced. It is the young who do not understand because it is something they hear of only. It is those that we are called to direct our thoughts to.

The state is trying its best to teach *ujamaa* through radio broadcasts, but for most of the people in the country it is like a teacher telling a pupil "we are told that the stone is black". So everybody must say that the stone is black while neither the teacher nor the pupil have seen the stone. Suppose that tomorrow that same pupil says that the stone is white. Who would be able to stand up and say no? Would it not be like the story of the Elephant and the Three Blind Men where the conclusions were all drawn from different angles though the beast remained the same?

Putting children to work together seems to be one of those few things the school can do about it today. But a pupil of what kind of society is the one teaching to work together? Do we expect a pupil to properly understand the meaning of working together in the sense of practical *ujamaa*, if he comes from and will return to a home which practises individualism? One might be thought to be biased, but perhaps one is right in saying it is only the children who are in the schools of the *ujamaa* communities who will fully understand and benefit from the teaching of the practice of *ujamaa* and at the same time be able to show the nation in the near future what are the possibilities as well as the limits of the new policy of education.

No kind of *ujamaa* education is necessarily effective if the pupil is going to return to a non-*ujamaa* community. But we can say that having the whole school own and work the same *shamba* and projects will definitely contribute to the education of the children. It introduces the children to the first steps of the meaning of working together and it is worthwhile even if only a few would put the ideas into practice at the same time in their lives. It should be remembered that putting the children to work together and to own the same *shamba* or project has to have an aim which must be first clearly understood by the children; otherwise we will have nothing more than a demonstration of work done together by children.

Having the children working in different groups, each group working independently, does not foster the meaning of working together in the *ujamaa* sense, and in Education for Self-Reliance it is said that each school should be a community of people working together for their own benefit. If we have these separate groups the school does not become a real community. We might succeed in stirring up competition between the groups and thus have more work done, but the overall result would not be a positive one. Also this competition might in future result in man to man competition which is not the ethic of a country to build an *ujamaa* society. There are for instance some block farms where people are living together but they are just like schoolchildren living together in school and split into competitive groups, each struggling on its own for survival and to defeat the other. What should people have in common – it should be a desire of people to live together and have a common thought and work.

The Teaching of *Ujamaa* and the Practice of *Ujamaa*

We do know that *ujamaa* is a way of life of people and can be found within that people. The fact that there are no clearly laid down principles which a people may follow if they choose to live the *ujamaa* way, makes it difficult to orally teach a person and expect a major success. In our case we have one and only one principle which is – living together in brotherhood and working together for the benefit of all. When it comes to teaching it we then have to begin to create the teaching material. This material must be based on a true interpretation of the principle as it is through the interpretation of the principle that ways and means will be found of teaching it. No doubt various methods of this teaching will come forward and it will be difficult to choose any one as there will be different expressions of the practice of *ujamaa* in different parts of Tanzania as is made clear in *Ujamaa Vijijini*.

In our school the people concerned have tried to formulate a few methods of teaching this subject which might be split into practical work, lectures, discussions and reading.

1. Practical Work. It is our practice that almost everything done in the school is done in the name of *ujamaa*, therefore on our timetable are six successive periods termed Practical *Ujamaa*. These Periods are basically intended for teaching the children some particular skill such as spinning, sewing, knitting, weaving, nursing, carpentry, building, farming, etc. It has not up to the present been possible to teach all those skills effectively because there is a lack of the necessary tools and equipment and particularly of the people with the skills to do the teaching. As a result much of the time is spent on farm work. It is not intended that a pupil who learns building work would not participate in farm work. Farm work is the basis of all life and development so that a builder of tomorrow might find himself sowing seeds. It is also a fact that the society that the pupil will be going to live in is a society of farmers and in order to be a part of that society it is essential for the builder also to be a farmer.

2. Lectures. These are given space on the timetable just like any other subject in school. For upper primary there are four periods of *ujamaa* lectures in a week for each class and in lower primary one period a week for each class.

a) Upper Primary
(i) Standard V – The teaching here becomes more difficult and more of it is an introduction to politics. We first start with the twenty nine basic principles of *ujamaa* which are listed out on a separate sheet attached at the end of this writing. This is followed by a study of Tanzania National Heroes part A.
(ii) Standard VI – The subject now ranges from the Tanzania National Heroes part B, to the study of the content and meaning of the Arusha Declaration and its implementation both as it has meaning for individuals and for the Nation.
(iii) Standard VII – We plan that at this stage much of the time will be devoted to the study of the policy of Socialism in Rural Development: fundamental economics of the *viambo*[3] and thorough review of the National Heroes part A and B.

b) Lower Primary
The main objective in all the lower primary standards is to help the children accustom themselves to think and work together. The content of the lectures is similar throughout the standards i.e. the teaching and telling of stories, songs, and plays of the revolutionary spirit, and of the idea of good and bad in terms of *ujamaa* behaviour.

3. Discussions. These are the pupil's own discussions and they vary from formal to informal. The aim of all these discussions is

---

3   Settlements, villages.

to help pupils to work and learn by understanding and without the necessity of being dictated to. Perhaps this is the most educative part of the whole teaching system on this subject as it is this which largely develops the group discipline. We feel this is one of the biggest differences between our school and most others. It is in general in schools for the pupils to be "told" and not be given a chance to contribute. Perhaps this is because the teacher has been assumed to be a person in possession of all the answers so that the pupil is always to receive and never to give. As a result the teacher has never learnt to trust his pupil while the pupil has always seen himself as an inferior person before his teacher with nothing to contribute to his own education.

These discussions can be divided into committees, discussion groups and the *Ujamaa* Assembly.

The Pupils' Own Executive Committee

This is on the pupils' side the supreme body, at the head of which sits a democratically elected chairman. The responsibilities of the Executive Committee are as follows:

i. To take care of the overall welfare of the children. This includes encouraging the sick to attend the dispensary, dealing with minor offences and checking undesirable manners in any pupil, issuing warnings in cases of bad behaviour or suggesting a punishment, such suggestions having to go for approval to the *Ujamaa* Assembly: to sort out any difficulties arising from feeding and to promote the cleanliness of the school and the children's persons.

ii. To plan the year's work and send the plan to the working committee for execution.

iii. To ensure that the working committee does its best to carry out the plan.

iv. To introduce legislation to the *Ujamaa* Assembly, study rules made by this assembly and check any undesirable rules.

v. To work hand in hand with the teachers on various matters affecting the children.

vi. To act as a financial committee by controlling all money gained by the efforts of the children.

The membership of this Executive Committee is as follows:

The pupils' chairman – who is an elected chairman. He presides over the meetings of both the Executive Committee and the *Ujamaa* Assembly: is the chief spokesman of the children and together with the manager he may be invited to sit in on some of the staff meetings.

The vice-chairman – who is also elected and his work is to assist the chairman.

The secretary – who is also elected. He has to put on record the discussions and important points decided on by the Executive Committee and the *Ujamaa* Assembly.

The treasurer – who is also elected and has the duties of keeping account of all the money gained through the pupils' work and of all expenditure of all this money.

The manager – he is an appointed official being the school captain who is ex-officio the manager and a member of the Executive Committee. This manager is the chief workman, foreman and work organizer of the activities planned by the executive. He has to be very energetic, of a strong character, intelligent and above all possessing the qualities of leadership. He is an extremely important post, as much of the success or failure of any of the activities depends upon him. He is also the chairman of the working committee.

The dresser – he is also an appointed person and is also a member of the working committee. His function on both committees is to help in solving the health problems of the children.

Besides the above there are six further selected members of the committee bringing the total number to twelve. They may be elected because they have particular duties in the school or because it is felt they are the type of people who can contribute to the general discussion of the committee.

B. The Pupils' Own Working Committee

This working committee is chaired by the manager and its work is:

- To execute the decisions of the Executive Committee, and the *Ujamaa* Assembly.
- To be in charge of all practical activities.
- To allocate pupils into groups to work on particular duties and to appoint leaders for these groups. After these appointments and allocations are approved, the working committee may not dismiss anyone from his duties or make changes without the consent of the *Ujamaa* Assembly and the Executive.
- To meet as often as possible to consider all work being done at that time.
- To act as a body of work supervisors to check any laziness shown in practical work by any pupil.
- To present an annual report of their activities to the Executive Committee and the *Ujamaa* Assembly.

Membership of the Working Committee: there is no limit to the membership of this committee as the size depends largely on the amount of work which is being done at a particular time. It could be termed a "manager's committee" as its members are appointed by the manager except for four members from the Executive Committee who sit on the Working Committee as ex-officio. These four are the Manager, himself as chairman, the chairman of the Executive Committee, the secretary and the treasurer. The chairman of the Executive Committee is present to advise the Working Committee on the best way to carry out its duties. Other members will generally be people who are in charge of various work groups and at present they are mostly school junior leaders (prefects). They are people as the following:

The *bwana shamba* – He is the next most energetic workman to the manager. He is at present in charge of all *shamba* activities but it is intended that in the future he will be in charge of all farm activities. His chief duties are:

- To supervise all *shamba* activities.
- To warn any lazy pupils and report on them.
- To know when to plough, sow and what is to be sown on each plot.
- To know when to weed, thin out and be able to report on any signs of crop disease.
- To report on all his duties to the Working Committee.

The gardener – takes charge of all gardening activities.

The storekeeper – is in charge of the food store and controls the issuing of the food and cleanliness of the store. He has to report any food shortage and to order new stock.

The mess leader – supervises the serving of the food and sees that all eating and cooking utensils are clean and kept in their right place.

The dresser – deals with all health problems and attends the sick in the dispensary.

C. The *Ujamaa* Assembly

This is a general assembly where all pupils sit to discuss their own problems. Its chairman is the pupils' chairman, who is a member of both the Executive and the Working Committee. The duties of this assembly are:

- To keep every pupil informed of all that is happening by questioning and criticism and by seeking information.
- To approve, amend or reject suggestions forwarded to it by the Executive Committee.
- To award punishments or issue warnings after consideration of the suggestions forwarded by the Executive Committee.
- To discuss and approve, amend or reject, activity plans submitted by the Executive Committee.
- To help the children to maintain a high sense of moral conduct.
- To question the teachers to obtain information.

This is a very important body and when attending its meetings it is possible to feel its power of sense of responsibility by the nature of the decisions taken. There is a maximum democratic element and the pupils feel very free to express themselves.

D. The Discussion Group

This is a group of selected intelligent children who are put to meet together to discuss any matters of education interest. It is appointed by the school authority and has twelve members. When they meet, other pupils may be invited but these have no vote. The group regularly invites member of the Association, visitors and teachers to talk with them on any point of interest.

The Role of the Teacher and Some Results of this Method

When all these committees and groups are set working one might ask that if they work effectively what is the part played by the teacher? These groups are really teaching aids as are tape recorders, pictures and diagrams, to illustrate particular subjects and they do not replace the teacher. The role of the teacher is not only still there but in fact becomes of much greater importance. Giving a child an exercise or a means of solving a mathematical problem is not the end of teaching. The important thing is the working side by side with the pupil which will help him to use that means to solve the problem correctly or at least in a satisfactory manner. In this case it is essential that the teacher should work with the committees, not as a member of them, or by telling them what to do, but by advising them on things which they are not sure of doing correctly. Here the teacher should be prepared to help, not by giving the right answers, but by giving them the means whereby they might find the right answer. Much depends on the nature of the question and there may be instances where the teacher might feel it worthwhile to give the right answer, but he should always refrain from spoon-feeding the children. It is even better sometimes not to give any answer if the question is one of which the pupils should know or re-member the answer from previous instances – pupils like all hu-man beings are often looking for an easy way of doing things.

In relation to these groups then it is the work of the teacher to be a guiding light, to generally refrain from coarse methods and to work by showing and explaining. Above all, politeness is essential in training children this way, rude treatment would not produce the desired results. This does not mean that the pupils should be treated as the President says "like eggs". Sometimes it is essential to be firm and there must be over everything a feel-ing of discipline.

Let us take an example from our experience. The children in our school have much freedom for thinking, deciding and do-ing things themselves. With these seemingly powerful organs in the hands of the children it is natural that the nature of the child might lead him to assume too much authority on his side. On one occasion the pupils decided to test their power by not agreeing to do certain things on logical grounds and by ignor-ing the school authority. This was really a time of testing for the teacher, because there is certainly nothing wrong if the pu-pils disagree with doing something when they have satisfactory reasons. But ignoring proper authority was something which showed a disdainful attitude and this could not be tolerated. It was accordingly necessary to show that the school authority must be respected and to get over to the children the lesson that in all situations in life there is some authority over us. On the other hand in the case of the work which they did not think should be done, we allowed it to pass, knowing definitely that the result would be unpleasant, but believing that through this the children would learn an important lesson for the future. We believe it is important to realize that mistakes are not all that bad. Mistakes are often regrettable but we should not forget that it has so often been that learning by mistakes can be part of a very effective learning, although sometimes slow and painful.

On occasion, therefore, it is important to allow mistakes to happen for the sake of learning.

Reading

We are not here talking of reading for pleasure or of the ordinary class readings. These are specially guided readings for exhortation purposes or for encouraging the correct spirit. These readings may be given before and after the *Ujamaa* Assembly, before and after any formal gathering of the children or in the mornings before starting lessons – this is part of what we call "*Ujamaa* Prayer". These readings are mostly selected parts of the speeches and writings of the President. They may also be biblical readings. It may be questioned why religious readings are included here but the truth is as many who know religious teachings well will agree that the Bible contains in it some excellent teachings for mankind. After all one can if he wishes show through the teachings of Jesus himself and Mohammed that they were socialists.

Attending Parents' *Ujamaa* Assemblies and RDA General Meetings

The children are also encouraged to attend communal *ujamaa* gatherings with the aim of sharing in the discussions of their parents, at the same time seeing and learning how their elders go about the business of solving their own communal problems. One of the duties of the pupils' *Ujamaa* Assembly is to choose delegates to attend the RDA general meetings, often it is the pupils' chairman and the manager. They do not attend these general meetings as spokesmen for the children but to observe although they can participate in the discussion if they wish. After returning they are required to report on the meeting to their own assembly after which they might be questioned and discussion might ensue. This is designed to keep the children informed of all that is happening and is planned for all the villages of the Association.

There is no doubt in my mind that in achieving its objective the school was highly successful, but this was in no way due to all of the ideas being carried out with efficiency. There were many difficulties quite apart from those caused through the lack of co-operation from the authorities in the earlier years. It was not possible to get a complete staff of people who quickly understood the ideas of the villages or who were easily prepared to join in and do hard physical work with the children. The idea of the children taking decisions on many matters for themselves was also hard for some of them to accept. On top of this the school was always growing more rapidly than the provision of adequate accommodation. Having found Toroka, who was an outstanding headmaster for such a school, he was then taken away for five months to do his term of National Service. When he returned from this, Mapunda, another member of the staff was likewise taken away for five months. There also continued to be outside calls on Toroka's time. He was appointed to a commission of the Ministry of Education on the curriculum for primary education in Tanzania. He was taken away for periods to assist in the party's programme of attempting of educate party leaders and government officials in the ideas of *ujamaa* village development. At times many of these difficulties led one to think that the whole programme would have limited success, and yet through it all the spirit of the children continued to grow. I am certain that the greatest part of this success was due to the fact that the whole of the programme was carried out within the context of an *ujamaa* village, that it was this surrounding atmosphere and indeed the atmospheres from all the other villages that the children came from which led to the success measured in the attitudes of mind of the children.

Some 350 miles to the east at Mahiwa was an institution called the Mahiwa Agricultural and Co-operative Training College which was founded with the object of providing an education for primary school leavers which would fit them to be better farmers in their home areas and guide them towards returning to those areas after their education. This was a very difficult objective to achieve in an establishment isolated from any promising experiment in rural development, and run by officers of the Agricultural Department. In 1968-69 Wayakile, who was then vice-chairman of the Association, was lent to Mahiwa to help them with a new experiment for their second-year pupils of living in simple accommodation on a small farm at Chipito some miles from the college, running the show themselves as a communal venture. It was quite obvious in talking to the members of the college staff at the end of this year that they were very impressed by Wayakile, not just as a person but also by his agricultural ability. But Wayakile told us on his return how so many of his efforts at directing the boys back to the villages were completely neutralized by the principal of the college who was actively working, mostly through the Ministry of Agriculture in Dar es Salaam, to find salaried work places for the boys when they finished their course.

As well as having Wayakile at Mahiwa, we had sent from Liweta two young chaps who had completed their primary education to be students at the college. These two were not children educated at the Association school at Litowa, but were two of the few who were already going through schooling when the Association was founded. Thus, although they were *ujamaa* village children, they had been formally educated in the schools where they would have come up against all the influences that would tend to lead them away from the countryside to the towns and to paid employment. At Mahiwa the staff assured me that these two boys were completely different from any of the other pupils, that they had a completely different attitude to field work and a much higher sense of responsibility. They were the only ones who would carry on with manual work when the staff was not there overseeing them. Wayakile told me that their performance at Mahiwa and confidence of what they were on about was extremely impressive as they were highly ridiculed by the other boys for their persistence in setting their eyes towards a life in their home village. This would suggest that by far the greatest influence on their attitudes was the fact that their home was in an *ujamaa* village, and also that they saw their village as achieving things worthwhile.

In the school at Litowa it was noteworthy that there was a proper respect for the members of the staff from the schoolchildren, although as time went on a number of the older children quite obviously had more idea of where they and their villages were going than some of the less able members of the staff. The fact that the children had considerable power in the school did not in any way detract from this, even where there were conflicts.

One such conflict occurred between Toroka and Victori Sangu who was the school chairman and therefore the children's own elected leader. The children's school manager, as Toroka wrote, was not elected by the children but appointed by the headmaster. This post was looked upon as a very important one. A boy by the name of Mahomedi from Mtakinini was appointed to the post. Mahomedi was a strong, capable boy but as time went on tended to become rather overpowering and as a result lost the confidence of the children. Victori representing the children went to Toroka to say that the children required a change and no longer had confidence in Mahomedi. Toroka's reaction was to defend Mahomedi and there followed a slightly heated exchange at the end of which Victori said "Mahomedi may be your manager but he is not any longer ours." Whereupon he turned about and walked away from Toroka who felt he had no choice but to make a change. This incident in no way affected Victori's or any of the other children's respect for Toroka or the staff or for that matter Mahomedi.

The end of 1969 was to bring the first children to the end of upper primary schooling with standard VII. For a year or two before this, there had been much discussion within the Association on how the children should be finally fitted for the work in the villages. It was decided, as a result of these discussions, that they should go on to different forms of practical training covering the many sides of agriculture, building, carpentry, spinning and weaving, childcare, health, plumbing, etc., needed in their villages. One of the biggest points of discussion was whether at that stage any of the children should be encouraged to go on to secondary education to provide future medical aides, nurses, doctors, accountants and so on. I was rather against this, feeling in particular that with the first children in the school it would have been a mistake to take the academically brightest (and the secondary schools would have taken only the academically brightest) as it was vital that these should go to the far more important jobs particularly in agriculture. There was, for instance, a tremendous need for really intelligent people to be trained to introduce and care for livestock. One of the most strongly argued points on the other side was the felt need for people with a higher education who would be able to put the case of villagers in national discussions. There was never any final decision on this as it was still very much under discussion at the time of the disbanding of the Association.

As the time drew near for the standard VII final examinations, on which any entry to secondary schools would be based, Toroka put an increasing emphasis on the children doing practical work rather than class work, almost as if he was trying to ensure that the children would not do too well in this final examination. However the reason that he gave me for keeping the children out of the classroom at this time was that it had nothing to do with its effect on the children, but with bringing home to the staff the unimportance of the examination system, and to make clear to them that their performance as teachers was not going to be judged on the results their pupils obtained in the examinations.

Some months before the end of the school year, the children's future began to be discussed with them and they were told the types of training that it was hoped to provide by the Association. They were each asked to give three choices of what they would like to do on completion of standard VII. Only the two children who were from homes near but outside of the communal village put as a choice to attend secondary school.

What choices the children had made were looked at in the light of the needs of the villages from which they came and their ability as evaluated by the staff. In some cases the children's choice fitted these criteria. In a number of cases it was necessary to make other suggestions. I remember how we noticed that in the Association we faced a position completely opposite to that in the country as a whole. There was much talk on the providing of work places for the stream of young people leaving school. Here in Ruvuma we had at that time seventeen villages, and some thirty six children leaving school in that year who would eventually return to work in those villages. This meant that most villages did not stand the chance of getting many more than two or three. This two or three was a negligible amount compared with the needs in the villages for people with a little bit more of the right education and training. Moreover, if things had continued, as the years went by there would have been an increasing need for more skilled labour. There was an acute shortage of school leavers.

The suggestions for what each child should be trained for were then taken to a third stage: the list was presented to a quarterly meeting of the Association, where the manager and one other from each village would discuss the list. No decisions were taken at this meeting but care was given to seeing that all these village leaders understood the process of making decisions. The village managers then took the lists and suggestions for training of their own particular children back to their villages for it to be discussed there. Any alterations were sent back to Litowa and the lists accordingly amended.

Now came the final stage when we met the children in standard VII to discuss the arrangements with them. This meeting took place in the school dining hall which had recently been completed and which was also used as a school hall. After explaining very carefully to the children what had happened since they had made their choices, although of course the majority, if not all, knew already, it was explained to them that this was the time when the final decision had to be made. A special bench was placed in front and on this the children from each village in turn would sit. With each group the needs of the particular village were discussed and then what was thought the best training for each child in turn was suggested. They could accept the suggestions on the spot, ask questions about them, make alternative suggestions, or think about them until a later date. All but three, after discussion, accepted the suggestions, these three preferring to think it over for a few days and come back with their thoughts. It was most impressive. It was a tragedy that these children were not allowed to continue.

A revealing incident took place towards the end of the five weeks' stay of some of the members of the TANU central committee at Litowa which involved the schoolchildren. The chairman of the school invited the committee members to come and speak to a meeting of all the children and they agreed to do so. The school hall was only some one hundred yards from the tents in which the committee members were staying. At the appointed time the children were assembled in the hall and as the committee members approached, the children all rose to their feet as a gesture of respect. The central committee members never entered the hall but from the doorway the most outspoken of them stood and for five minutes harangued the children as being badly brought up and lacking in respect. During this process the children remained standing listening. The members then returned to their tents. The children found this behaviour impossible to understand and Victori Sangu as chairman decided to go to ask why they had been treated like this. He took two other members of the school committee with him and walked over to ask for this explanation; he remained talking with the visitors for nearly an hour. Although only seventeen years old, Victori was an extremely impressive young man. He always behaved as a proper child of Africa with tremendous respect for those older than himself, and was very level-headed in his reasoning. It was only too obvious that, however much care he used and however much respect he showed, he was fighting a losing battle. One's knowledge of the world tells one only too well that the present central committee of the party and the Litowa schoolchildren could not live side by side.

12

VILLAGE INDUSTRIES

The economist Dr Ernst Schumacher writes:

> Agriculture alone, at the level of poverty, consisting as
> it does of scraping the ground and living with cattle,
> cannot develop the mind. Agricultural populations
> need the stimulus of non-agricultural activities, or they
> will stay at the subsistence level and increasingly tend
> to desert the land in the hope of finding a "better life"
> in the cities.[1]

In Rhodesia when we moved to Nyafaru, the company[2]
had taken over an existing farm and there was a small flock of
corriedale sheep. In Africa always far from the temptations of
shops, it was not often that I was tempted to buy Noreen birth-
day or Christmas presents. Seeing these sheep, however, and
knowing her talent in making things, I ordered from the UK a
spinning wheel, a pair of carders and a book called *The Weavers'
Craft*, and gave them to her as a Christmas present. This was in
1960. With the wool from the sheep she not only taught herself
to spin but very quickly produced pullovers and cardigans for
all our family as well as woollen vests for some, which enabled
us to "survive" the exceptionally cold winter of 1962-63 when
we were on holiday in England. Walks with the children had a
new interest searching for natural dye materials to give a good

---

1 *Small is Beautiful: a study of economics as if people mattered*, Blond &
   Briggs, London, 1973.
2 Nyafaru Development Company.

range of colours. Lichens, tree barks, leaves and wood, plants, shrubs and roots.

The farmhouse at Nyafaru was a large one and housed a small community of us. The spinning did not long stay as a pastime of Noreen. In fact it often became difficult for her to spin as the wheel was used by so many others. Weaving woollen mats followed, for which there appeared quite a demand, so that more equipment was obtained and one of the outbuildings was converted to a spinning and weaving "factory" employing half a dozen local girls. What was always evident as one by one all the local people came to have a look, was not that there was work for a few of their girls, but that here were "their" people making these mats, spinning this wool, knitting these jumpers. These simple accomplishments were sources of wonder. These were the Tangwena people very much in an economic backwater of Rhodesia, and literally scraping the ground and living with the cattle. Ian Smith's government felt it necessary to forcefully move them from their scattered homes purported to be on "European land" so remote that it was unsalable and unused.

When beginning work in Ruvuma we had discussed with the Litowa people the various possibilities of small industries and the greater variety of work that would come later as the villages progressed. It is not always easy for people to strive for such possibilities when they have never seen them and at that stage were only so many words, while the work to achieve them tends to be hard and very much the same from day to day. In the Ruvuma Region the land is covered with trees. When peasant farmers want to open up a new piece of land, the customary method is to cut down all but the larger trees from about three feet above the ground during the dry season when work on the previous year's harvesting has finished. With the larger trees most of the smaller branches are cut off and those branches, together with the smaller trees, are stacked around the stumps, left for a number of weeks to dry a little and then burnt together with all the grass on the plot. This kills the larger trees but the smaller roots generally manage to survive and quickly grow again when the soil is worked out after a few years and the owner passes to another plot. This method requires the minimum amount of work but is not suitable for a stable community or a developing agriculture.

By far the biggest job in the early years at Litowa was the proper clearing of the bush to make improved farming possible. It is surprising how many trees can grow on an acre and there are many acres. With this being the work day after day during the dry season, work on the crops during the rains, cutting poles, grass and building houses, all heavy work and connected with the basics of life, talk of other things being possible in the future would not necessarily mean much. As enquiries showed that it was possible to get wool easily and cheaply from Kenya, the idea was accepted that we should get a spinning wheel and teach one or two of the women to spin and knit as this was one of the easiest ways of demonstrating the idea. The results were quite amusing. Within a few weeks almost everyone, men included, when walking in the village were knitting as they walked. A few pairs of knitting needles had been given by the Community Development Department to teach the women to knit, but the rest could not await either their turn or for more needles. Needles were made out of shaped strips of bamboo, stems of grass or whatever else came to hand. There was not much doubt about the interest, but the work schedule did not leave much for the development of this at that time.

Other villages, such as Liweta, Matetereka, Ligoma, either hearing of it or seeing it when their members visited Litowa, wanted to send women to be taught how to spin. As a result the question was discussed at one of the Association's meetings. The leaders recognized the difficulties and dangers of trying too many things too quickly and that at present all equipment had to be imported, but from this time plans were evolved in Association meetings. The decisions were broadly that it was good for any village which wanted to take up spinning either for their own use for blankets or clothing, or for selling outside the villages where possible. In this latter case it was felt that selling should be organized through Litowa as colours from chemical dyes were more popular locally than those from natural dyes and these were expensive, although small quantities could dye large quantities of wool. It was better for dyeing to be done in one centre, and Litowa was the place where most expertise existed, with better facilities for marketing. It was decided that the greatest effort should be put into Matetereka village; its higher altitude made it a better place to keep wool sheep and a place more in need of warm clothing. It was decided not to hurry and that more success would be achieved in the long run if the village children at school in Litowa were taught the craft, taking it to their villages at the end of their training. The three villages which had suggested that they should send women to learn were the first allowed to do that even though they would have to return with no equipment on which to use their newly acquired skills.

With steadily increasing activities at Litowa there was always a shortage of accommodation, and with the school in temporary buildings (like the villages at first), it was not easy to find a place for a craft such as spinning and weaving which required equipment needing dry space.

In 1966 the first people moved from the original grass-hut houses to larger and more permanent buildings in the new Litowa village site. In 1967 we moved from our grass house to this new site. These new houses had ten-inch thick mud walls and thatched roofs. Ours was two blocks, one consisting of three bedrooms and the other having a kitchen with small dining room next to it and beyond this a large room which we called the school room. With our own children learning at home, each of course in a different year, it was best if they could be spread out a little so that the work of Noreen with one did not disturb the work of others. Pressure to push on with spinning and weaving training gave this room a dual purpose. We were given a number of spinning wheels by Oxfam for this training and into this room they went. People were interested to see weaving so that with *mpapa*[3] poles and bamboos Noreen built a simple loom on which the first woven blanket was made. This loom also went into our room and was later replaced by a Swedish loom donated by a teachers' association in the United States. As a result we were in a good position to see the interest that this little enterprise, carried on by eight school children – one boy and seven girls – created, and this was always remarkable.

This interest was not only amongst peasant peoples. Visitors who were government officials, school teachers, ministers, party officials, journalists and others were fascinated by these small efforts. On July 7th of 1969 these children took their equipment to Songea to the showground on the party's National Day and put on a demonstration of carding, spinning, washing, dyeing and weaving of the wool entirely organised and run by themselves. This again attracted the same fascination.

To us statements such as that peasant peoples need the stimulus of non-agricultural activities, are not merely academic pronouncements. This village textile industry was the work of eight children and yet whether visitors were shown this work by the chairman, the secretary, manager or any other Litowa member, it was always shown as a work of all the people of the village and the Association, as indeed it was. When we left it was still a part-time industry operated by the children during practical lessons, in after-school hours and at weekends. With the opening of a large wool sheep scheme in the highlands of the Kitulo Plateau south of Mbeya, it became possible to obtain the raw wool from within Tanzania and at a cheaper price. The rams in the flock were shorn twice a year and the second shearing we purchased for only 2.50 shillings per lb. There are very slight losses due to washing out the grease and dirt but this price does

---

3   Type of tree.

mean that people are able with their own labour to produce woollen clothing for themselves at a very low price. Moreover, hand-spun woollens are very hard-wearing. I have a pullover made in 1961 which is still like new.

As the children learnt to spin, all the yarn was usable. The first efforts were not of course high-class but were used for them to learn knitting, when they made articles to fit themselves. As soon as the spinning reached a certain standard, the wool was sold to schools for domestic science teaching and to a women's club, as well as to private individuals. Later blankets were also sold. This was because it was decided that the venture, even while it was educational, must be self-supporting and also able itself to purchase any additional equipment required. The Kitulo sheep sent some 200 lbs of raw wool not asking for payment for six months during which time the children earned enough through sales to pay for it. They also paid for the shipping charges on the Swedish loom and for all the soap powders for washing the wool and a number of other minor expenses. Odo Msambwa, the one boy learning who was the "manager" of the venture, spent a weekend at the end of the year going through the sales and expenses book and produced an impressive report and accounts for the annual meeting of the schoolchildren when the section leaders had to report on all activities.

Most of these children completed their primary education in September 1969. The new spinning and weaving building was almost complete and in November these children would have returned to learn and work full-time in this village industry. The disbanding of the Association in September put an end to these plans. Odo Msambwa was from Matetereka and his village sent him to Dar es Salaam where there was a small cottage industries training centre at which an Indian spinner and weaver taught his craft.

A similar interest showed itself in another very small effort that was tried in the last year with a product which is not much to look at – soap. The mission farm at Peramiho kept quite large numbers of pigs to provide themselves with meat and had considerable quantities of pig fat for sale to the surrounding people who used it for cooking fat. When, as part of their aid, the Americans sent large quantities of cooking oil for distribution at only the cost of transport from the coast, the pig fat did not easily sell and could be obtained at a ridiculously low price. We decided to try and make soap from it obtaining one or two recipes from overseas, all somewhat different. We had therefore to experiment.

Our first experiment was rather exciting but did not produce the right results. We used the wrong type of container so that our kitchen was very nearly inundated with an ever-increasing white froth, making us feel rather like the sorcerer's apprentice. We were soon able to make very good soap, and for some weeks were supplying all the requirements of the school when the American oil supply ceased and the price of pig fat more than doubled. One of the reasons for using pig fat had been that the school as well as some of the Litowa villagers had started keeping pigs. When Bagamoyo, the Litowa treasurer, killed a pig, he brought part of the fat for making soap; thus we had only to pay for the caustic soda. Just before the disbanding, the school killed a large pig and brought nine gallons of fat from it for soap-making. The point is not just that we had soap but it was soap that the people made – a very different thing.

These things showed people the possibilities for variety in village life but there were other more basic things which were already beginning to increase village activities. Particularly in Litowa and Liweta, carpentry was a growing activity and in both places had become an all-year-round activity, and not just for a few months in the dry season. In both cases it was mainly connected with village building and village needs such as cattle troughs, rabbit hutches, dispensary furniture and so on. In both villages also it had grown beyond this and they were dealing with Association building in the school and furniture for the school. Alongside of this developed the growth of sections producing timber from local trees by hand sawing. Although the Association was in business in Songea producing timber, the school buildings were being roofed with timbers entirely cut and erected by Litowa and Liweta villagers. Both of these villages were fortunate in having amongst their members men who had had some experience at carpentry, at Liweta to a rather higher standard than at Litowa. The villages had each selected younger members to work with these carpenters and so learn the trade, thus starting something in the nature of an apprenticeship. In the same way the area in which the Litowa and Liweta villages were situated was one where in the past many men had worked as sawyers for the missions. This skill now became useful for the villages which, while doing the work, were training others of their members in the same way as with carpentry.

This development of carpentry comes naturally in a village when the community reaches the stage where it is able to move on to more permanent housing and village buildings. Not all villages are as fortunate in having people with a little skill in these things and as a result, the teaching of carpentry was to be one of the subjects in the post-primary training course, so that after a few years young carpenters would be going into all the villages. Building too was to be taught, but as with carpentry there were certain skills in some villages which were growing of themselves. We will deal with this later.

13

LEARNING BY DOING IT YOURSELF

Although the villages of the Association did not receive much assistance from government, it is worth comparing the difference in approach of aid through the people's Association and aid from government. The large items of government aid were a grain storage building at Matetereka, a water supply at Liweta, and bridges over the Luhira river for Litowa and over the Liweta river for Liweta.

An adequate piped water supply is a great asset to a growing village not only in order to give plenty of water for domestic uses, allowing for greater hygiene – one tends to be very sparing with water when you have to carry all of it up from the river by hand or rather by head – but also for building, which is a great user of water. When the water is carried, its supply becomes a great user of scarce labour. On his first visit, Jimmy Betts, the Eastern African Oxfam field director in 1964, agreed to put forward to his committee in Oxford a request for funds to purchase the materials for installing a water supply. The committee agreed the funds.

The main work was the building of a dam at the top of a small rocky waterfall to get a good take-off point for the drive pipe of a hydraulic ram. Work could not start until after the rainy season when the river returned to its dry season level. This was not a bad thing as labour was most needed in the fields during the rains. Litowa had no fully trained builders but one member, an older man by the name of Karikenye, had done much labour on building sites, and learnt a little building. Another member, Lumumba, also had some experience. Having made out the plan and discussed it with the people, I wrote to the hydraulic ram manufacturers who agreed that the layout was feasible. A temporary sandbag dam was constructed (after some difficulty) to divert the river, and the dam wall was built by the two builder members. Much stone as well as sand and cement had to be carted down a very steep hill to a not very accessible point beside the waterfall. From this dam the water was piped to a header tank which would give a straight line for the drive pipe of the ram. This drive pipe had to pass down the side of a rock and be supported by a number of rock pillars built from the valley bottom. With a head of water of fourteen feet, the ram pumped to a supply tank 150 feet above the river from where it flowed by gravity down the centre of the ridge which was the future permanent village site. There was altogether about a mile and a half of water piping, and at the end of the rains the village had dug trenches in which this piping was later laid. The plumbing work was simple and it took only a little time to teach a group in the village to be able to do this.

While this work was going on, another group had been making bricks for building the storage tank. When the dam and installation of the ram and its drive pipe were complete, the builders moved up to build the tank. At this stage we had word that Jimmy Betts was again going to visit us and the people decided on an all-out drive to get the tank finished and water running to the village in time for the visit. This was achieved around midday on December 18th 1965 and it was a great event. Constructionally this last-minute rush was not a good thing as the hurried work on the tank led to a break of part of the wall the following year. However, the break in the water supply was only for a few hours as dealing with this emergency was a small task compared to the total installation. The people's own labour represented a considerable saving in cash and the total cost of the materials was only 38,000 shillings. The most important point was not the cash saving but what it added to developing a village organization. Dealing with the installation from the time of first discussing the idea and measuring up the river site until the first water came through, is practical organization, and through having done this, the capability of the people of the village had increased. This is quite apart from their sense of achievement at the results of their labours.

At this time it was suggested that government might install a water system for the Liweta village. We understand that according to government regulation they were not really able to carry out this installation as there was not the requisite number of people living there, but it was to be done in this instance owing to a special instruction from the President's office. The work was not carried out until 1969 – a long wait for a village wishing to have water to enable them more easily to carry on with improved, more permanent buildings. In each of the preceding years when we made enquiries we were told that the necessary finance was not available that year, but the work would be done the following year. In 1969 when we were beginning to believe that tomorrow would never come, the water unit moved in and quickly and efficiently installed the system. The cost we were told was 97,000 shillings. The standard of work was much higher than at Litowa. I feel that much of this higher standard is unwarranted and makes development difficult as works are divorced from hard economic reality. That the cost was two and a half times that of Litowa is an important consideration when there are many settlements in the region and available finances make it urgent to use resources to the best advantage. On top of the ordinary village needs and development, Litowa had a big school building programme for the Association, domestic water for 250 school children and for the school staff, as well as building and domestic needs for people brought to Litowa on the various training programmes. At times of peak use of water, as when brick making and building were in full swing at the beginning of the dry season, the water available barely satisfied the demand; but I feel this was a good thing by keeping the question of water supply constantly in mind. It also faced the people with the fact that their economic position did not make the "ideal" feasible.

The Liweta system can give something like three times the daily quantity of the Litowa supply while the needs are less. This is good in that it allows for future growth. I think that it is not possible to forecast how that growth will take place. The existing layout with expensive and permanent water points is suited to the existing temporary building. At present the village may feel that they will erect the permanent buildings on the same site but as the years pass and they begin to work on the new buildings they may develop other ideas. There is much advantage in the early stage of development to being able to see what is necessary from year to year and not just tie oneself down to rigid plans. When we first went to Litowa, one of the things I felt was how much the people wanted a plan and then how much they felt tied to it. I explained many times that I felt plans to be very necessary but that it was more necessary to be able to change plans. A permanent village plan for Litowa was made very early on in 1963 but it was not a rigidly fixed one and as developments were possible in later years, each was discussed in the light of the plan and whether the planned site was still the most suitable. The basic plan was still there but there were many changes made as time went on, and of course occasionally completely new items appeared such as the leadership training project which was not even thought of in 1963.

Having said all of this, I feel that the most important difference is that the Liweta people were having a supply planned and put in for them, and that this took away from them an important chance to develop themselves.

A somewhat similar situation occurred with the grain store at Matetereka built with government money. The plan was one taken from the standard drawings of the Ministry of Communi-

cations and Works which, although sound, needed alterations
in design to suit the conditions of Matetereka. The windows for
light and ventilation high under the eaves gave protection from
rain in most situations in the country, but with the high unpro-
tected terrain of Matetereka and the strong winds often accom-
panying rain, water found its way into the building. The village
was brought into certain parts of the work in that they were told
how many bricks were required and were asked to make them,
and asked also to supply stone for the foundations and sand for
the building.

The people of Liweta also wanted a storage building but as
it was not possible for this to come from government funds, they
had to get on with the business themselves. They had carpenters
but no bricklayers; they had savings to buy certain of the necessary materials, but not enough for the roofing. The Association
had a builder to help with the school buildings and the village
arranged to have this man help them where necessary, for example in setting out the building so that the villagers could dig
the foundations, helping with foundations and walls, and showing the villagers how to do the things that it was possible for
them to do themselves. The villagers negotiated a loan to buy
the galvanized corrugated iron sheeting for the roof. They had
to calculate how many bricks would be needed and make them.
The whole process necessary for producing the building was in
the hands of the village, and this much increased village ability
at many levels including the very important one of certain members beginning to learn various building skills.

The two bridges, for Litowa and Liweta, built with government funds, were both given out to private contract so that the
villages were not involved in their construction at all. One contract was given to the Benedictine mission and the other to an
expatriate contractor, both giving a good job of work.

14

RELIGION AND THE LOCAL MISSION

It is a point of interest to me to notice the position of religion
within a community. At St Faith's in Rhodesia, with the return of
the menfolk from the towns, the development of the communal
farm and the integration of the "professions" into the life of the
village – all producing a genuine community – there followed a
much increased church activity; church services and religious
functions were much more widely attended. As the steps were
taken by church authority, which one by one broke down what
the people had created, so step by step church services reverted
to functions attended mainly by schoolchildren and women.

When we moved from St Faith's to Nyafaru, we were only
a very small group of people but fairly quickly we became involved with the surrounding Tangwena people who were living on what was termed "European land". In particular we
worked with them on plans for developing a school. One of the
outcomes of this development was a request from the people
to use Nyafaru as a place to express their interest in religion.
As a result, very large gatherings were held; at first in the open
air since there was no building large enough. Here three separate religious bodies were represented and took part together
in a religious ceremony. The three bodies were perhaps highly
unexpected bedfellows: Anglicans, American Methodists and
the Watchtower. One group at one time would lead the singing,
another the prayers and the third the reading. Following these,
there would be discussions.

At Litowa, as many of the original people involved had
had rather unfortunate experiences of the church through work-

ing at the mission, there was considerable anti-church feeling, whilst at the same time some expression of their religion which grew as time went on. As the village developed into a community, the people felt very much that they should be visited regularly by a priest. But in Peramiho, which was the Benedictine centre of a very large diocese, there were considerable feelings against Litowa and a reluctance to become involved. I think in the first instance this reluctance was almost entirely due to the thought that the village was peopled with communists. Some time later there was an additional worry which reared its head when the church authorities visualized the possibility of numbers of new villages growing up, leaving their present well-established churches and mission centres outside these areas of new growth.

On the question of communism, many of the priests, both expatriates and Tanzanians, had some very strange ideas. Ntotera, one of the earliest members at Litowa and one who had to struggle very hard against his family in order to give up his work at the mission trading store at Peramiho where he was employed together with Ado, was married to the sister of one of the priests. It is a strongly held custom that when a child is born, as soon after as possible all members of the family should visit the parents to congratulate them. This particular priest had such strong doubts about Litowa that although in a good position to visit his sister, he did not visit for a very, very long time after her child was born, and then only after considerable persuasion. It came out then that he had some strange notions that at Litowa with people holding many things in common, they shared their wives. It took a long time for some of these strange ideas to die.

There were individual priests, and in particular Fr Gerhard, an elderly Swiss Benedictine father, who definitely had strong fears of communism at Litowa; but at the same time, as he was interested in improving people's agriculture, he wanted to help this new group starting there. He was the principal of the Teacher Training College at Peramiho and was responsible

for a large number of students coming to Litowa to assist with
bush-clearing. His assistance was not always as well thought
out as this and sometimes produced strong resentments. Very
early on in 1962 he had made it clear that he would be giving
the early settlers a gift. These people finding it very difficult at
that time to get the food for themselves necessary to be able to
keep on working, drew the conclusion that in all likelihood he
would give them a bag of maize or perhaps the money with
which to buy it. When he arrived they noticed that his car was
not carrying any maize and he intimated that he had a gift in his
briefcase which he was holding. It seems that he made considerable play of the fact that he had something inside for them and
they could only assume that it was a little cash. Eventually he
produced from it four cardboard cards each with three separate
pictures, the whole representing the twelve stations of the cross.
These pictures he had carefully made himself. There was very
great bitterness over this, as I saw when I arrived at Litowa in
March 1962 just after this had happened, when the people were
engaged in writing a sarcastic thank-you letter to him.

As time went on, Fr Gerhard often visited to say mass as
did another expatriate priest, Fr Benedict. Both produced more
resentment amongst the Litowa people basically because they
talked to them as if they were children. In spite of this the demand for their church continued to grow. Fr Maurus, the parish
priest and one of their own people, consistently ignored their
requests. Through all this time the villagers together held a Sunday morning worship and surrounding people began to join in
with them. Eventually, after increasing pressure from Litowa
as well as from some circles at Peramiho, Fr Maurus did come
to discuss with the people, but there was no real contact as he
had far too many preconceived ideas and fears. Very soon after
this, as is mentioned above, the auxiliary bishop, James Komba, came himself and arranged for Fr Stefan Mbunga from the
senior seminary to be the village priest and to visit every other
week. This was an extremely good choice. Some short time after

he had been attending, he felt the need to try and get rid of some of the strange ideas about Litowa held by his fellow priests and, with the approval of the abbot bishop, wrote a circular letter to all priests in the diocese. This was written in Kiswahili and what follows is a translation produced by Ado and Jennifer Leaning, our first Harvard volunteer, which had the complete approval of Fr Stefan.

Circular Letter "Litowa Farmers' Scheme"

To all priests in the diocese,

Many things have been said about Litowa. Some of them are true and some are not. Today I want to tell you some of the things which are true. I have been asked to do this by the bishop in the hope that, because members of Litowa come from nearly every mission station in the area, an account of the scheme and its people might extend our understanding of religious affairs in the diocese.

The Meaning of Litowa Farmers' Scheme

About twelve miles from Peramiho near the Luhira waterfalls and the Lupagaro mountains, a new village, Litowa, has grown up. Many people, from every corner of the Ruvuma Region, moved there voluntarily with the high ideal of developing a farming community based on African Socialism.

The village is similar to an Israeli kibbutz, in that the people live as a large family unit and together work the communal fields, so that the resources of the community are divided to serve individual needs. The people have decided to take little of the cash earnings for themselves until their farm has developed to the point where it is earning a reasonable amount of money, which will then be available for distribution among all the members.

The Beginning

Near the time of Tanganyika's independence a group of self-reliant young men from the region came together with the aim of building their country along co-operative lines. They went to the Litowa forest, which then was the home of lions, and there, in very poor conditions, using simple axes and hoes, they started clearing the bush. Having given up their profitable jobs, having left their homes, they were prepared to start an entirely new life. This brave band had to face many difficulties, including hunger which drove the chicken-hearted people away. Those who stayed now remember how they got comfort from trusting in God, how every night they came together and sang *Kaa nasi Bwana jua Linatua* (Abide with me . . .)

In 1963 an English agricultural adviser came to help the men with the agricultural work. By living together with his family in the village he helped the people in many other ways as well. He also helped to raise funds from overseas, because at that time the village was receiving no help from the government. Neither the government nor the church then understood what the members were really doing.

Their Situation Today

Slowly the government and church became aware of the possibilities of Litowa and began to show some interest. Although the government does not give outright grants of money, as it does at Mlale, the government-sponsored scheme, government officials help Litowa with encouragement and advice. Just recently President Nyerere gave 90,000 shillings to the Ruvuma Development Association to help purchase the milling business in Songea, which business will be of assistance to Litowa and other similar developing villages as a marketing and servicing centre. This was after his visit to Litowa when he stressed his desire to help. The church also helps to some extent, by providing a priest who deals with the spiritual needs of the people, and by giving them clothes, medicines, and so on.

A most impressive thing about the people of Litowa is their unity, their spirit of self-help, their willingness to undergo many present hardships for the sake of future progress. They share a courageous sense of love, a person does not think of himself. Fellowship and brotherhood are encouraged in the meetings and discussions they hold every week. They believe that a man and woman have equal rights. They strongly discourage polygamy. There is no feeling of superiority among those holding important jobs. They are guided by the Declaration of Human Rights. No one is admitted as a member of the scheme until he has served a probationary period and has found out whether he wants to stay or leave. He is free to decide: the members do not force him in any way. According to the powers held by the management committee a member who breaks the regulations can, after many warnings, be told to leave. Any person who wants to leave for a special reason is thereby allowed to do so.

School

The scheme feels a great responsibility in caring for the children of its members. Mothers who must work in the fields may take their babies to a nurse, who looks after the children during the day. Children of school age are sent to a dormitory where they will be looked after. Because the dormitories are not yet ready, the children now live with their families. Those who come from outside schemes board with different families in the village.

The Litowa school has 187 children and cannot admit more at present because the buildings have not been finished. It is registered under the agency of the Ruvuma Development Association, the organization co-ordinating all the schemes in the area developing along the same lines as Litowa. The Association has a secretary/treasurer, an advisor, and a committee formed of leaders of the various developing village projects. Mr Oscar Kambona is the president.

Although each scheme in the Association runs independently they all look to Litowa as a centre for advice, training and education. During their first holiday the school children at Litowa return to their parents: during their second they visit one of the other schemes to learn about the various occupations they might choose from when they leave school.

Sixteen Schemes

There are altogether sixteen schemes working on the same ideological basis as Litowa. The twelve well-established ones are: Litowa, Liweta, Luhira, Mhepai, Njoomlole, Ligoma, Matetereka, Mapinduzi, Mtakanini, Furaha, Kakong'o, Njaramatata.

Every scheme has its executive committee, headed by a manager, chairman and secretary/treasurer, which settles problems arising on the scheme. For important matters extending beyond the limits of one scheme, the Executive Committees consult with the chief advisors at Litowa, Mr Ntimbanjayo John Millinga, MP, and Mr Ralph Ibbott, the Englishman. Other advisers call themselves SERA or Social and Economic Revolutionary Army. These young men are revolutionaries not in that they seek violence or blood, but in that they are working to change the present poor living conditions of the people by helping to introduce the techniques of modern farming and the spirit of socialist unity. The main aim of the SERA members is to spread the spirit of love and concern among the people, by visiting the schemes and advising them how best to develop the methods to satisfy their basic needs. Some of the SERA members have studied at Kivukoni College, Dar es Salaam.

Because the example of Litowa and the ideas of village settlement are spreading slowly throughout every parish in the region, it is imperative for the parish priests to make every effort to understand and enter into the spirit of what is happening within the region round about them.

Religion

The total membership of Litowa has now reached forty. The residents who are not members are either still children or relatives of members. The aim of the village is to recruit eighty members. People of different religious beliefs, Moslems, Anglicans and Catholics all live amicably together. The Christians are now making efforts to build their own chapel similar to their grass houses, although progress is slow because the members must work in the fields from 7 o'clock in the morning until 6 o'clock in the evening for most of the year. In the next few years they intend to build an entirely new village of brick buildings. The map of the prospective village shows a place where a permanent House of God will stand.

In relation to religious matters, a priest can go quite easily to see the people at any time he wants, because they all live together almost as one family. It is warming for a priest to be able to feel one of a big family, able to talk freely and even eat with them. The villagers have a hospitable tradition of receiving a visitor by offering him food without expecting him to supply his own. Dr Ranz of Germany was astounded when the people refused payment for the nice small table, made by their own craftsmen, which they gave him on his first visit to Litowa.

During Christmas there were 130 communicants and just recently two marriages were performed. Religious teaching is carried on in the school and on Epiphany day the village held a big celebration for ten schoolchildren who were baptized and sixty-one who were first communicants. Now they are waiting eagerly for Easter Monday when they are going to receive 100 candidates for confirmation. From Saturday evening to Sunday, the members rest from their hard work and participate in all sorts of sports activities, show slides and films, sing African songs, dance and sometimes listen to tape recordings or the gramophone. All of them very much enjoy the new African songs composed for singing in the church.

In view of all this, how can we dare say that Litowa has no religious spirit? Why, if that is the case, did they ask for a priest? Their request shows that they strongly believe in creating a big family unit of people, all enjoying freedom, equal rights, and good health, all helping and living with one another as brothers. Their sense of co-operation has greatly lessoned fear, hatred, jealousy, laziness, violence, and meanness in the hearts of all the members. "Ubi caritas et amor ibi Deus est."[1]

Therefore the church must do everything possible to join with and support people with such a creative and hopeful spirit. The church must help them both spiritually and materially, so that these people, in their honest pursuit of development should be filled with a sense of eternal aims. "Per visibilia ad invisibilia."[2]

Fr Stefan Mbunga
27 February 1966
Senior Seminary, Peramiho
(Translated from the Swahili EAM/JL)

Stefan's view of the Association was clearly quite different from that of the majority of his fellow priests and I am certain that he came to Litowa not only as a duty to say mass but that he enjoyed coming.

From his earliest days as a priest Stefan had been interested in trying to make the music of the church into a music which sprang from the traditions of his people. He felt, and quite rightly, that the tunes brought over from Europe and the United States were not music into which the people could wholeheartedly enter. Before coming to Litowa, he had experienced considerable opposition to his attempts at Africanization of church music, and the battle to get the drums into the church was a difficult one. At Litowa he found a very receptive church con-

---

1   "Where there is charity and love, God is there."
2   "From the visible to the invisible."

gregation, and this Africanization added much to the place of the church in village life. To an outsider it was certainly an improvement, from the sound of people trying to copy European tunes with rather dismal results, to a wholehearted entering into religious songs with great enthusiasm and vigour. It was not so long after this that the battle was won for the whole of the diocese, and a ruling was made that the drums may be used in any parish where the people wished it.

Feeling against Litowa and the Association villages was fairly widespread within the church. Some time after the visit of the Israeli ambassador, I called to see him in Dar es Salaam. He was then very enthusiastic about his experience of visiting Litowa and Liweta, and told me that when leaving he had paid a visit to the Mtwara Region where, at another of the Benedictine missions some 400 miles from Litowa, he had come up against anti-Association feelings. He said he had tried to get over to them the fact that their thinking on this was based on much misinformation. Relations with the missions certainly improved and this was no doubt helped by the fact that *ujamaa* villages became national policy and the church authorities generally wished to keep in line with this. In spite of this, the Benedictine priests that one met occasionally when travelling around the region had very little idea of what an *ujamaa* community was and, apart from isolated individual missions, one felt there was little real interest born of understanding. This was shown by an incident which occurred on nearly our last day in the region.

Mention has been made of Fr Changula who was the regional TANU representative on the central committee of the party. Fr Changula was a priest trained at Peramiho, and, after serving in a number of posts, became the principal of the Peramiho Teacher Training College. He did not do too well in this post and was also becoming very anti-mission. From the time that he became a party official he also became very anti-RDA.

He wavered a little on this, at times seeming to become a little friendlier if it looked as if it might have been politically profitable to be friendly. Quite naturally a man of this character was not trusted by the village people and he played quite a leading part in the end in the destruction of the RDA.

There was at Peramiho a very likeable and hard-working Benedictine, Brother Edgar, who ran the tailoring section of the trade school. He was always friendly and cheerful and on good terms with very many of the people. Calling to see him for the last time before we left, I passed some derogatory remark about Fr Changula. Brother Edgar was completely astounded. He had assumed Fr Changula's anti-mission attitude was that of the Litowa people. He seemed unable to differentiate between different criticisms of the mission and classed all who had any criticism into one category. With his contacts and visits to Litowa, he was in a better position than most of the missionaries to understand these things, and yet he was right outside the situation of the people who related to the mission, outside of the many facets of their lives and struggles.

15

VOLUNTEERS AND EXPERTS
FROM ABROAD

When we first arrived in Ruvuma many small group initiatives of the people were spread over the Ruvuma Region. This was not special to the region but was a nationwide phenomenon. Within each of these groups were generally one or two individuals who were initiators prepared to try new paths and with the ability to persuade others to follow. The vast majority of these came to nothing. In the following years such initiators continued to appear, often ending in failure. There are two important reasons why so many of these failed. First, when people moved in to assist with advice, they did it in such a way that they took at least part of the group's leadership role and so prevented the group from developing its own leadership and organization from within. A community cannot be managed from outside; if it is, it ceases to be a community. Second, so often those who gave advice gave wrong advice.

A village community in order to develop needs considerable protection from outside interference and domination. Given this protection, there would probably be an initial period when leadership problems are worked through, after which with only a minimum of the right advice a community has a very strong natural growth. In my view it is unlikely that this little advice will be right unless it comes from those who choose to live within the limiting conditions in which the people themselves live.

Therefore, where people in the Ruvuma villages felt the need for outside knowledge, they had to bring it in with the utmost care. Many of the expatriates with knowledge in the region were in the Benedictine missions and so many of these had unfortunate "managerial" tendencies together with their knowledge. It was these expatriates that the Ruvuma villagers were used to and this made it hard to use advice from this source as it is not so easy for people to change existing attitudes towards those who have been in a position of domination over them.

When we were going to Tanzania in 1963 we were asked if we could take a young lad by the name of Brian Rée to be with us for a year before he went up to Oxford. This seemed reasonable on the understanding that he would have no particular function other than to live and work in the village with the people, so that they would see an expatriate with a different attitude who in no way sought to become part of their administrative machinery. This was very successful. It meant that the right type of volunteer could later come to work in the villages on specific jobs when the people's organization was sufficiently strong not to fear that the volunteer would in any way be taking over.

Starting at the beginning of 1966 we had a series of volunteers of different nationalities and from different organizations. The majority did useful work and were never in a situation where there was the danger of them taking more authority than was delegated to them by the village organizations. There were a number from the USA, some from an organization of Harvard students called Volunteer Teachers for Africa (VTA) and others from the American Friends Service Committee. With all of these there was a certain understanding of the philosophy of the villages and in the vast majority of the cases a fairly easy adjustment, probably through this understanding, to the rigorous conditions of life in the bush. These volunteers were mostly doing social-type work, particularly in relation to the nurseries for the children and helping the women. In another sphere there were four volunteers in succession developing and operating mechanical workshops for the Association, and training some of the young men in the villages. These found the adjustment to this new life much more difficult and two of them never succeeded. A young VSO volunteer started the work and had a successful year. It was carried on by a member of the Swiss Volunteer Corps who did two very effective years. This latter was a married man, and his wife worked well with the women and children at Liweta village where the mechanical workshop was established. His successor, also from Switzerland, was never able to adjust and had to leave. An earlier Danish mechanic recruited through the European Working Group also had to leave.

The Swiss Volunteer Corps also provided two nurses, and although the organization had considerable information about the project and the conditions, we felt that what they expected to find was so different from the realities that they never adjusted and so were not able to give very much to the people. On top of this they had a far too strong attachment to their volunteer organization, making it difficult for them to develop a loyalty to the Association. With the VTA, although one of their number was a co-ordinator in Tanzania, this never meant that their volunteers were so attached to their own organization that it prevented the growth of loyalty to the villages. Rather VTA was a purely convenient administrative arrangement.

We only had three technical experts and all of these were agriculturalists provided through the Swiss Ministry of Agriculture by Swiss Technical Co-operation. Here again the Association was very fortunate in that the first of these, Roger Pasquier, had a clear understanding of what his position should be and the necessity of working through the organizations of the Association and the villages. This was most important as he had certain monies at his disposal for use in his work with the Association. He also very quickly adjusted to the situation of Ruvuma, and while having tremendous enthusiasm, yet he understood the pace of events in a rural community. It was not quite so easy with his successors who found the adjustment much more difficult and took a much longer time to appreciate what was really happening. Nevertheless because Roger had worked so much as a servant of the Association, it added strength to the Association's organization so that it was very soon made clear to his successors where it was thought they were not treading the right path.

The real judgement of whether these people were doing effective work can only be made by the people in the Association. The people within such an organization, the work of which covers all the needs of their lives, know whether they are progressing, and there is no doubt that they welcomed volunteers and experts who could adjust and live with them. It has already been mentioned that towards the end of the life of the Association the recruitment of further volunteers to help was a high priority of the people, and what better compliment could be made than the summing-up of the discussion on this subject within the Association at that time: that the people looked forward to the time when their own experts would come to help them, but realized that at the present stage most of these experts spurned living with the people in the bush and would not really be interested in what was being done, thus would not be trustworthy and would always be wanting to go off to the towns. In the meantime they welcomed those with the knowledge who were prepared to come from overseas to live with them and pass on their knowledge.

There was never any question of the RDA looking for assistance from outside the country before trying for what was available locally. The villages were composed of people engaged in the practical affairs of their lives and for this reason their decisions were practical. When wanting new knowledge, they would look to those nearest before thinking in terms of overseas.

16

LITOWA – THE LEAD VILLAGE

In the RDA, although there was a common pattern, each village had its own character. There were variations in the ways of working; different types of people were leaders. Since the region was a large one, it embraced different climates, and quite naturally the rate of development was different from village to village. None of this is a problem, and it is not helpful to make comparative judgments among villages; yet people from outside constantly did make such judgments.

There was no reason why Litowa, the first of the villages, should have necessarily been the best, and it was not difficult to find ways in which other villages were "better". In spite of this, Litowa was a much judged village, and judged more harshly than other villages. This was extremely unfair. In the minds of officials, even when they had it explained to them many times, Litowa was confused with the Association. When people wished to attack the Association, they attacked Litowa. We made tremendous efforts in the face of this to explain that Litowa was only one member village of the Association on the same footing as all the others. But although amongst all the different villages there was a complete understanding of this, it was almost impossible to get an understanding outside the Association. At the end, when officialdom found it essential to tell the Association that it was disbanded, the minister of rural development made no attempt to call the leaders of the Association who were people from different villages but went to tell the people of Litowa. Some ten days later when they found that in a real-life situation certain matters had to be discussed about Association property, a group of officials again came to tell the people of Litowa. Yet the minister and some of these officials were amongst those who had been at the lengthy seminars and had had everything explained to them. The people of Litowa on this second visit thanked the officials for coming but said that they were only one village and could not speak for the Association. The officials simply refused to accept this and it took considerable time before they could be convinced of the necessity of meeting with what had been the executive of the Association. As always, Litowa received the attack on the Association.

By the end many had come to accept the idea that there might be communal villages with their own organization. The country had passed the stage of thinking only of block farms with individual peasant farmers and of villages based on this, but there was hardly the beginning of an understanding of the need or advantages of associations of villages; of the need for fully independent villages where people could take decisions unhampered by officials giving the wrong advice and orders, which prevented the natural growth of a true village leadership and the flowering of an independent village organization with confidence in itself.

In reality, as a village Litowa perhaps had a harder time than the others in its position as a centre for the Association, and it should be judged less harshly. The natural leader in the beginning was Ntimbanjayo and very soon after he was taken from the position of village leadership in order to work in all the villages. With the formation of SERA at the beginning of 1965, again a number of natural leaders of Litowa were taken away to work for the whole. This was a very big sacrifice and looking back with an understanding of the importance of leadership, it is amazing to see how well the village pulled through, particularly as Litowa membership was of rather a different nature from the others. The others were all composed of families who had come from the fairly immediate vicinity; whereas Litowa families were from the whole region with one or two from outside the region. This was because it drew from the Peramiho TANU Youth League, and since Peramiho was the church administrative centre, it drew in people from many places who came for employment there.

Starting the Association's school at Litowa was also a very considerable strain on the village. The need to grow food to be able to eat better so that people could work better and have a surplus to be able to increase the membership, was well understood. When the first children from one or two other villages came for schooling to join in with the Litowa children, these other villages were at an even earlier stage of development than Litowa and could not send food with the children. They were fed by Litowa, thus taking the village surplus. That they were prepared to make this sacrifice and were not put off by the brake that this imposed on their other developments shows their commitment to the schooling they were setting out to produce.

As time went on and the growth of *ujamaa* villages was more and more discussed in the country, a tremendous number of visitors arrived in Ruvuma, the vast majority of these coming to Litowa. They took up a very high proportion of people's time, particularly of the village manager and chairman, and on many occasions of the whole management committee. There were many other ways that cost much time and therefore progress to Litowa as the Association's centre. For example, the considerable organization involved in dealing with the building of the school fell on the Litowa manager because he was able and on the spot. To me, what was achieved despite all these drawbacks was impressive. It is because there has been so much highly emotional criticism of Litowa that I feel it is necessary to begin to put the record straight.

17

NJOOMLOLE –
THE VILLAGE THAT FAILED

One of the earliest groups we visited was Njoomlole (come and see) near to Ligera, some fifty miles southeast of Songea. This village consisted of members of the TANU branch of Ligera led by their secretary Rangimbayo Mhagama. The response to our visit from the group was very good and they very early took the decision to move into a new village and work together. The initial relationship was good but it did not last, and Njoomlole gradually became an important part of the opposition to the RDA. This was inevitable because of the character of Mhagama who, whilst in the first place discussing and seeming to understand the RDA ideas on village growth, began to work more and more as a sole boss in the group, not allowing proper discussion to develop. After he became a member of parliament, the rift grew rapidly wider.

Before our second visit we had asked if it was possible for villages which were seeking advice to have some outline of their plans so that we could discuss these with the people on our visits. Njoomlole produced the biggest plan of all with many duplicated copies and on quite a different basis from any other of the villages: where the others had a few down-to-earth ideas, Njoomlole had ambitious plans. These, however, were impractical and required large funds for their implementation. The amount of land they planned to cultivate was small and their forecast of the income they expected from it was much higher than was reasonable to suppose possible. This in itself was nothing to worry about as people had little experience of these things and it made a basis for discussion. On the visit this discussion was quite amicable. But soon afterwards it appeared that discussions here were not on the same basis as with the other villages. The plans were in fact those of Mhagama, and although we had discussed rather than criticized, the visit produced strong reactions from him on the grounds that the plans of a village were sacrosanct and should not be criticized. He began to write extremely lengthy letters of complaint to the Association with copies to a number of high officials. We found that this was a habit of his on many other matters also. By doing this he created an embarrassing situation. We had explained to him at some length why the plan did not make sense. Mhagama sent it unaltered to government with a view to getting money. Ntimbanjayo and I were approached by government whilst attending a conference in Dar es Salaam as to our views on these plans which the ministry considered to be ill-conceived. It transpired that they were under the impression that these plans had the approval of the Association.

Back in Songea we arranged a meeting to try and discuss with Mhagama, but it was impossible as he insisted that as a prerequisite to a discussion, the constitution of the Association should be changed to conform with his suggestions. It seemed that he wished for a system with many committees. The other officials of the Association could only take the view that the constitution allowed for amendment in the usual way and any propositions would have to be made to a general meeting and have the proper approval there. It was impossible to get beyond this stage and with the constant friction, the member villages of the Association felt it better that Njoomlole should cease to be a member. They only wanted those who were members willingly. For years afterwards Mhagama kept bringing the division up and carried on a permanent feud against the Association.

Njoomlole did in fact make rather a good thing as far as money was concerned, out of being in opposition to the Association, as the government was always looking for places to build up in competition to the RDA villages to show how much better they could do things. It is certainly one way of doing things, to keep a small village happy by continually bringing in money, but it was not the Association's method. The aid to Njoomlole increased very rapidly towards the end and during the time of the central committee opposition, bigger aid than ever was given. At the time of the Association's banning, we heard it announced on the radio that Njoomlole had "earned" 300,000 shillings. Of course the money was not earned, some of it came from the Ministry of Rural Development and some from the second vice-president's office. Both the minister and the second vice-president were strongly opposed to the Association, and on top of this the second vice-president was born near Njoomlole. In the Association very little money went to individual villages. Funds raised were for projects of common use to all the villages such as the school, Association business enterprises, the mechanical workshops and so on. In the six-and-a-half years, what the Association raised directly for the seventeen villages would hardly have totalled 300,000 shillings. The largest sums went for the installations of village water supplies.

It should be noted that one of the accusations of the minister of rural development against the Association when it was banned was that its villages were not large enough, and yet Njoomlole's membership was about the average size of the RDA villages.

Quite naturally, we did not again visit Njoomlole but a number of visitors who had been there told us that the atmosphere was quite different from that in the Association villages and that at a village meeting there, all questions were answered by Mhagama. Mhagama also played his part in the final destruction of the Association by feeding stories to those wishing to make their case against it. The pattern that those at the top employed in trying to make a showpiece out of Njoomlole to set against the Association, followed a pattern that local officials had used before (for example with the tobacco-growing block farm and the village of Kakong'o), except that now it was on a much more lavish scale with the much larger resources of central government.

Although Njoomlole had its share of conflicts, they were of a different nature to those of the RDA. The villages of the RDA, after the first year or two of their existence when they were not understood by those around, built up good relations with the surrounding people and also with the branches of TANU. Njoomlole had bad relationships with the surrounding people and, in spite of the fact that its membership was originally the party branch committee, even their relationship with the branch became very bad later on. It appeared that Mhagama had complained to the second vice-president that the branch was not giving any assistance. When he was to visit Njoomlole, it was arranged that he first call at the Ligera party office and proceed from there for the last three miles to Ligera together with the party officials. It seems that this did not suit Mhagama and Njoomlole, as on the day of the visit a party of them met the second vice-president's party a few miles out of Ligera and took them direct to the village by another road without picking up the party officials. This demonstrated to the second vice-president that the officials were not interested as they were not in attendance at Njoomlole for his visit. Expressing his anger, he sent the police to Ligera to get the party officials and made them run on foot the three miles to Njoomlole. The RDA villages never had this sort of relationship with the party branches; their troubles were always with officialdom, which existed away from basic levels of day-to-day life. The Mhagama ruse did not in fact succeed in its purpose, as later on the second vice-president heard the truth of the story and sent his apologies. Such apologies were hardly likely to make the Ligera party branch any more enamoured of Njoomlole.

On another occasion Njoomlole was virtually at war with the local Co-operative Primary Society[1] and as feelings ran high, the regional commissioner in visiting the area to deal with the troubles, felt obliged to be accompanied by an armed force. Again this type of conflict never arose with the RDA villages.

---

1   Primary collection of produce from different areas.

18

THE RDA'S LEADERSHIP

During the preceding account, much will be gathered of the development of leadership throughout the Association and its villages, particularly with regard to SERA. But more needs to be said of Ntimbanjayo Millinga, the first leader.

In an article on the Ruvuma Development Association written by Grif Cunningham, principal of Kivukoni College, for the July 1966 issue of *Mbioni*, the college magazine, he wrote: "A unique set of circumstances prevails in the RDA, for the founder and chief sustaining drive behind the settlements is undoubtedly Ntimbanjayo Millinga, MP for Songea South. Millinga has provided a genuinely charismatic leadership from the very beginning in 1960 and has by his messianic zeal created a small group of disciples who have learned well from their leaders."

This leadership of Ntimbanjayo is extremely important and much of development of this type depends on the right leaders. The fact that the right leadership grew up at different levels as time went on, owes much to the example that Ntimbanjayo set from the beginning. He always considered himself one of the people. He was a person whom it was impossible to bribe either with money or with women. Very early on in the growth of the Association he had developed a clear picture of the sort of path that he would take in order to further the ends of his fellow villagers, and every step that he took at a later stage was taken only if it fitted in with this picture. However much work he was involved in, he always found time to spend working with the people in the villages, and this was never simply a token five or ten minutes' work. He was capable of making public speeches. He could talk at length to the villagers on ideas of development. He was also able to chair an Association meeting keeping himself very much in the background and encouraging discussion and ideas to come from the delegates. He had a very quick brain and was able quickly to see what was necessary. On top of this he developed considerable courage to be able to stick to his course whatever opposition he met. This was harder for him as he worked on a wider scale and often had to meet opposition alone while the villages met it as a community.

It is difficult to say just why people have particular qualities, people being such complicated creatures. His background would not have looked too likely. He had a very powerful dominating mother who became so difficult that she gradually isolated herself from society. His father appeared to be a rather gentle man who, perhaps through the difficulties with his wife, had retired from this world and taken to a life of tramping. His formal schooling had been only a primary one, eight years, in schools of the highly conservative German and Swiss Benedictine missionaries, part of this in the junior seminary. Beyond this, he had a short time on a course of nurses' training and then the eight-month course at Kivukoni College where I met him. None of this perhaps accounts for what he was able to achieve.

His way of operating was such that he always encouraged the growth of leadership at many different levels, and because of his example, this leadership also had a high level of honesty and a commitment to the work in the villages and the Association. At these different levels of leadership were people of vastly different backgrounds, and as the Association developed they were of course assisted by the ethic which developed in the movement. It is also important to note that the successful products of the first leadership training course also had the same qualities. They might have been vastly different characters, as with Bernardo at Mbambara who was a highly intelligent, slightly built and very energetic young man with a considerable townee background; or Ludovic Mgimba at Ndivo with a much more rural background who was quiet, almost retiring, and yet had an amazing ability to lead the village of which he was a member. But they shared the honesty and commitment to the villages and the Association.

Probably one of the things which helps in this type of development is that by its nature it is an expanding process with constant new openings, so that there is always room for those with initiative and drive to be able to find outlets. Generally leadership struggles did not exist, after the initial ones in those villages founded by unsuitable leaders. Each of these was removed by the villagers.

19

THE OPPOSITION

The first opposition we encountered was not very serious or worrying, since it was from expatriates who were not to be in the country for much longer. The start of opposition that mattered was probably from Haule as regional commissioner in 1964. For an understanding of this I feel it is essential to realize the complete differences in approach of a man such as Haule and that of Ntimbanjayo. The latter worked by patiently explaining his ideas to the people, encouraging them and working with them. Perhaps a story will show Haule's different way of working.

One of the previous regional party leaders was trying to start a farming project on the main road to the west of Songea, near to the boundaries of the Songea and Mbinga districts. Haule as regional commissioner agreed to meet the surrounding people to suggest that they join the project. He was to arrive at midday and the divisional executive officer of the district council was to call the people together at that time. Knowing that exact time-keeping was not usual, this man called the people together much earlier and by midday the people had already been there several hours, but no commissioner arrived. The hours passed and by five in the evening with everybody still waiting, the council officer decided that something must have prevented him from fulfilling his engagement that day and so sent the people home. Around six o'clock the commissioner arrived, was furious to find nobody there, returned immediately to Songea and had the police arrest the unfortunate officer and put him in prison for twenty-four hours. It is probably inevitable that this sort of person, in a position of considerable power, would wish to have a man like Ntimbanjayo and his ideas out of the way.

Much of this dictatorial behaviour came when officials were having adverse reactions from the people or were not finding it easy to implement the plans they were working on. Often commissioners in this situation are posted elsewhere when their fears lead them to behave too badly towards the people. At the time when Haule was trying to have Millinga made area commissioner in Tunduru, he had probably received warnings from central government and seemed a very worried man. Ntimbanjayo as chairman of the Songea town council had left Songea to attend a meeting in the north of the Association of Local Authorities of Tanganyika. He travelled three days by bus through Tunduru and Lindi, and arrived in Dar es Salaam on the first leg of his journey, to hear that he had been appointed area commissioner in Tunduru, and was to fly back to Songea on the first available plane. While waiting in the capital he saw Vice-President Kawawa, explained his position and feelings to him that he wished to remain with the people of Litowa and the other villages of the Association, and received his authority to turn down the offer. Also through a personal assistant of the President, he received word that the President would accept Ntimbanjayo's decision.

On his arrival at Songea airport he was met and taken to the commissioner's office where he explained that he had to refuse the offer. Haule would not accept this and a long meeting ensued at which Ntimbanjayo tried very carefully and fully to explain. When he arrived at Litowa that evening he looked worn out and told us that it was impossible for them to understand what he was saying. To him it was so simple: he felt committed to work for what had started with the people at Litowa and only to accept offers of positions from which he felt he could further these ends. He told how he had explained again and again and in the end had wept from a complete inability to get over such a simple idea to them. Minutes of this meeting were recorded in the files in the regional office.

After leaving the commissioner's office, the administrative secretary came out and very seriously warned Ntimbanjayo that he had better accept or else his life would be made very difficult. He had tried to argue his case and had not mentioned his talk with the vice-president in Dar es Salaam. The following day he had to return to see Haule and I offered to go with him if he thought it would be helpful. He welcomed this, and the following morning we travelled to Songea, but on meeting Haule we were told that he had a very busy day and would not be free until the evening. We were quite prepared to wait, and he agreed to see us when all other business was over. On this day a group of the Nigerian army were giving a demonstration in the Songea showground as part of a farewell tour around the country.[1] We watched the show and waited until Haule had finished entertaining the officers.

When we eventually met we saw he was worried and upset. We started by my repeating the same arguments as Ntimbanjayo had gone through on the previous day at some length, which were listened to without interruption for perhaps twenty minutes. The reaction was not what we expected. Haule, looking even more worried, complained of feeling ill and having pains in his head and chest. I happened to have aspirins in my pocket and to get back to the subject I felt it best first to offer these. After sending for water and taking two aspirins, the discussion continued with Ntimbanjayo, feeling that no argument would get anywhere, telling Haule of his call on the vice-president and that he would accept Ntimbanjayo's refusal. This changed the whole atmosphere. Haule immediately recalled that the letter of appointment sent from Dar es Salaam for Ntimbanjayo to sign had stated that he should sign if he accepted the post. All that

1   They were in Tanzania at Nyerere's invitation following the 1964 attempted coup. They stayed until a new army was trained.

was necessary then was for him, the commissioner, to write to the vice-president's office notifying them of Ntimbanjayo's non-acceptance. Clearly his fear was partly that Ntimbanjayo's refusal would reflect badly on him in Dar es Salaam at a time when he was already under pressure from that quarter. The meeting ended with all in the best of spirits.

This did not change Haule's position on the Association. Some time after this, Ntimbanjayo had to accompany Haule to a settlement he had prepared for rehousing people flooded out by the exceptional rise that year in the level of Lake Nyasa. He thought the journey, some 100 miles, would be a good opportunity to talk on the Association and allied matters. However, Haule's reaction to the first overtures showed a refusal to address those things. Otherwise, the day was notable in that the people were resisting the move and while the commissioner felt it necessary to force the people to move, custom prevented this. It was his home area and his own parents were involved. It was impossible to force them to move.

Changes in area or regional commissioners always seemed to change the emphasis in a district or region. A new commissioner seldom seemed to carry on the projects started by his predecessor; he would want to make his own name. It became more and more obvious to us that very little which could be called development would be brought about by these people. When Peter Walwa, who was the next regional commissioner, arrived, I am certain he knew of the President's growing interest in Litowa and the other villages of the RDA. Largely for this reason, I believe, he involved us in much that he did and on the surface there existed good relations and much discussion. Inevitably there were differences of opinion which on the surface always appeared good-hearted.

His big project was to start the Regional Development Fund through which he was going to tackle one of the big problems facing the region: the building of feeder roads to make the marketing of crops easier. There were to be other smaller projects: the establishment, for instance, of a fund to lend money for corrugated iron roofing in the Songea township where thatched roof fires were a constant problem. This was particularly the case at that time when a group of the disaffected showed their dissatisfaction by tying a matchstick to a lighted cigarette and both to a length of string with a stick on the other end. This was thrown on to the top of a thatched roof when some minutes later, after the culprits had disappeared, the cigarette fanned by the breeze had burnt down to the match head which ignited, setting fire to the roof of the house.

I was asked to be the treasurer of the Fund, but pointed out that since I was out of town it was not very practical, particularly with a project such as the roofing where there would of necessity be much dealing with individuals in town who would have to make regular repayments. However, the work of doing this and all the everyday book-keeping was given to the executive officer of the district council and I was made treasurer to produce some sort of accounts at the end of the year. The money for the Fund was easily come by – each of the three district councils was told what contributions they had to give; likewise the two co-operative unions; all traders (who were predominantly Asians) were "asked" to contribute a sum equal to the cost of their trading licences. In practice no new licence was issued until this was paid. There were one or two other sources. The biggest part of the expenditure was for the feeder roads and this was dealt with very simply by the purchase of three Caterpillar tractors at something over £5,000 each. One would be given to each of the three district councils and would be used to build these roads. The whole idea was a fantasy. The district councils were finding it increasingly difficult to collect the money to carry out the commitments they already had without having these expensive machines to run. If they could not organize the people on a self-help basis to build these roads, it was unlikely that they would be able to cope with using these machines. They had no proper facilities for the maintenance and repair. However, the regional engineer, an expatriate, backed up the idea and these three great machines were purchased amidst great excitement within the small area of the regional offices. One was later used to clear away the rubble of houses demolished to make way for a national housing project in Songea, and one was hired out to the Mlale settlement to do some work on roads. Otherwise they stood around idly, an embarrassment to Walwa's successors.

Before all of this I had discussed mechanization with Walwa. Early in 1965 we had a visit from Leonard Elmhirst and another of the Dartington Hall trustees, Peter Sutcliffe. At a meeting with Walwa, Elmhirst pointed out that looking around, we could see that the main form of transportation was the heads of the women in the region. He felt that one of the greatest steps to progress would be the introduction of the donkey. Walwa was shocked and said with great surprise, "But Mr Elmhirst, this is 1965."

Regional commissioners are powerful people, at the head of the administration and of the regional party organization. Few were willing to contradict them, yet there must have been many who knew that buying these machines was getting nowhere. The first of the tractors was due to arrive at about the same time as the President's visit, and frantic efforts were made to hurry it up to be there before his visit, including to find a driver who could operate it. At the Songea showground a pile of earth was deposited in front of the platform where the President and his group were seated. The Caterpillar tractor came forward fitted with an earth scoop and, rather shakily, with a novice driver, scooped up a load of earth, turned and dropped it into a lorry standing by.

I was interested to know the President's views and on his visit to Litowa the next day, while we were discussing with him and his party in our kitchen, I brought up the subject of machines. He laid his hand on Walwa's arm, laughed and said that "Our friend Walwa couldn't wait. He wanted his big machines now. Well, he couldn't have them." It probably could have been said with a little more respect for Walwa's feelings!

The National Housing Corporation was to build a number of houses in Songea; this was also entered into with energy by Walwa. He visualized the road in from the airport lined both sides with better houses, and very good it would have been. From what I had heard, there seemed to be very little considera-tion for those in the old houses, the people just being told to get out as the pulling down was starting at a given date. Not think-ing that anything could be done in the situation, I nevertheless questioned Walwa on this but was told that in Africa they didn't have to worry about such things: the extended family of African society took care of all that!

However, there are limits beyond which people will not go. In his enthusiasm Walwa had organized the pulling down of all the houses in the road. After this was started it came to light that the project was only to build houses half way along the road. Those on whose houses the demolitions had been erroneously started were naturally rather annoyed and some of the old men amongst them attacked Walwa so that he had hurriedly to retire to his Mercedes and drive back to his office.

There were at this time a number of different types of set-tlement in the region. There were the village communities of the Association; the large investment settlement agency pro-ject at Mlale; the farming project for training National Service men on the farm purchased from an Asian company at Kitai; the much-assisted block farming tobacco-growing scheme near Namtumbo; and the resettlement village for those flooded out from the lakeside. We were asked by Walwa to write a short paper giving our views on each. This was a difficult thing to do as we had been particularly careful to keep away from Mlale and from publicly voicing criticisms of its concept. Mlale was al-ready showing signs of cracking, visible not only to us but also, together with many other similar projects of the agency in other parts of the country, to the members of a research team from Syracuse University who were at that time studying them. What we wrote tried to get over one main point: our belief that the whole of development in these rural areas was dependent on the growth of rural communities and a growing rural organization. We felt this could only happen when these communities engaged collectively in the real activities of their everyday life. We discussed whether this was taking place in the different settlements.

We were then told that there was to be a regional conference to discuss which type of settlement was most suited to the Ruvuma Region. The Association was asked to send three representatives. I was asked if I would give a talk on the organization of the RDA villages. On Mlale, their deputy manager was asked to talk, and there were one or two other speakers. We were informed by the community development officer that this meeting was designed as an attack on the Association, that an attempt would be made to lead the meeting to say that RDA communal villages were not wanted. We were surprised to see on arrival that an amazing number of priests had been invited, mostly Roman Catholic priests, including some expatriates. Walwa opened the conference with a speech on the dangers of communism and we could only suppose that the Roman Catholics were supposed to react to this and that this was the reason they had been invited.

Things did not go well for Walwa.

After the talks, the floor was open to comment. The first to speak was a Tanzanian priest who went out of his way to show that he was sitting on the fence, and no other priest took any part. This first contribution was followed by a most delightful speech from an old Anglican, Father Kakongue, who had been several times to Litowa to be with the children from Association villages who were Anglicans. Not having any idea what was behind the conference, he stood up and said that he had been to Litowa and he had been to Mlale, but when at Litowa he had never felt anywhere else so near to the Kingdom of Heaven. It set a good tone for the rest of the conference. I believe minutes were produced in the regional offices but I never saw these, although I was told they bore no relation to the feelings expressed in the conference. A few days afterwards we heard that Walwa was being posted elsewhere, and nothing further was heard of the conference.

This will make it easier to judge whether we might have steered a better course on this journey. The generally held concepts of what those in authority felt was development are important to note. It tells us much about what the Association faced.

In the last few weeks of this period Walwa had another idea in which I was involved. He decided that the region should build a presidential lodge in which the President could sometimes come to rest, with accommodation also for some visiting president, so that they could confer in the peace of the Ruvuma countryside. There was no money available for such a project and I felt the President would not want it, already having other such places. The regional engineer, whilst making out provisional plans as asked, approached me saying that in his job he could not question the move, but asked if I would be at the committee meeting, as he felt the project was not possible with the presently available resources. It was not a thing I wanted to do but I did raise in a cool way a number of obvious objections. It was a small committee and all the other members were government officers. During the whole time of my raising mild doubts, not one of the other members of the committee said a word, although I knew that most were dubious about it and knew that there was no money available. This was a very common situation. The feelings of the regional commissioner were seldom questioned and often people were reluctant to put a point of view until they first knew his. This is hardly the atmosphere for discussions on development. I feel a similar situation existed with the President and those around him, even though very often they would act afterwards in a way opposite to that to which they had agreed in his presence. In the case of the presidential lodge, the committee decided that on the design it was necessary to get knowledge of the full needs with regard to such things as bodyguards' accommodation, and the President's office should be written to. In this way Nyerere came to hear of it and wrote thanking the people for the thought but saying that he would rather any available money was used for a community project for the people of Ruvuma.

I met Walwa again some three years later in Dar es Salaam when I had gone to the national assembly to meet Ntimbanjayo. Walwa came over to me and pressed me to go to Bukoba to advise him on his plans for *ujamaa* villages. It was the time when these were all the rage and commissioners were vying with each other to see who could have the most. Walwa was, it seemed, still wanting to have people around him who would provide a suitable smokescreen to cover up what he was actually doing. He was using dubious means to get people into villages, but there were other difficulties and he was not just moved from his post but dismissed from the service.

He had been on the same course as Ntimbanjayo at Kivukoni College and one day told me how surprised he was that Ntimbanjayo had become a leader, as at college he had not seen anything of the stuff of leadership in him. Walwa no doubt thought himself a born leader as I was told that, after completing his college course, since there was no job awaiting him, he made a nuisance of himself around the party offices until they recognized his ability by giving him a post!

When Edward Barongo became regional commissioner he had been in a difficult position. Previously he had been a junior minister but in the general election of 1965 had not been returned by his constituents. Not all members of the national assembly were elected; a large number were appointed by the President. He had appointed one or two key ministers who had failed to gain the confidence of the electors, but we heard that he was reluctant to do this in too many cases as it would be going against the wishes of the people. We also heard that Barongo's friends in the party spoke for him. At any rate, after some delay he was appointed Regional Commissioner in Ruvuma.

The great emphasis of Barongo's reign was the enforcement of the regulation in Songea that the growing of fire-cured tobacco was compulsory. In my view the vigour with which this was done did much to widen the rift between the administration and the people of the district. Before the planting season, all regional and district officers as well as party leaders went out to all parts of the district telling people to grow tobacco. Several months later, when the crop was nearly ready to harvest, these same officers were again sent out to round up those who had failed to plant, in effect turning the whole of the administration into a temporary police force. Community development officers acting in this capacity were hardly likely to be very effective afterwards in helping the people in other spheres. People who were caught might have been given a prison sentence or been forced to work on roads. During these raids many peasant farmers who had not grown tobacco disappeared into the bush with their bed rolls. Tobacco production increased enormously but there was no improvement in the price the grower received.

Ntimbanjayo was in a difficult position, wishing to remain in discussion with Barongo and not create a situation where the dialogue ceased. In the area around Litowa where little tobacco had been grown before, and where the agricultural staff was quite unable to deal with the education of all the new growers in the techniques of growing tobacco, much work was put in by many people with very little financial return and sometimes no return at all. Ntimbanjayo spent days patiently going round explaining to a number of new growers what to do with the tobacco to try and get over the point that the agricultural department could not cope with what was thrust on them. Strict authoritarian rule by commissioners was a fairly common phenomenon in Tanzania, but Barongo was nevertheless criticized nationally for the methods he was using when the matter was raised in the legislative assembly where, it seems, he confidently expected Ntimbanjayo, as a member for Songea, to defend him. Ntimbanjayo was not in the assembly at the appropriate time and Barongo was for weeks extremely bitter about this. His whole emphasis was on money. Towards the end of his time he produced and circulated a pamphlet with a picture of himself and an account of what he had done for the region, in which he claimed that later on people would look back and be thankful, and say that they had Barongo in their pockets. He told the people of Litowa that there were one or two individual farmers who were getting up to 2,000 shillings a year for their tobacco. Reinhold Nungu, the treasurer of Liweta village, who was a very well-established farmer on his own before becoming one of the leading people of Liweta, when told of this, said immediately that in the RDA villages people were moving ahead much more quickly than those farmers Barongo was talking about who, even in terms of money, were employers of labour and paid out to their labourers a very large part of the 2,000 shillings. Ntimbanjayo remarked how in the areas where tobacco grew well, and the people had more money, there was little of development. The money was spent – in his phrase – on beer, women and bicycles, and they started each season in the same situation as the previous one.

He was never able to get over any of these points to Barongo, and there probably never was any hope of that. As in the case of Walwa, the difference in approach made it difficult to find any common ground, but where with Walwa there was the pretence on the surface, with Barongo the differences were out in the open. He was always keen to tell the people that the government is strong. At Ligera, to the southeast of Songea, when there was a little trouble worrying the people, he went to meet them accompanied by armed men. There is, I think, little that people detest more than having to discuss a grievance at gunpoint. During the meeting no one could even go out into the bush to relieve himself without an armed escort.

Barongo's battle against Ntimbanjayo and the Association, and his desire to split villages from their connections with other villages, was only the more noticeable part of the battle, particularly by openly calling the leaders of the villages to a regional party meeting. A generally worsening attitude to the Association amongst officials made it easier for Barongo to wage his war against us. The reasons were various.

There was an increasing lack of discipline amongst government staff, and organized villages tended to show up this indiscipline. Although in some spheres villagers had access to outside advice through the Association, they always expected assistance from their officials and were encouraged within the Association to work for this. They seldom received it, and at times this became a point of discussion – the Association was made up of villagers keen to get on with their village development and they were as a result not content to leave things unsaid.

The results of this indiscipline among officials were more evident in other contexts, but as long as only the results were talked about and not the reasons, nobody involved was worried. For instance, the position of the district councils was getting increasingly difficult. Their main burden was the cost of primary education. Towards the end of 1967 Mr Mhina, the assistant chief education officer responsible for primary education, having visited Ruvuma, reported on meeting the regional commissioner that "He kindly welcomed me to the region and briefed me on what education problems there were in the region, namely that Mbinga was almost bankrupted and Songea was still experiencing problems in paying teachers." With the increased tobacco crop, it should have been possible to collect the local tax, but the position grew worse rather than better. It was no doubt more difficult to combat tax evasion with a growing rift between people and officialdom, but the main reason, I am sure, was a growing laxity on the part of the tax collectors who would often return to town after having collected enough to cover their own salaries. Later on the problem was "solved" by abolishing the tax and introducing a general sales tax which would be collected at central government level; the district councils were then financed entirely by central government. This pays the teachers and prevents the closing down of bush dispensaries, but the underlying problem of official lack of discipline remains particularly important when the general direction in development is towards using officialdom more and more in the regimentation of the people in order to achieve "results".

Another growing reason for officials' dislike was the increasing knowledge of the villagers through their practical work, which was more real than the increasing theoretical knowledge of officials. When officials feel themselves superior to the people, it is galling for them to realize that the people have knowledge they haven't. As a result such knowledgeable villages are best not visited. This was stated quite bluntly by one of the assistant commissioners in the Ministry of Rural Development when he met Ntimbanjayo in Dar es Salaam after having visited the RDA with his minister Peter Kisumo. He pointed out that the standard of agriculture in some of the villages was quite high, particularly at Liweta where it would, he said, "be difficult for an agricultural officer to face the village *bwana shamba.*"

This same assistant commissioner also asked how Ntimbanjayo knew that I wasn't a spy! In one of his visits to Ruvuma, Ntimbanjayo said that one of his joys in getting back to Litowa was that there were so many things to talk about, whilst in the top circles in Dar es Salaam in which he moved, talk of spies was an overriding subject. Having expatriates was making it more difficult for the RDA; yet the people of the Association continued to wish for people with knowledge from outside to help them. At the end of the Barongo period, the time was nearing when Roger Pasquier would be returning to Switzerland. (He would have liked to stay longer but during his stay his wife's health had been poor and he felt that for the sake of the family he should return home.) The people not only wanted a successor but with the increasing work to be done they wanted more, not less, outside help. The Association asked the Ministry of Agriculture to request two agriculturists from Switzerland; we knew from our contacts that Swiss Technical Co-operation would have been willing to provide these.

There was also a strong desire in officials to be able to enjoy town life. The peasant existence is a hard one, particularly with the breakdown of much of the old tribal organization. Many officials started from this background and from the day they first went to school they felt themselves on the road that would take them away from this hard life. Having achieved their objective of a town-based life, it is not easy for them to accept as part of their work, the going back to live and work with peasant people. Yet in reality, all aspects of development desperately need those responsible for rural development to be rooted in the whole atmosphere of rural life in order for their thinking to be in any way practical. A new officer may appear to have the right ideas but after a time a number of things tend to lead him into opposition to the RDA villages. A lack of discipline, a liking for being in the towns, a dislike of working with people of some knowledge and experience with whom it is necessary to discuss, instead of with unorganized people who can just be told.

One such case was Makamo, the new rural development officer who came with Kisumo, his minister. Officially a large part of his work was supposed to be with these communal villages, and I feel that when starting work in Ruvuma after our discussions with the minister, Makamo had ideas of doing great things to help. He told us that as a first step he would spend about four days in each of the larger villages of the Association. He said that he wanted to learn from the people and that when he visited Litowa, which he would put first on the list, he would like to talk with me. It was in fact some time before the first visit took place and was after much enquiry from the Association about when it would be. The visit was fixed for a Monday and we expected it to last most of the week. He did not arrive until midday, complete with camp bed and bedroll, and immediately asked if he could spend the afternoon meeting with the village management committee. I told him that I would welcome talking with him as he had asked, but that I preferred to do this after he had discussed with the people.

That afternoon the members of the management committee gave up their work time to discuss with him. He had prepared a file with many headings such as History, Agriculture, Health, and under each heading a list of questions. The time was spent by him completing this file from the answers of the village members. He planned to gather similar information from all of the villages. The following morning at 10 o'clock he came to see me to say goodbye as he had to leave, it being necessary, he said, to take one of the members of his party to the doctor at Peramiho.

Some weeks later there was to be a quarterly general meeting of the Association to be held at the Ntakanini village. These meetings usually lasted three days. It was an ideal opportunity for Makamo to learn much about the villages and the Association and, as was usual, he and other officials were invited. (Agricultural and development officials were always invited but almost never attended.) In this case Makamo attended for part of one day. A little later he paid a very short visit to Matetereka, and that was the end of the plans to learn all about the villages and to assist them. A new man falls down on his aims and thus drifts into the ranks of those who are just not interested in or who are opposed to the villages. It is easier to oppose.

The pattern was not always the same. Our divisional executive officer of the district council – Mahekula – was a man with whom we had always got on well, although he had not been engaged very much in assisting us. With the official policy of encouraging communal villages and as this talk permeated government and party, Mahekula approached us to say that he wished to be more involved. He told us that in other areas at the beginning of the decade he had spent much time in encouraging people to live closer together, recognizing that they could do more to help each other than through living isolated lives. However, he said that through seeing things this way for himself in the past he had so often got himself into trouble with authority that with a growing family he had felt that he should play it safe. He told us that with much of what he thought now official policy, he felt he could come out into the open and that he would like to assist the Association wherever he could be useful.

The people of the Association immediately took him up on this. With the general mood of the people in the area at that time, it seemed unlikely that much could be done to encourage more people to join the villages even though many of the villages badly needed a larger membership to increase the rate of development. This was particularly true of Litowa because of the extra work done there, in what was the centre of the Association. One simple immediate answer appeared to be for Litowa and Luhira Goliama across the river to join together, and this suggestion had been put forward before on one or two occasions. Because the Association was made up of the village people, to effect this could not be forced or rushed. Each community had its own leadership, each slightly different ways of working and so on. Mahekula was a respected official and from experience the people trusted him to speak carefully. Since he offered to help, he was asked if he would call the people of the two villages together and speak to them on the possible uniting. He did this after he had first discussed the reasons for such a move with the Association leaders. Some months after this the two villages did join. This was primarily because of work on the idea done over quite a period by people in the two villages concerned, but I do feel that this meeting with Mahekula helped.

However, Mahekula's judgment on the situation was not quite accurate. Official policy or not, in his last weeks Barongo was making a determined effort to get rid of any officials who befriended the Association. He banned one local party official called Pilis from the region. As well as publicly speaking for the Association in political lectures in the region, Pilis had also been criticizing Barongo's implementation of compulsory tobacco-growing, so that his banning was not only on the basis of his support for the villages. Barongo had also taken steps to get rid of Mahekula but was himself moved before he could act against him.

At the end of Barongo's reign, we appeared to have quite a number of silent supporters amongst the ranks of the officials, but I came to feel afterwards that this was primarily because they were fed up with Barongo and secretly sided with those who they felt were standing up to the man. The majority of officials were not personally involved with the Association and the relevant issues involved probably had little if any interest for them. Apart from the area and regional commissioners and for a while the education department, the worst was the agricultural department. This may have been mostly because Munthali, the regional agricultural officer, was so set against the Association. For instance, his staff had prevented a small village of only five families from joining the Association. This small group at Mtimputipu had been farming communally for a number of years and had asked visiting agricultural officials very early on if they should join the Association. The officials warned them against it, saying that the Association would take all their money! What these villagers said when they eventually came to join was revealing. They were a group of co-operating peasant farmers looking for advice whom the agricultural department could have helped considerably. We found afterwards that they were a very hard-working group of families, and the simplest of advice and assistance would have taken them far. After relating what they had been told about the Association, they then said that they had been discussing amongst themselves and noticed that while the villages of the Association were progressing, they themselves remained stationary, so that they had decided to ask to join the Association feeling that it was better to lose their money if it meant that they progressed!

During the last period of the Association's existence we were much involved with national rather than regional and district officials, and here we found greater understanding but also often greater enmity. Those with a real interest in the *ujamaa* villages and a fairly good understanding of them often also knew that the struggles of the villages for political freedom were one with the struggles in the country generally. Our major contacts were with just a few ministries and we could only judge by these, but in both the Ministry of Education and the Ministry of Rural Development we had many friends and found many who were willing to discuss frankly. Both had unsympathetic ministers. Those who were interested in the villages were the ones willing to talk with the people and did not behave as superiors. They were also perfectly willing to talk with me so that I did not feel that they put me in any special position. Those who were opposed did not want to talk either to the people or to me. The visit of the teacher training college principals demonstrates this. The Association's answer to their report was written by Toroka, commissioned to do it by the executive committee which also asked that I put it into good English and make any additions I thought fit. (Both are published at the end of this chapter.) In such instances I always took much trouble to keep the precise meaning of the writer and would generally make no additions, but in this case the penultimate paragraph is mine, added because I happened to have heard a remark of the President on the problem of theft in the towns; he said that those thieves were poor people who stole in the night because they were starving and were not the people we should worry about, we should be worrying instead about the daylight thieves.

Not many people put their criticisms into writing as Mwowo has done in this report but his tactics were fairly standard. A fleeting visit, a few questions, an attack on Litowa, a praise for some village other than Litowa, an attack on expatriates and a bit of high-sounding advice. We know that the talk of a class society developing at Litowa was told to people, including the principals, before they reached the place; friendly visitors told us this. Others heard these tales and went off to spread them, never coming to Litowa to see for themselves. As far as Mwowo was concerned, Toroka's assumption that the story was based on the two different types of housing which existed was true, as we have since heard of him telling of this once he became ambassador for Tanzania in Paris. In the more spacious houses that the principals saw, only one was for a member of the school staff and two for officials of the RDA; one of those was the same house as the teacher, as they were man and wife. Toroka himself was still in the old village and was not to leave for the new house he was building until a week or two before he was moved by authority to Kigoma. Most other teachers were also building houses for themselves in the new village. These were being built by the teachers using their salaries to pay builders, but on the understanding that the houses when finished were the property of the village as were all the other houses. This was a way of the teachers sharing their salaries with the villagers, a beginning which soon was to grow, with teachers applying for membership of the villages and prepared to discuss the handing over of their salary to the villages. It would be hard to find any other place in the country where the school staff so associated themselves with the farming parents of the children they were teaching.

However, having alighted on a story, the enemies of the RDA stuck to it, continuing to use it even when they knew it was a lie. Some central committee members staying for their five weeks at another village paid a short visit to Litowa during that time and again used the different housing as a weapon – this time also as an attack on me. By then there were only a handful of the old houses left and even some of those few were occupied by people such as the staff of Ntimbanjayo's department involved with its education programme. Towards the end, all the tales against the Association were so far off the truth that

Ntimbanjayo, reading some of the central committee members' reports, told me that it seemed that every one of the people's best achievements was written down as its exact opposite.

These stories reached the President of course, and at the first seminar with the central committee in February 1969 he asked the Association representatives what they had to say in answer to people who came to him to tell him that there was no progress in the Association. This was answered very ably by Ngairo who said that he had been born in a village not very far from Litowa, a village which existed long before he was born and still existed, but not only was there no progress in this village – it had in fact become poorer. When he was young there were cattle in the village, now there were none; the crops were poorer; many young men left for the towns. He said that Litowa had started from the bush only eight years before and now there was a village with greater security for the people, with improving food and housing conditions, with a dispensary run by the village, with a piped water supply, a carpentry shop, a village store; with a dairy herd growing; with a school which was directing their children towards carrying on with village development, and where older children were already working in the village, and so on.

I am certain that the main point of opposition was always the fact that in the villages the people were organized and ran their own affairs, but there were several additional reasons already mentioned. Taking away a government contract for maize flour and for timber was by no means all for political reasons, but also because in dealing with the Association, officials could not obtain bribes to augment their salaries. In the case of the sawmill, the contracts for the timber for the Ministry of Communications and Works (Comworks) were put out to tender and in June 1969 the contract was awarded to a bogus company. There was in fact nobody other than the Association which could supply the quantity of timber required in the time required. Everybody concerned knew this but it would be possible for an individual to collect from many hand sawyers enough timber for a few local purchase orders on which a number of people could get their rake-off. This in fact happened. While it was happening, Comworks officials privately approached our people to say that we should go on preparing timber as in spite of the tender they would have to come back to the Association to supply their needs. With the flour contracts, they were given to a trader at a higher price than those tendered by the Association, and our people had no doubt why the contract went in this direction. In the region it was illegal to move food crops from one district to another, and it was not easy for the Association to get a permit to buy beans for school-feeding from the Mbinga District. It was very easy to buy from an Indian trader in Songea beans in any quantity which he had bought from Mbinga, and he could promise delivery at any time knowing that he was in a position always to get a permit to pass the road barriers.

At one of the national seminars for administrators, the Ruvuma regional official was overheard one evening in the bar telling his fellows how they had "taken the timber contract away from those RDA people". Possibly the dislike of the Association and the desire for a rake-off were working together. In the case of the flour mill the political aspects were certainly involved, as one regional commissioner had put forward a plan to use regional development moneys to buy a grinding mill for the Songea district council in order to try and put the RDA out of business.

When officials brought forward the accusation that development in the villages in the Association was too slow, I don't believe that this was always a manufactured reason. I am certain that many officials were looking for quite unrealistic strides. There was I think much more realism than in 1963 when an area secretary told me that with the start of the Village Settlement Agencies project at Mlale, it would not be long before many people were prepared to come into such villages, as they saw the first settlers buying their cars! It is probable that Kisumo believed that large-scale development would happen, based on the government resettlement in the Rufiji where groups of over a thousand families were put together into villages and told to co-operate.

In the middle of 1969 when visiting Mahiwa I had had a discussion with the members of the staff. The most talkative member there obviously had great dreams of what development was and the villages of the Association did not reach his dreams, obviously a great disappointment to him. And yet in all the areas around him nothing was happening, and just previous to our discussion he had been conducting me around the college vegetable garden – an utterly miserable one compared to any in the RDA villages.

On the other hand, some did see the realities. A week or two before the disbanding, a surveyor of the land planning unit who several years before had been engaged in a survey of the Liweta land at which time he had lived in the village, approached the village leaders to say that he would like to give up his work and become a member of Liweta village. This is in spite of the fact that while engaged on the survey he had had to spend a few hours up a tree when, while walking on his own over the land, he had suddenly come face to face with a lion. After the disbanding, the district police commander told me of a new man who had first seen Litowa when sent there by the party to collect property of the Association; he said that he felt that if such places grew, people would soon be wanting to go to live in them and be leaving the towns.[2]

It is perhaps necessary to say that our experiences with officialdom were not because we were an awkward lot. In fact seeing experiences elsewhere, I feel that the people in our villages

---

2   After being back in England for over six months, whilst looking at coloured slides of Litowa, our fourteen-year-old son said that it was strange to see them now because the people looked poor but while we were there we thought the people rich as we compared them with those in the surrounding areas. It is important to get our perspective right.

were more reasonable and receptive towards government than many. At Somangile outside Dar es Salaam, a group absolutely under the control of the party and the agricultural office and not allowed to grow anything but cotton for cash on the scheme land, had after discussions with Ntimbanjayo decided to grow some maize to feed themselves. This was a vital step. When this crop was knee-high the agricultural officers had forced them to cut down the whole crop with *pangas*.[3] It is not surprising that the members were a surly crowd.

When we were in Dar es Salaam for a conference towards the end of 1966, Ntimbanjayo had decided to invite two of the leaders from this group to visit Ruvuma. We stopped at Matetereka on the way down to Songea and immediately the Matetereka village manager took these two visitors and conducted them around the village and farm. After this tour of about an hour they were noticeably different people, seeing for themselves the Matetereka people in charge of their own affairs. Mbambara and Ndiva too could relate many such stories of the despotism of officials. To my mind one of the greatest requisites for development is that the people developing should have power over their own lives.

Joint Report by a Party of Teachers' College Principals
Litowa-Liweta, Songea

Sunday 24 - Friday 29 November 1968

Present:

EK Meena – ACEO (TE) Leader of the party
S Tunginie – Principal, Butimba Teachers' College
JAT Muwowo – Principal, Dar es Salaam Teachers' College
HD Sembuche – Principal, Katoke Teachers' College
JA Ramadhani – Principal, Korogwe Teachers' College
LW Swai – Principal, Marargu Teachers' College

---

3   Cutlasses.

JM Franken – Principal, Morogoro Teachers' College
M Chengula – Principal, Peramiho Teachers' College
Hon J Millinga, MP – Litowa *Ujamaa* Village
Fr Chengula and Mr Millinga arranged accommodation and the programme for the visit.

1. The Origin of the Meeting

The idea to visit Litowa was mooted at the principals meeting in July 1968. It was generally agreed that it would be of value for the principals to visit a living example of an *ujamaa* village in order to gain an insight into the life and practices of such a society. Principals, it was felt, would then be better equipped to talk on this subject with the students in their colleges.

2. Visits and Impressions

The party first visited Liweta. Most of the founders of this *ujamaa* village are old people. They are all experienced people and have all travelled extensively outside of the region so that, in a sense, the idea of living together was born out of real personal life experiences. The people have tremendous confidence in themselves and in the kind of society they have decided to build for themselves. The overall picture is that all are villagers and all are workmen. They plant tobacco, maize, groundnuts, beans and such-like crops. They have facilities of tractors and ploughs.

The main concern of the villagers is that their children have to travel to Litowa, some four miles away, for their higher forms of primary education. They consider this is a waste of time and also a set-up which does not help their children to be fully incorporated into the life and activities of their *ujamaa* village.

A French couple lives in the premises to assist with the necessary repair work of all machinery and farm implements.

3. Litowa

This is the parent *ujamaa* village in the Ruvuma Region. It was founded in 1960. But the policy and general organization of Litowa is, in many ways, different from that of Liweta. The farms and all projects are totally communal: also we discovered some unfortunate signs of a class society developing in the *ujamaa* village. They, too, have an expatriate couple advising the villagers in the organization of the village.

The general concern of the villagers was that they were not given opportunities to develop a very different primary school programme appropriate to an *ujamaa* village life – make the course more practical and productive and generally give a course which heavily orients the children to life in the *ujamaa* village. It was felt that courses on such topics as the geography of Canada – some work of which was found on the blackboard – was irrelevant and not quite meaningful to a child in Litowa. In this sense, the party agreed that the current experimental books English for primary VI and VII were not suitable for our primary school programme, the themes of children applying for jobs in towns, photographs depicting people smartly dressed in suits and ties and also equipment like a refrig, electric cookers and irons were not helpful to the existing government policy that children in primary schools should be educated to live in the villages.

4. General Recommendations and Summary

i. It was generally agreed that Liweta, which was an off-shoot of Litowa, was a better organized *ujamaa* village and generally succeeded in putting across a correct meaning of a typical *ujamaa* village as should be understood in Tanzania.

ii. The party questioned most strongly the advisability of employing expatriate staff to advise in any way the functioning of an *ujamaa* village in Tanzania. These projects, it was felt, touched most fundamentally TANU's policy on the basis of rural development. As such, the party did not believe that there could be room for an Englishman or Frenchman in this kind of work. The fear was that most of these expatriates might well end up writing books or theses for higher degrees on the failures or successes of the endeavours of our people. Utmost attempt must be made to make use of our own local technicians and advisers. The party believed that these are available.

iii. Schools in *ujamaa* villages should be given opportunities and should be encouraged to try out educational practices such as would orient the children to live creatively in the villages.

iv. Assistance to *ujamaa* villages from the Ruvuma Development Association and from the regional development committee should always be forthcoming so as to give encouragement to the endeavours of the villagers. There should be a well organized machinery for marketing the crops from the *ujamaa* village farms, efficient facilities for repairing the farm implements and also constant advice from the agriculture office and also visits from party officials to give encouragement and necessary guidance to the villagers.

5. Other Visits

a) On the 26th November 1968, the party made one long trip to Lituhi and then along the shore of Lake Nyasa to Mbamba Bay and then back to Peramiho. This was a journey of some 300 miles by Land Rover.

The landscape is extremely beautiful and has great potential for tourism and agriculture. By making this trip, the party was also able to size up the magnitude of the border issue with Malawi.

b) On 27th October 1968, the party of the principals was taken round to see the various establishments of Peramiho including the tailoring school and the garage workshop. The saying being repeated at Peramiho is a statement, we understand, which was made by His Excellency the President, Mwalimu JK Nyerere while on a visit there: that "*Peramiho ina kila kitu isipokuwa Jela ya kufungia watu.*" [Peramiho has everything except a jail to freeze people out.] There couldn't be any more complete summary of the organization of Peramiho than this. It seems to us that Ruvuma Region is PERAMIHO and its outer missionary stations! The success of any social and economic development programmes in the region may well depend upon, we feel, the closer involvement of the Benedictine fathers at Peramiho.

An Answer to a Joint Report Issued by a Party of Teachers' College Principals on their Visit to Liweta and Litowa on 29 November 1968

Ruvuma Development Association
Litowa, February 1969

1. The Idea of the Visit

> ... it would be of value for the principals to visit a living example of an *ujamaa* village in order to gain an insight into the life and practices of such a community. Principals, it was felt, would then be better equipped to talk on this subject with the students in their colleges.

2. Visit and Impressions.

a) Liweta.

> ... the main concern of the villagers is that their children have to travel to Litowa, some four miles, for their higher form of primary education.

Any one reading such a statement would automatically be led to think that the children of Liweta have to walk some four miles every day to and from Litowa for school. If the party thought so, they did not understand aright for the children from Liweta stay in school as boarders. Even these children whose home is in Litowa stay in the school as boarders. All children who go to school in Litowa are boarders except seven. They go home during some of their holidays, but not walking as the Association provides transport. Besides Liweta is not four miles from Litowa but eight miles. It would not be possible for the children to walk daily. Also, Liweta children and all others do not come to Litowa only for their "higher forms of primary education", but for a full primary course.

They consider this a waste of time . . .

Liweta and the other villages of the Association built the schools at Litowa of their own accord, and together with the other villages decided upon the set-up of the school. They did so and are still doing so for understandable reasons. Because they feel that the school is theirs and it would not matter where they build it. Liweta like all the villages in the Association has a feeling of oneness – a feeling of taking part in a common struggle which in the end would lead men to a common end. This end being a better economic life on an *ujamaa* basis. That is why they joined together in an Association. Apart from this the people of Liweta know that they cannot have their own school for the simple reason that there would not be enough children in the whole area to fill up a single classroom of thirty. The ministry is well aware of this. Even so, how could they have it while the district council is already struggling on its death bed? How could the Liweta people complain?

> . . . and also a set-up which does not help their children
> to be fully incorporated into the life and activities of
> their *ujamaa* village.

We consider this a statement which would cause division and which the visiting party imposed upon Liweta by exploit-

ing their ignorance. The programme of the school and its organizational set-up is geared to reflect an *ujamaa* village. Therefore
none of the children of Liweta are going to lose through entering
school at Litowa.

> ... A French couple lives in the premises to assist with
> the repair work of all machinery and farm implements.

The white couple living at Liweta is not French but Swiss.
They were brought in and put there by the Association because
the Association's garage is at Liweta. They work not only for Liweta but for all the fourteen villages of the Association. As you
read this the mechanic may be out in other villages repairing
grinding mills or servicing farm machinery. He has nothing to
do with the organization of Liweta, is not involved in the daily
village discussions or the organization of the work in the village,
neither does Liweta direct his work, other than asking for his
services when they have machinery to mend.

b) Litowa

> ... the policy and general organization of Litowa is in
> many ways different from that of Liweta. The farms
> and all projects are totally communal ...

The organization of the two villages does not differ in any
fundamental way at all. We are sure that the party did not find
that at Liweta there was a manager and at Litowa a *jumbe* as
communal heads! What may have appeared as a difference to
the party is the fact that at Liweta there are one acre plots allocated for each family for their own personal use. This is not a
fundamental difference for they also exist – although not so big
– at Litowa and in fact in every *ujamaa* village in the Association.
The apparent difference is that at Litowa these areas surround
the houses of each member while at Liweta they are well out
in the fields. They were put there, not as a gesture of a good

basis for an *ujamaa* society, but as one way of getting more land cleared for the future use of the community. The size of these is diminishing each year and it is the intention of the village in future to have much smaller plots around each house as soon as they are able to build permanent houses.

> . . . also we discovered some unfortunate signs of a
> class society developing in the *ujamaa* village.

We are surprised to note that the party was able to see a class society developing in a two-hour stay in a village. If such a class society is growing it must therefore be outstanding to be seen by people who do little more than drive through the village. We can only guess what may have led to this "discovery". If you enter Litowa from the main bridge you notice that many houses are old. This is the old village where many houses were built in the early 1960s. The party may have assumed these houses to be for the village members. As you go up the village from there you soon find newly built houses with better solid mud walls, good grass thatch, looking quite spacious and with gardens around them. Were these assumed to be the houses for the teachers or of higher authorities in the village or RDA officials living there? If these were the assumptions they were wrong ones as these houses are for the villagers. It is the permanent village and gradually as more houses are built all villagers will be living there, all in the same type of houses. Further than these is the people's church, dispensary and new school buildings, all with iron roofs. The school could not be a sign for a class society, neither could the church or the dispensary, for these are communal public buildings.

> They, too, have an expatriate couple advising the vil-
> lagers in the organization of their village.

The white couple is Ralph and Noreen Ibbott who live at Litowa with their family. They are in the same sort of position as

British VSO or American volunteers in our secondary schools. As with those at Liweta, they are here not just for Litowa but for all the villages and the Association. It is the RDA which brought them in not Litowa. They do not take part in the organizational work of the village and have never done so as this is the work of the villagers themselves and still is. Ralph Ibbott's part is as an adviser on development.

c) Peramiho

> . . . a statement, we understand which was made by
> His Excellency the President Mwalimu JK Nyerere
> while on a visit there that, "Peramiho ina kila kitu
> isipokuwa Jela ya kufungia watu."

It appears to us that many people, such as these party members do not understand Mwalimu's language, although it is often very simple and so took this statement to be a high honour for Peramiho. Many people are deceived by seeing magnificent buildings and large workshops and take it to be development. We believe that this statement was said in mockery and meant that all this was not for the good of the people. These fine instruments are for filling up the bellies of a bunch of foreigners under the flag of religion. One only has to look at life a few paces from the mission where apart from the African shopping centre there are people still living in abject poverty, people who have no good shelter and whose children have no future. There are many examples to explain Mwalimu's meaning but all show that these fine things mean nothing because they have effected little change in the life of the people.

> It seems to us that Ruvuma Region is Peramiho and its
> outer missionary stations.

> If we accept this statement, then Dar es Salaam could be
said to be the whole of Tanzania. It is either a deliberate insult to

the people of the region or an attempt to ignore completely the efforts of the people in this part of the country. The party is saying that there can be no Ruvuma without the missionaries and their stations. How can a few individuals who are prospering amongst so many poor be said to be the whole region.

> The success of any social and economic development programmes in the region may well depend upon, we feel, the closer involvement of the Benedictine fathers at Peramiho.

This is subversive writing. If the party really means what it says then it is suggesting the betrayal of the efforts of the poor into the hands of a few foreign interlopers. Development does not depend on a few individuals, but depends on the efforts of everyone. We feel that the party is either ignorant of the basis of development or has acted under the direction of a foreign master. It is difficult to believe that in the case of this group of educated people it could be ignorance for the basis of development of our people and the country has been made clear so often in many speeches and particularly in the Arusha Declaration, in Socialism and Rural Development and more recently in Freedom and Development. These same Benedictines who the party recommends using for the development of the Ruvuma Region, came here over seventy years ago and if they have the development of the people so much at heart, what have they been doing? Before independence, was not this region known as the Cinderella of Tanganyika, and used by the colonialists as a detention camp? The Benedictines were here then. It would take a miracle for this conservative group to become dedicated to the development of our people.

General Recommendation and Summary 3 (ii)

ii. The party questioned most strongly the advisability of employing expatriate staff to advise in any way the functioning of an *ujamaa* village in Tanzania. These projects, it was felt, touched most fundamentally TANU's policy on the basis of rural development. As such, the party did not believe that there could be room for an Englishman or Frenchman in this kind of work. The fear was that, most of these expatriates might well end up writing books or theses for higher degrees on the failures or successes of the endeavours of our people. Utmost attempt must be made to make use of our own local technicians and advisers. The party believed that these are available.

This paragraph also proved that the party has refused to understand the facts of our development or is working for an anonymous master. Previously they were recommending the close involvement of the missionaries. Are the Benedictine fathers not expatriates? Perhaps the party means that they are more refined expatriates than those honestly involved in the development of our country and its people. However, on pages eight and nine of the Arusha Declaration "Teach-in", the President has this to say on expatriates:

> But it is not only capital which we must welcome from outside; it is also MEN. Few things make me more angry than a refusal to accept and to work with people from other countries whose participation can make all the difference between our plans succeeding or failing. It is not being selfish to refuse to carry out the directions of a foreign engineer, a foreign doctor or a foreign manager; it is just stupid . . . , but if the implementation of a particular policy requires someone with good educational qualifications or long experience, it is not very sensible to allow that policy to fail through pride.
>
> We must look at this question of employing expatriates scientifically and without prejudice; we must assess the interests of our development as a whole, not the interests of a particular person who feels that he would like the high post concerned but is neither ready

for it nor prepared to go on learning from someone else.

It is further made clear in *Utekelezaji Wa Azimio La Arusha* [Implementation of the Arusha Declaration] on page 2-3 paragraphs 2-5.

It is the same difficulty we face in our villages and indeed the same problem with *ujamaa* villages all over the country. There have not been enough people from the government sector, amongst party officials or the missionaries with a proper interest or understanding wishing to help. From 1963 to the present, effort after effort has been made to get assistance from the government offices in Songea, but little or nothing has come of it in spite of all our struggles. For the future we still look forward to help from every quarter as understanding grows amongst our people.

Summary and Conclusion

If the aim of the visit was to study the practices and life of *ujamaa* communities then this aim was not achieved, as it is not possible in a two-hour visit to each of two such villages. Such remarks as that Liweta is an offshoot of Litowa is not true. Litowa has never had an offshoot, nor is there any village in the Association with an offshoot. Each village started and developed as a completely separate unit, although they all have many things in common.

On the question of a school for the Liweta children, it is disappointing that the party did not understand the conditions necessary for a village to have its own school even when the villagers maintained that they could not have their own, the visitors insisted that they could and talked as if they had come to solve the villagers' problems.

If at Litowa they could see a class society developing after looking at school classrooms and a bridge in the course of construction and sitting outside one house talking on education, all in the space of two hours, then they either knew of its existence before or they are superintelligent. When parents at Litowa expressed their concern on the curricula of the school, they did not do so just for their own children but for the children in all the schools in the country.

If the party can see garages and workshops in Peramiho and decide that Ruvuma is Peramiho and that the success of development in Ruvuma depends on the Benedictine fathers – this is saying that the success of development does not depend on our people's efforts, but will be achieved by bringing Chinese or Germans. The party failed to understand that the Benedictines are on the whole a very conservative group, yet some of the party members were supposed to be modern revolutionary Catholics. The Benedictines failed to understand the *ujamaa* villages in their early stages and opposed them.

The party appeared to have their conclusions before their visit and did not need to stay long. *Ujamaa* societies have very intricate systems of organization and practice which cannot be understood at a glance. As a result this party which only had a glance ended by writing untrue and insignificant things. There were for this reason people at Litowa who expressed their dissatisfaction when the party on arrival appeared to be in a hurry – one refused to talk to them. Study does not mean calling people together and flinging a couple of questions at them, but detailed observation and discussion – this the party failed to do. We believe that many of the party members have higher degrees. Did they obtain their degrees on a thesis written after two hours' cursory study? Are their degrees then worth more trouble than the people?

The visit with a serious purpose was at the expense of the people of the country – the poor – and we feel that the failure of the party to treat it as serious made it a misuse of public funds. Is not this daylight thieving? Why the sightseeing tour of the Nyasa shore? Why even the tour of Peramiho?

The Association has often been accused of not accepting criticism or other people's ideas and advice. This visit is an example of so much we have to put up with from visitors. Are we to take any notice of what they say when there is no real interest, perhaps even dislike of *ujamaa*, and it is said by people without practical experience? People in the villages and the Association will always accept serious discussion, criticism or ideas. It is only through this selection of whose ideas are accepted that we have been able to exist.

20

PRESIDENT NYERERE AND *UJAMAA*

I think it is necessary to say something of President Nyerere, since he was much involved with the affairs of the Association, particularly towards the end. I don't pretend to be passing a judgement on Nyerere, merely to say how he appeared to us in relation to rural development.

In the situation in Tanzania it is doubtful whether something of the nature of RDA and its villages would have been allowed to exist for more than a year or two without the backing of the President. There was perhaps no escaping this, particularly as the country developed towards and became a one-party state, with an administration in the regions and districts where the government administrative head was also the party secretary. As head of both government and party with this set-up, the President constitutionally had tremendous authority and there was little other protection when the regional boss attacked.

If it were not for Nyerere, Litowa would never have come into existence and I would never have been in Tanzania. From before independence he had begun to call to his people to come together, as a result of which Ntimbanjayo started at Litowa. Soon after this, he called through government for the establishment of village settlements for which purpose the Village Settlement Agency was started. There was probably a considerable difference between the original ideas of Nyerere on the settlements and how they turned out after those ideas had gone through the machinery of administrators and experts. When it was apparent from research by the Syracuse University Village Settlement Project which reported in August 1966, that these settlements were failing,[1] I am certain that much of the quick decision to call a halt to the project and think again was the initiative of President Nyerere.

From this time, a new approach to rural development began to grow and many realities were squarely faced. The new ideas appeared to come from State House. It was impressive to hear these ideas from Nyerere speaking and to read them in his writings on rural development which were published in the next few years, particularly Education for Self-Reliance, Socialism and Rural Development, and Freedom and Development.[2] He saw the need to start from where the people were, and explained this on one of his visits to Litowa by saying how often in his travels he was confronted by people with plans of what they were going to do who were waiting for the money to come along in order to be able to make a start. He likened them to people coming to a river without a bridge and sitting on the bank waiting for all the water to pass by before they could cross. He recognized that the beginnings would be slow.

On the same visit, Grace Chips as head of the Litowa school gave a report on what the school had achieved in the past year and finished by saying that it was very little. Nyerere contradicted this and said that it was progress, we were going forward. While many were after their big machines to get things done rapidly, he said that the country was not ready for them. Along this same line, he read René Dumont's book *False Start in Africa*[3] and we were told he ordered copies for all of his ministers to read. He also invited Dr Schumacher, the apostle of intermediate technology, to visit and report on Tanzania. Nyerere spoke against despotic officials, so that during Barongo's dictatorial tobacco-growing reign, when he came to Songea to open the new regional administrative block, he made what must surely have been his shortest speech, before hurriedly unveiling the plaque:

1   With the exception of Kitete.
2   *Freedom and Socialism*, pp 267, 337; *Freedom and Development*, p 58.
3   See Further Reading.

294 UJAMAA – THE HIDDEN STORY

"This building is meant for development, not for ruling." He understood that co-operation had to be with the assent of the people and that it was a gradual process. So we read in Socialism and Rural Development:

> . . . socialist communities cannot be established by compulsion.
>
> Viable socialist communities can only be established with willing members . . .
>
> *Ujamaa* villages will have to be established, and will grow through the self-reliant activities of the people. They will be created by the village people themselves, and maintained by them. It must be done from their own resources.
>
> . . . we should gradually become a nation of *ujamaa* villages where the people co-operate directly in small groups and where these small groups co-operate together for joint enterprises.[4]

And so on.

About the same time as publishing this last writing, the President placed Ntimbanjayo in the party youth league headquarters with a responsibility towards settlements and economic activities of the youth league and a year later moved him to the party headquarters as secretary for *Ujamaa Vijijini*. From then, as has been described, he began to push the issue at various levels. With the many speeches on *ujamaa* and the establishment of *ujamaa* villages becoming official policy, it became inevitable that every area and regional commissioner entered the competition to see who could have the most *ujamaa* villages, few of which bore any resemblance to what was written in Socialism and Rural Development. It seems strange that a man who had shown so much understanding of the need for slow,

---

4   *Freedom and Socialism*, pp 356, 364, 365.

steady growth should have handed over his policy to party and government officials on a national scale when he had so much experience of how these people operated. It seems to me that it is in fact very easy for politicians who live away from the realities of rural life to get carried away by ideas in spite of starting with a very good knowledge of the situation. The various facts involved are never put together and considered as a whole in order to study how to go forward. The idea leads completely.

When a group of us met the President after the first seminar with the central committee in 1969, two of his statements showed the confusion. There were many people in all parts of the country coming together into groups, as Nyerere asked for in his many speeches. When talking of training leaders of these groups by sending them to Ruvuma, he said very realistically that the people of the country knew very little and if we could ensure that their horizons were made just a little wider then we would have achieved something. A few minutes later I heard him say that at the time of independence many people came together in groups and we failed to be able to help them so that the groups collapsed. Now they were again coming together and he said that this time we must not fail. He had the experience to know that there was not the ability to deal with the number of these groups which were appearing. It was this point which I had attempted to talk on at the beginning of the Kivukoni seminar for the central committee.

Again, he was aware that the vast majority of officials knew no other way of working with peasants other than through coercion, and that this also applied to the members of the central committee. It was reported back to us that at the Handeni seminar of the central committee, Nyerere had dramatically told them that they were not going to bully the people as long as he was there. If they wanted to bully the people, he had told them that they would first have to shoot him. Many times he had talked to people about those things and knew how difficult it was to change attitudes. In Freedom and Development he said this very clearly:

> The *ujamaa* village is a new conception, based on the post-Arusha Declaration understanding that what we need to develop is people, not things, and that people can only develop themselves. The policy is, in fact, the result of learning from the failures which we have had, and from the successes of those small groups which began and grew on a different basis.[5]

Yet when he told us to go ahead and through Peter Kisumo get the volunteers from overseas, and we later came back to him asking if he would act as Kisumo never would, his answer was that these people (i.e. those like Kisumo) acted as they did because they didn't understand and that it was only through the continuing dialogue they would learn – we were to continue to battle for the volunteers. As he was working with those people it is hard to believe that he did not understand that there was no possibility of changing Kisumo's attitude and that he was working to destroy the RDA.

I feel that in fact during this time his thoughts were developing on lines different from those on which he had written in the year or two before. Impatience was beginning to take over. This seems an old story. More recently in China, there appeared to be a very great change from the way the peasant was helped and encouraged to take small realistic steps towards cooperation in 1949 and the years following, to what was called "the great leap forward" in 1958 – only nine years later. I would guess that in 1949 the realistic and to my mind very successful approach was possible because the whole of the communist movement in China had had to be very close to the land and the realities of life through the Long March and years of survival against great odds, fighting the government of their own

---

5   *Freedom and Development*, p 67.

country as well as the Japanese. They must have been largely a government of farmers but it took only nine years for the bureaucracy to grow and for the decisions to be "political" rather than practical.

In Tanzania in 1969 a large resettlement plan was put into effect in the Rufiji valley for people who had been flooded out. Nyerere decided that with this going on, those resettled should be put into *ujamaa* villages and should co-operate together. These new villages were quite large, many with over a thousand families, and in the Tanzanian situation it is not possible to imagine putting such numbers of people together and getting them to farm co-operatively. Ntimbanjayo was asked to go there and found immediately that there was hardly any sign of the land planning unit having set out the land to suit co-operative working. Such a change could not be instituted in the middle of a large operation when there was not even the understanding in the planning unit of what would have been necessary. In the year after this resettlement there was an almost complete failure to do any farming at all on an individual basis, let alone co-operatively. Things were made worse by a difficult season. There was considerable hardship through lack of food and food provided by government often arriving late and inadequate in quantity.

The saddest part to me was that having appointed Ntimbanjayo, a man with practical experience, he never allowed him to use that experience to develop the work, but used him only as a tool to try and implement things his way.

Consequently, since the disbanding of the RDA things have moved further still from the philosophy of *ujamaa* as a growth from the people. During 1970 there was a new move to settle some 875,000 cattle-owning people around Dodoma into co-operative village units. The thinking behind this appears to be that through the normal agricultural extension methods, it is the more forward peasants who take up new ideas and so become better farmers than their neighbours, and gradually move into a position where their neighbours become their employees and are exploited by them. This classic situation becomes one difficult to change, and in order to prevent it, the people must straight away be moved into co-operating units.

After the Rufiji resettlement, it is hard to understand how the Dodoma plan can have been put forward, but the answer comes that through Rufiji the lesson has been learnt that the village units that were set up were too large for co-operative working, and the Dodoma villages will be smaller – around 250 families instead of a thousand or more. How wonderful it would be if rural development were as easy as this. How hard for the people of Dodoma in a country where you would be hard put to find a few dozen agricultural officers able to run a co-operative farm suitable for only a dozen families. In such a bureaucratic exercise as resettling such vast numbers of people, many must suffer. This exercise is the idea of the same man who less than three years earlier wrote that "socialist communities cannot be established by compulsion."[6] In practice, it seems, such a sad exercise is acceptable once it is on a smaller scale – a few dozen villages of less than a 100 families each – and there is not that much machinery for great coercion. An exercise where much might be learnt.

Compulsion has of course always been the rule for officials and it is not changed by one or two presidential writings and by government or party posters. Such happenings as were always there must still go on, so that only recently I heard that a group of peasants in the south-east of the country were questioning the certainty of their food supplies if they moved from their plots to a communal farm as they had been ordered; they received the answer that decisions had now been taken and there was no longer need for argument.

One hears of the great exponent of democracy being a complete autocrat in his own home. I feel there is something of this

6   Socialism and Rural Development, *Freedom and Socialism*, p 356.

with Nyerere's advocacy of village democracy: he tried to work towards it by running the country as a one man show. Producing a set-up where the villager has a real say is no easy matter, and it may be possible for one man with the ideal through strong central rule to encourage and protect peasant organizations until they are strong enough to hold on to power. However, I am certain that such a person would have to build up a strong team to work with him at the top to see things through. The right people did, I'm sure, exist, but they were not going to come along through the party or civil service machine. Perhaps with Nyerere it was his schoolmaster background, but whatever it was he seemed to me to be unable to build up a team around him and in the end he gave away much of his power to the central committee. It would be hard to find in Tanzania a more disappointing body than this. However, it is not as straightforward as this. Nyerere believed in the party, and on an issue where there were differences of opinion in the highest body of the party, he as President, despite all that we from this side might read into the constitution in relation to his powers, would be bound to accept the majority view. Not to accept it would be as unthinkable as a British prime minister ignoring a parliamentary vote and putting a law onto the statute book which the House of Commons had defeated.

At the local level, much of the RDA progress was due to Ntimbanjayo's ability to build up a team, both a team of villages as well as a team of more educated leaders. He would talk easily at all levels feeding out ideas, while at meetings in the chairman's seat he could sit back and let the people decide, sometimes almost appearing to be asleep. He helped create a situation where people could express themselves and so they came. Toroka in a similar way in the school was prepared to encourage and feed out ideas while the children learnt the management of their affairs. Ngairo had not learnt these ideas; Wayakile who followed had.

In terms of the whole of Tanzania the few villages of the RDA were almost nothing. Perhaps Nyerere's idea of "forcing" whole populations into co-operative villages would get somewhere. I doubt it. To me, everything must start from what is possible with available resources. I have never yet seen signs that the agricultural department is able to work out a reasonable plan for one co-operative village. The attempt of the department at Litowa to do just this in 1969 was pathetic when the village, together with many others, had been there so long – long enough for officers to come into and gain experience if that had been their intention.

Understanding that other problems apart from agricultural ones also need looking into, had not really begun. At Ligoma in 1969 where we had been unable to visit for some time, government Land Rovers were visiting three or four times a week and no officials attempted to understand the social problems that needed help before agricultural advice could be effective. Left to these officials, the village would have gradually disintegrated while they continued their frantic rushing in and out with advice.

The idea of having all Tanzania's peasant people turned into co-operative farmers in a few years just is not possible. A number of co-operative villages such as in Ruvuma can be something of importance where little in the way of growth exists. They can be genuine centres of growth because they are dealing with the basic realities of life, and there is no reason why they should not eventually grow beyond villages into small towns and so begin to produce a foundation for development which could bring a proper balance between town and country; but this can only happen when there are many prospective towns like it. Moreover, because of their communal beginnings one would expect the participants to play a full and proper role in ongoing development.

The RDA had not much more to start on than Ntimban-jayo's ideal and my ten-year apprenticeship in Rhodesia. In spite of this, it was not only possible to have an association in Ruvuma of communal villages very much controlled from within, but with other genuine *ujamaa* villages growing in other parts of Tanzania, it would have been possible to begin to develop a national association of the villages as well as their local associations. Such a body governed from the bottom would have been able to organize much of what was necessary to assist the proper growth of the village communities.

It is hard to see any other genuine centres of growth. There are local government centres, missions, government settlements, district training centres, projects of the UN agencies, but none of these seem to be centres capable of providing a foundation on which to build. Looking at villages like Matetereka, Liweta or Litowa, they all had a potential of growth in many directions. The party has largely put paid to this potential, but I feel that even before this, Nyerere had moved onto a path which was different from that of the Association, and that this inevitably meant a setback for the people of the RDA.

21

EPILOGUE

When the Ruvuma Development Association was banned by TANU's central committee, my job as an adviser to the RDA came to an end, and our family – four children, my wife and myself, had to quickly pack up and return to the UK.

It was not politic for me to have contact with my Tanzanian friends at that time. It might have been dangerous for them, and also it might fuel the story that was being put about, that the RDA was foreign-led. But I was able to take my personal papers with me, which made it possible to respond to a request to write this story of the RDA.

A few months before the banning, Fred Wood, a representative of the education department of the Commonwealth Secretariat, visited Litowa with special interest in the school. At the same time, David Bowdrey, a mechanic who had helped the RDA before, also visited. When they arrived at Songea, their passports were taken and they were told they couldn't visit Litowa. To get their passports returned, they had to get out of the region within (as far as I remember) twenty-four hours. Their visit to Litowa was therefore brief, but it did happen.

About six months after returning to the UK, I got the following letter (dated 19 March 1970) from the Commonwealth Secretariat:

> ... I now write to confirm that we should like you to write an account of your work in Africa during the past few years with such analysis and reflections as you are moved to make. I know something of what you have been doing with the RDA but I gather from my col-

league Mr Wood that some of your earlier experience
might also be of interest to us.

Rural development and the education of rural communities is of central interest to all who are concerned
in the business of development but the problems it presents have for the most part remained unsolved. The
RDA seemed to point the way to a particularly fruitful
method of proceeding. In spite of its sudden disrup-
tion we still have hope that the lessons it had taught
to those who have been closely associated with it may
still prove of value both in Tanzania and in similar situations in other countries.

We would hope that with your other commitments
you could complete the job in six months or so and we
would offer you an honorarium of £400. We should
of course wish to publish it, if it proves suitable for a
wide audience, and in any case to circulate it to people
concerned in the problems of rural development.[1]

That is how this book came to be written.

Tanganyika became independent when the vast majority of
its population were peasant farmers. President Nyerere thought
then what was later expressed in the Arusha Declaration:

The truth is that in the villages the women work very
hard . . . The energies of the millions of men . . . which
are at present wasted in gossip, dancing and drinking, are a great treasure which could contribute more
towards the development of our country than anything
we could get from rich nations.[2]

It was generally known that Nyerere's plan to begin to address this had been on the one hand to develop a "model" gov-
ernment-planned village in each region of the country. On the

---

1   The letter was signed by HW Springer, Assistant Secretary General.
2   *Freedom and Socialism*, p 245.

other hand, he called for members of the TANU Youth League to form groups to work the land co-operatively. It is hard to see how without this call the RDA would have come into existence.

Nyerere always backed the RDA. For example, the regional commissioner for Songea was made chair of the RDA to express the government's backing for it. When later it appeared that the same commissioner was reluctant to call meetings of the Association, it was Nyerere who over the chair's head gave the RDA permission for a change in its constitution, so that the running of the villages was entirely in the control of the villagers and out of the control of the commissioner. Later still, when the Association felt that the educational curriculum in the country was not suited to lead to school-leavers carrying forward the development of these rural villages, it was Nyerere's influence that allowed for an experimental curriculum and structural changes in the RDA school. When the Association had the possibility to purchase the Songea grain mill and timber sawmill, and the government was not forthcoming, it was Nyerere who assisted with a sizeable amount towards the cost with what we were told was his own money – delivered in cash.

He also took steps to spread the RDA methods of development by having Ntimbanjayo Millinga, the RDA's leader, go first to the TANU Youth League headquarters and then to the TANU party headquarters, with the remit of spreading *ujamaa* villages using the RDA experience as a model. This was followed by seminars for senior officials and national executive members held at Kivukoni College, and in the towns of Sumbawanga and Handeni. In these cases Millinga brought in leading members of the RDA to help with the instruction.

Nyerere's policy, and officially the policy of TANU, was *ujamaa,* or African socialism, and according to his writings the RDA communal villages were *ujamaa* villages. In the second half of the 1960s we received many visitors. Some of these had come as a result of having asked Nyerere about his *ujamaa* strategy and were told by him to go to Ruvuma and see for themselves. Then there was the sending of the members of the central committee to spend time in the *ujamaa* villages and work with the people.

During that period, when Nyerere was attempting to educate his top party leaders and government officers, Millinga, because of his position in the TANU offices, had spent much time with Nyerere. In the late 1990s, the academic David Edwards, then an MA student, was helped by Millinga on his fieldwork in Ruvuma for his thesis "Matetereka – Tanzania's Last Ujamaa Village".[3] Edwards records comments by Millinga that add to our knowledge of the happenings during those times. He writes that:

> According to Millinga, the brain behind the movement to disband the RDA was the minister for regional administration and rural development, Peter Kisumo. He paid very good lip service to the President. He would say, "*Ujamaa* is fantastic!" But behind the President's back he was very open about his hatred of socialism, *ujamaa* and the RDA.

Again at the seminar at Matai in Sumbawanga, Edwards quotes Millinga as saying:

> The topic under discussion was nothing to do with *ujamaa*. Leaving the room the minister [Kisumo] said to me, "Why do you keep talking about *ujamaa* villages!" The remark was so out of context that I was quite taken aback. The minister went on: "I assure you, as long as *we* are in power, *ujamaa* will never succeed! We will make sure it fails!" I went to Mwalimu [Nyerere] later in the day to ask him why this remark had been made, out of the blue. But Mwalimu has many faces and

---

3   (Now Dr) David Edwards, Centre of African Studies, Occasional Papers No 77, Edinburgh University, 1998, p 15.

moods. He said "OK. Thank you for telling me that."
And that was all.

Similarly, Millinga tells that at the close of one of the sessions at the Handeni seminar when they "were discussing something completely different, and then at the close of the session, all of a sudden, the prime minister and vice-president [Rashidi Kawawa] said

> The development of this country will be brought about by the people of this country, and no foreigners! The RDA will disband itself!

His and other hostile references to foreigners were an attack on the support work I and others were committed to. Nyerere was very clear on how welcome those who really could help were.

This antipathy towards the RDA that developed through the 1960s and resulted in its destruction in September 1969 came from the top: from the central committee, government ministers and with rare exceptions the top civil servants – what amounted to the whole political establishment. The RDA would not have been allowed to exist as long as it did had it not been for Nyerere's commitment to it. The question is: why was the antipathy so great? I have been asking myself this question for many years.

Despite all the President's efforts, the decision on the NEC was a 21-3 majority to ban the RDA. I heard later from Ntimbanjayo who was present that the members had told the President that when they went to the villages, the villagers had planned to kill them: one said by a rock being rolled down a hill, and another by getting a bull to attack him. The President told them they were talking nonsense.

But perhaps with a twenty-one to three defeat, he really had no choice but to agree with them on the Association's banning. Ntimbanjayo later said to me that Nyerere told them that this was a thing that he wanted very much, and now the party would have to take the responsibility for seeing to it. They of course assured him that they would. Did he not know that anything they would produce would be unrecognizable as the *ujamaa* of his writings: *ujamaa* villages formed by the villagers and run by them? He knew very well of the difficulty of finding people for the positions of power who would go along with the *ujamaa* practice of his writings. That was why he wrote those things in the first place. But the bureaucracy wanted to control and command.

Back in Britain, I wrote at some length to the President (see Appendix II) and received a letter back from Joan Wicken, his dedicated personal assistant, in which she says that my letter has been seen by the President who

> clearly believes that the action taken in relation to the
> RDA was the right action, and he does not accept that
> it is contrary to the ideas of *ujamaa*. He says that it
> is necessary that the nation as a whole should move
> forward under the aegis of TANU, and that it is neces-
> sary to organize ourselves on a national basis. (Dar es
> Salaam, 10 December 1969)

Some months later, on 6 April 1970, Joan wrote us a personal letter. She had always had a great interest in the RDA. She said that after the banning she had a tremendous row with the President in which they both lost their tempers. She regretted this because she had

> made it impossible yet to get a discussion of the issues
> and clearly he believes some most peculiar things. But
> as he has been told these by people he trusts only time
> will put them straight.

Joan Wicken died in 2004. I think we shall never know what those "peculiar things" were.

A president always has to be aware that anything he says can soon become public knowledge, and the lack of response to my letter was perhaps the sort of thing that I might have expected, but it was a non-response after he knew what Kisumo had done on the day after the NEC meeting. That day Nyerere had left on a foreign trip. So Kisumo hurriedly flew to Songea to put an end to the Association. Two months later Harold Miller, the secretary for relief and service of the Christian Council of Tanzania, wrote that he had had a lengthy conversation with Emil Ndonde from Litowa about his impressions on the demise of the Association. Emil Ndonde has a degree in law. He went to Litowa soon after the break-up of RDA and became a member of the village. Miller wrote me that according to Ndonde's account,

> the President rebuked Kisumo on the action taken vis-à-vis RDA for he apparently didn't know the full story until after the visit to Canada and the USSR. According to him [Ndonde], the President had agreed that the RDA needed some changes, but it was not the President's wish that the RDA receive the treatment it had gotten. And the President was deeply frustrated by your leaving, for he had not apparently expected that.

Harold Miller wrote again in August 1970 to say that Ndonde again came to his office and was on his way back to Litowa having completed his five months National Service. He tells that several weeks before, the Ruvuma regional commissioner had asked the office of Vice-President Kawawa for permission to detain Ndonde, Millinga and others connected to the now disbanded RDA. Permission was refused as no one was prepared to face the President with the request. In June 1972, Carlotta Johnson, a friend of ours, wrote an account of an hour's meeting she had had with Millinga who, on the subject of Ndonde, said that the President had just given him a very good job. "The terms of service allow him to go to the village whenever he wants to. He will travel with the President. He is not a civil servant."

I heard further from Harold Miller in February 1970 that Kisumo, one way or another, had been able to transfer Millinga to Kivukoni College as a lecturer, but when the President got wind of this Millinga was quickly restored to his office in TANU HQ.

When Kisumo had rushed to Songea after the NEC vote against the RDA there was no proper planning of the action that was to be taken. For instance, there was nothing done to transport the schoolchildren from the other villages back to their homes. The Matetereka children had a walk of ninety miles. Many things considered Association property were confiscated – the Renault Roho car, the Peugeot 404, mohair goats, sheep and ducks, etc., that had been introduced by the Swiss agriculturalists, the school maize grinding mill, spinning wheels and weaving loom, the Songea grain milling business, the timber saw mill and more. I would imagine that this action taken by Kisumo probably had no legal basis. (Apparently the Roho had its engine stolen and the Peugeot its gearbox while parked at the police station.)

According to Ado Mgimba in a letter I received at the end of 1971, there were groups of people in Mtwara who wanted to form an association to be able to buy a cashew nut processing plant. He says that Nyerere told them that if they wanted to form an association they should first go to Ruvuma and meet the people of the RDA to see if they might wish to form their association again. The resulting delegation met with the RDA leaders who had been collected from all over the region, apparently overnight. This was the first time these leaders had been together since the disbanding. They were told that the government wanted to return their property to them. In Carlotta's account of her meeting with Millinga, he also mentions this meeting in particular in relation to the saw mill. He said that they were given three alternatives by the vice-president: to sell it and give the money to the villagers; to let the district development council run it; or to give it back to the villages. He went on to say that Kisumo told the delegation that they should not let the villagers choose the third alternative. But the villagers were in total agreement that it was the third alternative they wanted. Over the next months nothing happened and Millinga said that so much had been stolen and the one machine left was not working. Mgimba wrote that after a long time of struggle some things – the school grinding machine, the mohair goats, ducks, sheep, spinning wheels, loom and other things – had been returned to Litowa, and various other things to other villages.

During the period following the President's defeat by the NEC, I think it may be said that he was on the side of Millinga rather than Kisumo. It brought to an end his long struggle to "educate" the top levels of TANU and the government bureaucracy in getting them to encourage communal groups to set themselves up and assume full responsibility to organize their own development. I think it had been an impossible task, and disaster followed for the burgeoning *ujamaa* villages across the country. Nyerere set up a small group of expatriates he trusted and gave them the task of producing two plans, one for development that would produce growth on the lines that Millinga was working on, and the other for gathering the whole rural population of the country into villages by government diktat: so-called "villagization". It was this last alternative that Nyerere decided on and which was put into operation in the mid-1970s. The people were told that this was necessary so government could provide proper services for them such as schools and clinics. In practice it caused considerable problems, in particular food shortages, and it resulted in a fall in the popularity of the President. It was the exact opposite of the *ujamaa* he himself had advocated and urged and supported and pointed to in Ruvuma as the way he thought Tanzania should develop. Yet villagization is taken to be Tanzanian *ujamaa*, discrediting *ujamaa* and hiding the history of the RDA.

Presumably the group he set up would have pointed out the type of legislation that would have been necessary for the implementation of the villagization option. This resulted in "An Act to Empower the Government to Control and Regulate Utilization of Land." Its short title was "Rural Lands (Planning and Utilization) Act 1973". It was enacted by the parliament of Tanzania on 27 July 1973. It is highly significant that it was only given assent by Nyerere on 23 July 1974: he spent almost a year thinking it over.

This Act was a most draconian measure. Under Section 4, the President can declare any area of land in Tanganyika to be a "specified area" which could be reserved "for the establishment of an *ujamaa* village". The section also allows for any existing right to such a "specified area" to be revoked.

The minister given the powers under the Act was "the minister for the time being responsible for regional administration" who could "delegate to a public officer all or any of the functions under this Act."

It was the end of the road for *ujamaa* villages as they had been created by the RDA. In the case of a few of the older and larger villages such as Litowa, under the villagization scheme these became new villages, with a large number of families from elsewhere brought in. The original families were outnumbered. The smaller *ujamaa* villages simply disappeared, their inhabitants having been taken elsewhere to be part of new, larger villages. Amazingly, Nyerere had destroyed what he had spent so much time and energy proposing, encouraging and supporting. Perhaps it was just a hope that if people were brought together there might be some progress. Could he really have thought that?

While we were in Dar es Salaam waiting to fly back to the UK, I heard for the first time that the aid agencies and others were saying that the RDA and its villages were perhaps the greatest grassroots project in Africa. Yet after the banning, almost all of the NEC members and a great majority of the TANU bureaucracy will have wished that the RDA would be forgotten. In 1962 at Litowa the fourteen young men and one older man brought their then reluctant wives to the village of Litowa. By 1969 in that Ruvuma Region, there was an association of seventeen villages working on a communal basis. They had developed a school at Litowa with a curriculum for the children of all the villages that suited the RDA's development as a society and a productive unit. They had purchased and operated efficiently the grain mill and timber sawmill in Songea town, the regional capital, whose profits would go into village development. They had a mechanical workshop at Liweta village to serve the needs of the villages and to train mechanics. They had set up a cadre of a few of their more experienced members to be available to help and advise villages whenever requested. Then there were enterprises developed at Litowa and followed by other villages as they increased in size: there was a clinic with one medic having spent a few months at the government hospital in Songea, which provided a first aid-type service – people in the area also made use of this; a young children's feeding scheme along with a children's day nursery for parents working in the fields; a piped water supply (without electricity) at Litowa and Liweta with others under construction or in planning; the beginnings of small village industries in joinery, wool-spinning and weaving, and experiments in the possibilities of producing glazed ceramics.

There were regular Association meetings with all villages attending. This was in a region about the size of Switzerland and before the days of mobile phones or landlines and only one short strip of tarmac perhaps a couple of hundred yards long on the main road in Songea town. From the beginning the management was entirely by the people themselves. With the communal working, everyone was involved and responsible and benefitted not only from their work but from their individual and collective responsibility, decisions and achievements.

Beyond Ruvuma, in many parts of the country such villages were developing. It was an exercise that attracted attention beyond the borders of Tanzania. It was the result of real, hard work and commitment over many years by those villagers. They deserve a place in their country's history. Most of the time, their achievements were despite the lack of assistance from politicians or officials, with the occasional exception of honest and strong-minded individuals.

Anyone reading Nyerere's three key essays[4] will get a clear impression of the type of development in the rural areas that can truly be called *ujamaa:*

> *Ujamaa* villages are intended to be socialist organizations created by the people, and governed by those who live and work in them. They cannot be created from outside, nor governed from outside. No one can be forced into an *ujamaa* village, and no official – at any level – can go and tell the members of an *ujamaa* village what they should do together, and what they should continue to do as individual farmers.[5]

Such were the villages of the RDA – the villages that were so disliked by almost all of the political leadership of the TANU party and most of its government officers in the Ruvuma Region.

It was not only in his writings and seminars that Nyerere tried to educate those people to his ways of thinking. I mention in Chapter 20 how on his visit to Ruvuma for the opening of the newly built regional administrative building, he tried to make his point about government coercion with what was probably the shortest speech he ever made at such a ceremony: "This building is for development not for ruling."

There was a build-up to that which I well remember. Ado Mgimba and I went to the Songea airfield for the President's arrival. The small government plane was a single engine able to take four or five people. Everything was ready for the President,

---

4   Socialism and Rural Development, Education for Self-Reliance, and Freedom and Development.

5   *Freedom and Development,* p 67.

a line-up of the great and the good of Ruvuma along which he would walk, shake hands, possibly chat, with the car at the other end. He climbed down from the plane with a very stern face, no smile, no wave, walked along the waiting line stopping for no one and straight into the waiting transport. Everyone got into town as quickly as they could and waited for the ceremony. He arrived, still with the same stern expression. The regional commissioner made the usual sort of speech, in particular thanking the Americans who had provided the money for the building, and introduced the President, at which point Nyerere made that shortest of speeches pulling aside the cover over the memorial stone and marching straight into the building. A great piece of theatre. The regional commissioner had not got any reflected glory from the welcoming of the President.

Enforced villagization is so obviously the antithesis of the original *ujamaa vijijini* that Nyerere put so much energy into explaining and urging. Yet *ujamaa vijijini* is used to refer to those enforced villages which did not in the least resemble the RDA. If I mention today that I was involved with *ujamaa vijijini,* people only know *ujamaa* as villagization, and it would take too long to explain the fundamental differences in chance meetings. I cannot mention it. I have seen, for instance, an article on Nyerere and *ujamaa* based on fieldwork done during the 1990s which included an interview with Nyerere where the researcher has shown complete ignorance of the Ruvuma Development Association. A footnote talks of the failure of *ujamaa* in practice. In my understanding of what *ujamaa* in the villages was, it did not fail. It was highly successful and it was about to spread. That is why it was killed.

Again, why were politicians and government officials so opposed to the RDA villages? In the beginning when the RDA was first formed it was not like that. Very early on we were told of other groups which had made a start and we were encouraged to visit them. Those who were seriously prepared to enter into full-time working to start the development of a new communal village formed an association and the regional commissioner was the chairman, not to control it but to denote official approval and backing. In these RDA villages the communal way of working and organization of their society meant that there was much discussion on all the problems they were facing. This led to them finding answers to those problems. With a very high death rate of children under five in the region, they wanted to say to death, "Stay with the old folks, keep away from the children," and this led to a children's feeding scheme and then a day nursery. Then again there was the worry that if their children were sent to school they would develop the desire to go to the towns rather than continue the work their parents had started. This was addressed by the development of their own school which the children were involved in running, with a curriculum that prepared them not for a job in the city hierarchy but for the continuation and development of the work of their community, and of their own work as part of the school.

Chairing a meeting of such villagers was not the same as making speeches elsewhere. (This may have been why it was not possible to get the regional commissioner to call a meeting of the RDA. This may seem hard to believe of a man in such a position of power but it was a common problem.) In 1969 when members of the NEC were sent by Nyerere to live for a few weeks in *ujamaa* villages, the inability of those in such positions to enter into a dialogue with even the school children was truly amazing.

At Litowa an invitation had been given by the school for them to talk to the children. As they approached the school hall the children respectfully stood up. The NEC members never entered the hall but stood in the doorway, harangued the children and then went back to their tents.

On the same NEC visit I well remember the time when we were having our evening meal in the adjoining room to where the Matetereka village schoolgirls had come after classes to carry on with their wool-spinning. There was suddenly this loud tirade at those girls from the woman of the NEC. There was probably no place in Tanzania where it would have been easier to talk to children or adults than in the RDA villages, *but that was not what the NEC had come to do.*

Another example of attitude, this time amongst officials, was when I was in Songea with Mgimba: we heard that there was a meeting going on in the authority offices drawing up a plan to assist Litowa, presumably on the instruction of Nyerere. Amazing that no one from Litowa had been invited.

In the region they always had considerable notice of a presidential visit. This resulted in a great effort put into one of their schemes to prepare things to impress the President. I think they resented the competition from Litowa. I remember Millinga being frustrated by this attitude and asking why they were unable to show off the RDA villages to visitors and the villages themselves taking the credit for what they had accomplished.

What was the thinking of these people? The Arusha Declaration, and in particular Part Five: The Arusha Resolution, may have been Nyerere's work but it was fully subscribed to by the TANU party. Following this, in a meeting of the national assembly, Vice-President Kawawa promised that answers to any questions on the Arusha Declaration submitted by members would be provided. Nyerere's answers were published in the Kivukoni College journal.[6] This states that many questions were received. Unfortunately almost all the questions related to . . . qualifications for leadership. There was not even one question on Socialism and Self-Reliance.

John Saul writing on the 50th anniversary of Tanzania's independence quotes a report in *The Nationalist* newspaper in 1967, the year of the Arusha Declaration, of a public speech given by Nyerere when he warned that the people should not allow their freedom to be pawned, as most of their leaders were purchasable. He warned further that in running the affairs of

6   *Mbioni,* Vol IV, No 11, July 1967.

the nation the people should not look on their leaders as saints and prophets.[7]

At the same time, there always seemed to be one or two officials who were different and enjoyed a good relationship with the RDA villagers. Life could not always have been easy for those few.

Right through the 1960s and into the 1970s Nyerere seemed to have a strong and continuing wish to be able to get these gossiping, dancing and drinking men across the country playing their full part in the development of Tanzania. Changing the patterns of living of a people is not a thing that can be done quickly, particularly when government officials put their own interest above the interests of those they are paid to serve. Twice the President suggested that if Millinga came up with someone suitable as a commissioner who would work along with the RDA he would welcome it. Twice Millinga did just that, but on both occasions Nyerere was facing a situation elsewhere, where it was necessary to dismiss a commissioner and Millinga's suggested candidates went to those other places. So Ruvuma missed out. Towards the end, his answer was that it was necessary to keep up the dialogue. He kept up the dialogue nationally in a big way but to no effect.

---

7   "Nyerere called on the people of Tanzania to have great confidence in themselves and to safeguard the nation's hard-won freedom. Mwalimu warned that the people should not allow their freedom to be pawned as most of their leaders were purchasable. He warned further that in running the affairs of the nation the people should not look on their leaders as saints and prophets.
"The President stated that the attainment of freedom in many cases resulted merely in the change of colours, white faces to black faces without ending exploitation and injustices, and above all without the betterment of the life of the masses. He said that while struggling for freedom the objective was clear but it was another thing to remove your own people from the position of exploiters."
Quoted in Tanzania: Fifty Years On (1961-2011): Rethinking *Ujamaa*, Nyerere and Socialism in Africa by John S Saul, in *Review of African Political Economy*, Vol 39, March 2012, pp 117-125.

So often with so much opposition there were those who bravely stood out against the majority. So it was that with the central committee members, the RDA had one supporter. David Edwards quoting Millinga records:

> After further argument, Mwalimu had only one supporter – the oldest member of the committee (over seventy years old), Mr Selemani Mhigiri. Mhigiri said "This is very strange. These people are making progress for themselves, for the pride of this nation. It makes me disbelieve these stories. Let them live in peace." There was an uproar.[8]

Elsewhere in the country possibly some fifty groups were developing on the same basis. The RDA was the villagers, not some outside authority. It was a Tanzanian creation, not a foreign construct. The banning of the RDA was an attack on the villagers. Why could the RDA not just be ignored by the authorities? Might they not then, with those villages springing up elsewhere, have been a useful example of development through honest hard communal work in the country? Without the rush for a big result, might more have been achieved in the end? But those who wanted to destroy the RDA had a very different agenda. For them, villagers – adults and children, young and elderly – working hard and planning and building their future collectively, were the enemy.

---

8   Edwards, p 17.

APPENDIX I

Constitution of Ruvuma Development Association

1. ADDRESS

The address of the Ruvuma Development Association shall be P.O. Box 48, Songea, Ruvuma Region, Tanzania.

2. OBJECTS

The purpose of the Ruvuma Development Association hereafter called The Association, is to encourage and promote economic, social and cultural development within the Region on a pattern which might be said to fall within ideas growing under the terms "*Ujamaa*" and "African Socialism". A basic tenet of these concepts is to be that all development shall grow from the wishes of the people and shall not be brought about through planning from above. To this end The Association has as its objects:

a) To encourage the establishment of villages such as that in existence at Litowa where a group of people have come together to build a close village life and together work the land as a single large-scale farming unit. Such villages are hereafter termed communal farming villages.

b) To give advice to such villages on all aspects of development, to encourage the participation of Government Departmental officers, to bring into the Region experts where necessary to assist these villages by any other possible means.

c) To assist the development of a group of understanding people from within those projects with which The Association is connected, to be called the Social and Economic Revolutionary Army, who are most able to quickly increase their understanding of the development of African Socialism and who are prepared to give up their membership of any group so as to be free to visit developing village projects with which The Association is working to give advice and help forward development of the lives of the people. This Social and Economic Revolutionary Army, hereafter called SERA, will be soldiers of peaceful development helping to bring about the Social and

Economic Revolution necessary to enable people to lift themselves from the clutches of the enemies of ignorance, poverty, and disease.

d) To encourage, as becomes possible, the development of small village or cottage industries, or such other industries as may become possible to be operated within the communal farming villages or together by a number of such villages.

e) To assist with the marketing and sale of agricultural and industrial products of the communal farming villages by assisting in the establishment of companies or other organizations which may prove necessary for this purpose.

f) To investigate the possibilities of processing within the Region of agricultural products and where necessary assist in the establishment of businesses to introduce such processing.

g) To set up, or assist in the establishment of companies or other organizations which might set up services within the Region necessary for the maintenance of the communal farming villages.

h) To promote educational facilities for the members of the communal farming villages, SERA, and others connected with The Association as may be desirable and necessary to further the development of the work of The Association.

i) To promote medical facilities, community centres, communal activities, and any other necessary or desirable social services to perform any of the functions of a benevolent or friendly society, for the benefit of the communal farming villages, SERA, and others connected with The Association.

j) To encourage people outside the work of The Association to benefit from the services provided and to enter into the new life being developed, to make use of marketing and services arrangements assisted by The Association, where this is possible and will not be at the expense of the progress of development.

k) To pay all the costs, charges, and expenses of the promotion and development of The Association.

l) To appoint Trustees which shall be incorporated under the Trustees Incorporation Ordinance to purchase, take, lease, or otherwise acquire any immovable property acquired by The Association.

m) To purchase or otherwise erect, maintain, reconstruct, and adapt any buildings, offices, workshops, mills, plants, machines, for the purpose of The Association.

n) To draw, accept, make, endorse, discount, or negotiate bills of exchange, promissory notes and negotiable instruments.

o) To donate, advance, and lend money upon such security as may be thought proper, with or without interest, or without security therefore, and become a grant or surety in respect of the indebtedness of its members.

p) To raise funds from membership fees, loans, donations, and any other means.

q) To invest the monies of The Association not immediately required, in such manner as from time to time may be determined.

r) To provide for the welfare of persons working in The Association or any of its associated communal farming villages or other associated organizations, and of the wives, widows, and families of such persons by grants of money, pensions, and other payments or means.

s) To subscribe or contribute from time to time to any charitable, benevolent, cultural, or education object which does not conflict with the principles of The Association.

t) To enter and carry into effect any agreement for joint working in the business or for sharing of profits with any other similar association, business, or co-operative society.

u) To do all such other things as may appear to be incidental or conducive to the attainment of any or all of the above objects.

3. MEMBERSHIP

a) The membership shall consist of:

   i. Those twelve communal farming villages which were in existence at the time of the coming into effect of this Constitution, viz: TYL Farmers' Scheme, Litowa, Liweta Farmers' Association, Njoomlole Farmers' Scheme, Ligera, Matetereka, Ligoma Settlement Farm, Mapinduzi Farmers' Scheme, Luhira Farm, Mhepai, Njaramatata, Mtakanini, Furaha, Kakong'o.

ii. Such other communal farming villages which may be admitted in accordance with this Constitution.

iii. All members of SERA.

iv. Any advisers connected with the work of The Association whose membership the Executive may feel beneficial to the work of The Association, for the duration of their term as advisers.

b) Members shall be admitted after election by the Executive. The Executive shall have the power to refuse any application for membership without giving any reason for such refusal. All elections to membership by the Executive shall be confirmed by the next General Meeting of The Association.

c) After election as members by the Executive such members shall be treated as members of The Association until the next General Meeting when, if confirmed, they shall have their name entered in the Register of Members which shall be kept by The Association. Each member shall be given a Certificate of Membership.

d) Application. Application for membership shall be made in writing and shall be in such a form as the Executive may from time to time require.

e) Termination. Membership shall be terminated:

i. In the case of a communal farming village:

(a) When such village ceases to operate from any cause.

(b) By withdrawal under this Constitution.

(c) By expulsion by a three-fourths majority vote at a General Meeting of which at least fourteen days notice has been given that a motion for such expulsion will be one of the items of business at such Meeting.

ii. In the case of members of SERA by:

(a) Death or insanity.

(b) Withdrawal under this Constitution.

(c) Expulsion by a two-thirds majority vote of a meeting of SERA.

iii. In the case of Advisers by:

(a) His ceasing to become an Adviser for any reason.

(b) Withdrawal under this Constitution.

(c) Expulsion by two-thirds majority vote of the Executive.

f) <u>Withdrawal</u>. A communal farming village may withdraw its membership after giving three years notice in writing to the Secretary of The Association that at the end of that time it shall have paid all its debts to The Association and any penalties which The Association shall in General Meeting decide should be paid on withdrawal.

g) A member who is a member of SERA may withdraw from The Association at any time provided that he gives at least one month's notice in writing to the Secretary or in the case of a SERA member being a member of the Executive of The Association provided that he gives at least six months notice in writing to the Secretary in both cases provided he gives notice before another member of SERA as witness and is not indebted to The Association.

h) An Adviser may withdraw from The Association at any time provided that he gives at least one month's notice in writing to the Secretary provided that he is not indebted to The Association.

i) <u>Expulsion</u>. A communal farming village may be expelled for:

i. Failure to pay any sum due to The Association within twelve months of written notice given by or on behalf of the Executive calling upon it to make payment or after judgement has been given in favour of The Association by any competent court.

ii. Any serious action which the General Meeting may consider is likely to defeat, frustrate, or hinder the objects of The Association as defined in the Constitution, or when such communal farming village changes its mode of working so that the General Meeting considers that it no longer follows the objects of The Association. In such cases membership shall cease at such time as the communal farming village had fulfilled all its financial and other obligations to The Association.

j. A member who is a member of SERA may be expelled for:

i. Failure to pay any sum due to The Association within twelve months of written notice given by or on behalf of the Executive calling upon it to make payment or after judgement has been given in favour of The Association by any competent court.

ii. Any action which may be considered by a two-thirds majority vote of SERA to be disloyal or contrary to the interests of The Association, or likely to cheat The Association or deceive its members, or to have allowed any such action to be done on behalf of SERA or The Association.

iii. Any action which a two-thirds majority vote of SERA may consider is likely to defeat, frustrate, or hinder the objects of The Association as defined in this Constitution.

4. DEBTS

Any debt owed by a member of The Association to The Association may be recovered from any sum due to him from The Association.

5. FEES

a. Members of SERA and Adviser members of The Association shall not pay any membership fees.

b. Communal farming villages which are members shall pay no membership fee on joining or in the first year of development. During the first two years of the operation of this Constitution it shall be one of the duties of the General Meeting to produce a plan of payment of annual membership fees by communal farming villages. Such plan shall take into account:

i. That new villages, in their first few years, need all their resources to be directed into the production of food for use within the village and into work which will bring its reward in the future rather than the present and during this time they shall pay no fees.

ii. That The Association exists for the growth of a fuller life for the people through the development of these communal farming villages and it is these villages which therefore have a duty to sustain and expand the work of The Association and to cover all the overhead costs of The Association.

6. GENERAL MEETINGS

a) The supreme authority of The Association shall, subject to the provisions of this Constitution, be vested in the General Meeting.

b) The General Meeting shall be held as soon as possible after the date of the annual audit, and in no case later than three months after the date of such audit, this meeting being known as the Annual General Meeting.

c) The General Meeting shall also be held at other times when summoned by the Executive, or at the written request of not less than one-fourth of those entitled to attend the General Meeting.

d) Each communal farming village shall be represented at the General Meeting by two of its members one of whom shall be their Manager. On a village becoming a member of The Association the Secretary of such village shall notify The Association of the name of the Manager and the other member who will represent them, and of any subsequent changes in their representatives. All expenses incurred by representatives shall be the responsibility of the village sending them.

e) All members of SERA and Adviser members of The Association shall be entitled to attend the General Meeting.

f) All those attending the General Meeting under clause 6 (d) and (e) shall have one vote.

g) The presence of at least one-half of those entitled to attend shall be necessary for the transaction of any business at a General Meeting, provided that if there is no quorum present within half an hour of the advertised time of the meeting, then the meeting shall stand adjourned to the same time and the same place on the same day two weeks following at which meeting the business on the published agenda for the original meeting shall be dealt with, and any decisions made shall be binding on The Association, whether or not a quorum is present. Notice of any adjourned meeting shall be sent to members not less than seven days in advance, but non-receipt of such notice by any member shall not invalidate the proceedings of any adjourned General Meeting.

h) Except for amendments to this Constitution and expulsion of a communal farm village, business before a General Meeting shall be decided by a simple majority of member voting.

i) Where the Executive think it beneficial, persons who may be able to give useful advice or persons to whom it is wished to show the workings of The Association or any other persons may be invited to the General Meeting. Such persons may with the permission of the Chairman join in the discussions but will not be entitled to vote.

Amendments to this Constitution and Expulsion of Communal Farming Villages

Amendment to this Constitution and expulsion of communal farming villages under this Constitution shall require the votes in a General Meeting of three-fourths of those entitled to vote for the time being under this Constitution who shall have voted in person or by written votes at such General Meeting called in accordance with this Constitution.

Business Reserved for the General Meeting

The following business shall be reserved for the General Meeting:

i. The election, removal, and suspension of members of the Executive subject to the provisions of this Constitution.

ii. The consideration of the annual statement of accounts and balance sheet and the auditors' report.

iii. The consideration of the annual statement of the Secretary on the work of the Executive.

iv. Amendments to this Constitution.

v. Expulsion of communal farming villages from membership of The Association.

vi. To appoint trustees of The Association for the purpose of holding any immovable property acquired by The Association.

vii. Any business referred to a General Meeting by the Executive

viii. In the case only of equal voting the Chairman of the General Meeting shall have a second or casting vote.

ix. All business discussed and decided at a General Meeting shall be recorded in a minute book and the record shall be signed by the Chairman of the General Meeting which confirms the record.

7. THE EXECUTIVE

a) The General Meeting shall elect a Secretary and a Treasurer who shall be ex-officio members of the Executive and four other members of the Executive from amongst those entitled to vote at the General Meeting. Two members of the Executive shall retire each year and their places shall be filled by election in General Meeting. Those to retire shall be the ones who have been longest in office since their last election, but in the case of more than two of such persons having been elected to office on the same day, the ones to retire (unless otherwise agreed by them) shall be determined by lot. A retiring member of the Executive shall, subject of the provisions of this Constitution, be eligible for re-election.

b) The Executive shall elect annually from among their members a Chairman and a Vice-Chairman. The Chairman of the Executive shall, ipso facto, be Chairman of The Association.

c) The Executive may invite any person to attend their discussions where they feel such persons can give useful advice. Any such persons have no vote in the deliberations of the Executive.

d) Any vacancy in the Executive shall be filled by co-option by the rest of the Executive to cover only the unexpired portion of the term of office of the person who has ceased to be a member. If the Annual General Meeting is delayed the existing Executive shall hold office until such Annual General Meeting is held.

e) A member of the Executive shall forfeit his membership if he:

i. Ceases to be a member of The Association.

ii. Is convicted in a court of law of any offence involving dishonesty.

iii. Is removed from office by a General Meeting.

iv. Resigns from the Executive in writing.

f) The Executive shall have meetings at least once every quarter at which all members shall attend before any business shall be transacted except when such attendance is impossible through illness or for any cause which the other members of the Executive agree is beyond the control of the absent members.

g) Other meetings of the Executive shall be held whenever the Secretary shall feel it is necessary to summon the members. Business shall be transacted at these meetings when all those whom it is reasonable to suppose they could attend are present. Business at these meetings shall be confirmed by the succeeding quarterly meetings.

h) The members of the Executive shall receive no payment from The Association for their services as members of the Executive.

i) The Executive shall conduct the ordinary business of The Association and shall exercise the ordinary powers of The Association except those reserved for a General Meeting and subject to this Constitution and in particular shall have the following duties:

i. To observe in all its transactions this Constitution.

ii. To maintain or cause to be maintained true and accurate accounts of all monies received and expended, of all goods bought and sold, of all goods and assets of The Association and of all business transacted by The Association.

iii. To examine the accounts and sanction expenditure subject to any general direction of a General Meeting.

iv. To keep a register of members and of people entitled to vote correct and up to date and to supervise the maintenance of all records required to be maintained by this Constitution.

v. To prepare and lay before the Annual General Meeting income and expenditure accounts, profit and loss accounts and audited balance sheet.

vi. To elect new members to The Association and issue membership cards.

vii. To call special and Annual General Meetings in terms of clause 6 above.

viii. To arrange the terms on which the business transactions of The Association shall be conducted and to ensure the safe custody of The Association's goods and property.

ix. To arrange for the incorporation of any trustees appointed by the General Meeting to hold immovable property acquired by The Association and to instruct such Trustees in the exercise of their duties.

x. Subject to any special conditions or reservations imposed by a General Meeting and to powers delegated by the General Meeting of the Executive to officials of The Association and to this Constitution, to appoint, suspend, and dismiss employees and to ensure the faithful discharge of employees' duties.

xi. Subject to the provision of clause 7 (i) (ix) above, to handle all contracts and legal matters on behalf of The Association. All contracts to bear on behalf of The Association the signatures of two members of the Executive one at least of which signatures shall be the signature of either the Chairman, Secretary, or Treasurer.

xii. To acquire on behalf of The Association shares in any registered co-operative society of limited liability or in any limited liability company and to appoint delegates to such society to represent The Association.

xiii. To open and maintain in proper order one or more bank accounts in The Association's behalf with recognized commercial banks and to arrange for the signatories for the signing of cheques and other negotiable documents connected therewith on behalf of The Association in accordance with the provisions of clause 7 (i) (xi) above.

xiv. To negotiate loans from members or non-members.

xv. To suspend members and recommend suspension under this Constitution.

xvi. To pay from the funds of The Association to members of the Executive and to members of SERA reasonable expenses, on such scales as the General Meeting shall approve, incurred solely in the execution of their duties on behalf of The Association.

xvii. To cause the books of The Association to be audited annually.

xviii. Generally to carry on the business of The Association.

xix. In the conduct of the affairs of The Association the Executive shall be responsible severally and collectively for any loss sustained by The Association by any acts contrary to the law or to this Constitution.

8. THE SOCIAL AND ECONOMIC REVOLUTIONARY ARMY (SERA)

a) The Social and Economic Revolutionary Army shall have no importance in itself but shall exist in order to serve the developing communal farming villages through example, advice, and assistance, and to help where possible all the efforts of The Association to assist these villages and develop industries and services for their necessary development.

b) SERA shall to a large degree act as the messengers of The Association, keeping the Executive of The Association informed of the development, problems, and needs of the villages and making it possible for the Executive to efficiently serve these villages.

c) The membership of SERA shall at no time exceed two for every one communal farming village which is a member of The Association with the exception that should SERA at any time have the maximum permissible number of members and any village shall in any manner cease to be a member of The Association the membership of SERA need not be reduced.

d) The following people shall be members of SERA at the date of the coming into operation of this Constitution: Ntimbanjayo J Millinga, E Ado Mgimba, Sangu Wayakile, Matupo Bwanaliko, Mrs Defrosa Bwanaliko, Bagimbaya J Mhagama, John Ngairo, Mahindi Lighanga.

e) New members shall be admitted only after serving a probationary period of at least twelve months and then by a majority vote in writing of at least three-fourths of the existing members of SERA.

f) It shall be one of the beliefs of SERA that the economic improvement of its members shall keep as far as possible in line with the economic development of the people with whom they are working in the villages. At the time of the coming into operation of this Constitution the members of the villages are poor and have only just started on a road which can lead them out of their poverty. At this time therefore the members of SERA shall receive no payment for their services to the people. It shall however be a point of discussion within SERA and The Association as to how SERA members may benefit from any success which attends their work in the betterment of the lives of the people with whom they work. All such plans emanating from SERA shall be laid before the General Meeting for approval.

g) All members of SERA shall meet together to discuss any business and look into their method of operation and to discuss whether methods used for development are correct or can be improved on and to discuss matters of their organization and to keep each other informed of the whole of development within the work of The Association at least once every quarter. All members will be expected to attend. Absence of a member will be allowed only through illness or through any cause which the other members of SERA agree is beyond the control of the absent member.

h) Other meetings of the whole or of part of the membership shall be held whenever the Secretary of SERA shall feel it is necessary to hold such a meeting.

i) SERA shall select from amongst its members a Chairman, Vice-Chairman, and Secretary-Treasurer who shall be the organizers of SERA. One of these organizers shall retire each year and his place be filled by election of the SERA members. The one to retire shall be the one who has been longest in office since his last election but in the case of more than one having been elected to office on the same day, the one to retire (unless otherwise agreed by them) shall be determined by lot. A retiring organizer shall, subject to the provisions of this Constitution, be eligible for re-election.

j) Members of SERA shall attend meetings of the Executive of The Association whenever the Executive may summon them to such meetings.

9. REGISTERS

The following registers and documents shall be maintained in proper order and it shall be the duty of the Secretary of the Executive to see that this is done:

a) A register of members of The Association showing name, address, membership number, date of admission and date of termination of membership.

b) A register of persons entitled to attend and vote at a General Meeting of The Association showing name, address, whom they represent, date of commencement and date of termination of such entitlement.

c) A register of members of SERA showing name, address, membership number, date of admission and date of termination of membership.

d) All such cash books, ledgers, and other books of accounting as may be necessary to give a clear and accurate record of all financial transactions of The Association and of the financial position of The Association at any time.

e) Minute book for all General Meetings, for all meetings of the Executive and for all meetings of SERA

f) Such other records and registers as may from time to time be required

10. DISPUTES

Any disputes not resolved by the Executive or in General Meeting or in meetings of SERA in regard to this Constitution or the business of The Association between members or past members of The Association, or persons claiming through them or between such persons and the Executive or any official of The Association or between such persons and SERA or any member of SERA, shall be referred to an arbitrator appointed by the Registrar of Societies and approved by the parties concerned. Any decision of the Arbitrator upon these disputes shall be carried out by the Executive.

11. GENERAL

Every member of The Association shall accept and faithfully comply with this Constitution and with all amendments thereto.

1965

APPENDIX II

Letter from Ralph Ibbott to President Nyerere

2 Sherwoods Road,
Oxhey, Watford,
Herts, England

31 October 1969

President Julius K Nyerere
The State House
PO Box 9120
Dar es Salaam

Dear President Nyerere,

I was asked by a number of people in Ruvuma to write you expressing the thoughts we had had over the past weeks in our conversations, and my own feelings, and particularly to stress their loyalty
to what they believe were the aims of TANU. They were shocked by
the accusations against them and were worried by newspaper reports into feeling that you might believe some of these accusations.
The people know their own difficulties and failings but find it hard
to understand why criticism takes the form of crude false accusations rather than of critical discussions.

Mervyn Jones – a journalist writing mainly for the *New States-
man* – wrote me in 1966, "I feel that you are fortunate to be working
in Tanzania where your ideas would be sympathetically received by
the President. From what I have seen in the poorer countries of Asia
and Latin America, any such development which really involved
the people would be killed immediately."

We have always stressed to our supporters and interested
friends that the existence and growth of these village democracies
depended on your protection. To me it is only this distrust of any
genuine coming together of peasant peoples by those in authority
that makes sense of any of the happenings during the short history
of the Ruvuma Development Association. Any genuine discussion

or objective looking at things does not enter into it. The truth has no importance against the fact that the ordinary people must not be allowed to organize themselves.

It seems in fact that almost every possible angle of the work in the Ruvuma villages has been taken by the members of the central committee and interpreted in a way opposite to the truth. The main charge, that the Association was against TANU is however the most ridiculous and at the same time the most interesting. The first reaction of the people here when being told this was one of complete disbelief – these people must be joking. There are probably few places where there were people with a greater loyalty to TANU. I understand that when the central committee members told this to the people of Matetereka, the manager speaking for the people said, "We don't understand what you are talking about, you had better go away." There could be no other reaction.

Litowa village grew out of TANU and during the whole of my stay there one of the strongest impressions has been of the people feeling that they are TANU and have been trying to express the policies of TANU. In the last years this feeling has not lessened but in fact has grown, and grown considerably for reasons easy to see. Such writings as Education for Self-Reliance, Socialism and Rural Development and Freedom and Development have been understood, and made the villagers feel that they were on the party's road. The placing of Millinga in the party headquarters with the purpose of spreading the ideas of *ujamaa* increased this feeling, and sending people to Ruvuma so that – to quote the Litowa chairman – "we can show them the correct way" gave them an increased feeling of being an instrument of the party.

The various intrigues against the Association by party officials about which the people knew, never took away this basic belief that they were the instrument of the party, showing others the way. It was the official policy of the party which gave them this belief. If there was a plot, it was against the RDA and because of the positions of the plotters, had to succeed.

Another much repeated criticism of the RDA was that they would not co-operate with or accept help from government. Again the opposite is and always has been the truth. The Association has always been going out to ask for government to help but it has always been that most departmental officers have not wanted to help villages with their own organization. There always have been the exceptions but these exceptions only spotlight the problem in that officers who co-operate are often ostracized by their fellow officers. In 1965 for instance, the requests of the Association met a good response from Edward Mwakabonga, the district, and later acting regional community development officer, and this good relationship continued for the whole of Mwakabonga's term of office. It was through him that Grace Chips came to Litowa as a community development worker, who later resigned from the department to go back to teaching in order to be able to make Litowa her home where she has ever since been a most valuable member of the community. As a result of his assistance, Mwakabonga found himself the odd man out in the administration so that rather childish things occurred such as not receiving an invitation to a sundowner party for a visiting minister.

This applies not just to Litowa but to all the villages. Matetereka villagers are great workers and very easy to work with. They have repeatedly asked the agricultural department for advice, particularly on the veterinary side, with very little result until they wrote on the subject to the area commissioner. The result seems to have been a visit from veterinary asking why they were trying to get them into trouble! Again here at Matetereka we find the exception in Mr Mayemba, the Maweso branch chairman of TANU, who spends much time at Matetereka and lives with the people for long periods, which is much appreciated by them.

Of recent times the question of co-operation has been an important one with development money available through regional funds specifically for *ujamaa* village development. In the Association the chairman pointed out that many government officers were new in the region and district and stressed the need for the greatest care in discussions so that it would not be possible for people to continue the lie of the Association not being co-operative. I believe this was a very necessary approach although from experience in Rhodesia I knew that people who are intent on breaking up an organization have no respect for the truth so that whatever one does in such circumstances has little effect towards saving an organization against those with the greatest political power.

The first steps in assisting the Association were when a group of surveyors were sent to Litowa with rather vague instructions and asked the Litowa manager for five members to work with them over the next weeks. The manager asked me to talk with them and find out exactly what they were to do, pointing out to me the difficulty of being asked without warning for five workers when the month's work was already fully planned. This I did and then by agreement with the surveyors I went to discuss with the regional director of agriculture. This was a first meeting with the new man and I felt as we have done so often in such circumstances that he had been told "things" about us making for initial awkwardness. However this soon disappeared in conversation and he was able later to meet and discuss with the secretary of the Association the survey priorities in the villages. Following this a team of people from different branches of the department of agriculture – veterinary, fisheries, beekeeping, forestry, etc. – were sent to stay a week at Litowa for planning with a view to aiding the village. Mr Kikwa, the leader of the group stayed for the whole week, few others stayed beyond the first day returning for the rest of the week to the joys of town life! The resulting plans tended to be very unrealistic. For example, one of the items on which most was to be spent was for livestock, buildings, etc., to produce one pint of milk a day for everyone at Litowa. As nearly half of these people were children from other villages this would have meant that Litowa was to put nearly half of its dairy effort into charitable works – very commendable but just not possible.

Following this pretence of a week's stay at Litowa, government officers held a meeting over two or three days to discuss the plans for Litowa. No one from Litowa or the Association was invited to the meeting. Some of us attended by hearing of it by chance as it was starting, through the regional veterinary officer when we came to collect medicine for livestock. There has been nothing at any time in these discussions with government from people of the Association that anyone could complain about.

One of the suggestions for help was that the department of agriculture should place a field assistant at Litowa to live with and help the people. Before I left I heard that a field assistant from Maposeni had been instructed to move to Litowa but that he had refused to go!

I would suggest that there was no question of the Association not co-operating with government. In the face of indiscipline and lack of a sense of duty in government staff and lack of any correct approach to the Association and the Litowa village and the doubtful nature of the plans they produced, the people of Litowa and the Association behaved extremely carefully and correctly.

It could be that when members of the central committee talk of plots against them that they look upon anything in the nature of a meeting to discuss their proposed visit as a plot. Yet no real organization could do anything but meet and discuss such a visit, and neither could they fail to discuss the most serious statement of the second vice-president at the Handeni Seminar that "the RDA must stop." If it is suggested that the resultant meeting of the Association's committee was a plot, then it can only mean that those who suggested it are people who will not allow any discussion amongst the people and who desire to have absolute rule.

Mr Toroka, I understand, reported to the committee on the Handeni seminar and Mr Kawawa's statement was discussed, the meeting deciding that they felt that they could not take any action as it was a statement of an individual at a seminar and not a decision of the party. On the coming of the central committee members, the meeting understood from Toroka that they were coming to Litowa, Liweta and Matetereka to live and work with the villagers, to see the workings of the villages and to learn of their difficulties. The committee members certainly did not come in that spirit but I feel that Toroka's interpretation of the proposed visit was a correct interpretation of the official reason.

As a result of this the three villages were informed and told that they should make their preparations for receiving the committee members. At Litowa for instance the village selected four families, each to take in one committee member. In all cases the accommodation and food would have been good. After these preparations, regional officials arrived and said that they had come to collect the TANU tents to put two in each village for the committee members. The Litowa manager said that he could not speak for Njoomlole but in the other villages tents were not necessary as preparations had been made by the villages to receive the members. The next we heard was that in Songea they said Litowa had refused to allow the officers to take the TANU tents. A TANU official was sent out to Litowa and he went back satisfied that Litowa had done no such thing. I understand that this official has now been dismissed. The tents were then erected and at Litowa the central committee members refused the houses and spent the whole time in the tents preferring the cold at night in the tents and excessive daytime heat, to the more pleasant conditions of the houses they were offered.

I was personally very keen to gather impressions of these TANU leaders because of certain reports from the seminars which worried me. In particular to hear that they put forward a settlement that they visited while at Handeni where it was planned to develop it as an *ujamaa* community although at the time of the visit there had not yet been implementation of communal working or proper village "self-government", in preference to Mbambara where communal working is a fact and the villagers are fully involved. This was worrying because it was what we had seen so often in Ruvuma, and so suggested that in this new central committee the attitude of mind was the same as with the regional commissioners we have had at Songea, nearly all of whom have now been removed from their positions in party and government. At a time when in many places we were meeting increasing numbers of people with a growing understanding of and interest in *ujamaa*, it seemed that the top body of the party was made up of what we can only call reactionaries, of the type of people who before we had found to react against any attempt of education in what was socialism. This fear was more than confirmed during the members' stay in the Ruvuma villages. However the people tried to explain themselves and their organizations, but I am never quite sure how much of what the committee members "learn" is out of fear of the people and how much from a sheer inability to understand anything. There is nothing on which there is not confusion, so that they say they were told lies at Handeni as Millinga said the school and spinning and weaving belonged to Litowa and now they find they belong to the Association. One knows that Millinga said no such thing, but on these simple details there is never an admission of confusion but always an accusation of being told lies. On other things one cannot but believe that misrepresentations are deliberate. I was told some things in the report of the visit to the RDA villages of those committee members who stayed at Njoomlole. The visit to Ibbott's house where they saw the wooden machine where his wife makes blankets. She has never made anything on the loom and it is really impossible for anyone not to see the pride in achievement of the children in their weaving work. The seven children concerned took all the spinning and weaving equipment to the Saba Saba show in Songea by themselves, my wife being in Masasi, and very successfully demonstrated the work. They saw the filthy dirty houses of the villagers. There are very few of the old houses left and Litowa has the highest standard of housing of any of the villages in Ruvuma and new housing progresses very well. At Matetereka they met the "chairman who is also the manager" – a suggestion perhaps of a one-man show. But the statement is not true. They say they saw ten acres of poor coffee. There are thirty-five acres all together at different stages of growth, the earliest plantings now coming into production. So it goes on.

Some things which on the surface appear quite ridiculous, are yet, I believe, what people really feel and have a relevance to the situation. Thus we heard from "reliable sources" that Mr Chengula, our Ruvuma representative, said the people of Litowa had arranged that he should go out herding the cattle so that Simba (the bull) would kill him. Genuine communication between people when such fear exists on one side is impossible.

I think a similar attitude of fear exists amongst the central committee towards the party cadres. This interests me personally as I had feared that in the present situation, these young people being trained as village cadres and faced in their job amongst the villagers with the opposition of those with great political power, would tend to associate themselves with those who hold power rather than with the villagers. From my enquiries it seems that those who attended the various seminars, felt the opposition present there to the growth of village democracies, and their reaction was to wish to work harder for the organization of the villagers. To me a most hopeful sign if selected young students can be given a short course in village socialism and then, with little practical experience, when faced with opposition to the idea that is coupled with political power, can stand more strongly with socialism.

The opposition to the idea of village socialism is in the highest places. I was told by one of the Association people at the Handeni seminar that towards the end of a lengthy discussion on the cadres, the second vice-president in, as it were, an aside to him said, "But if we have these cadres, where will we be?" Not an opposition based on opposed ideas of political philosophy but rather from a groundless instinctive fear. The opposition from Mr Kisumo, the minister of state, however, seems to me more "deliberate" judging by such open remarks as when he said to Millinga, "You can't win. The only way you could win would be by taking over the power from us." Also in correspondence with me, his letter was a very conscious misinterpretation of my letter and obviously designed with the object of trying to get rid of me. There is also, however, the blank refusal to discuss, such as when one of our new teachers, talking from experience when Mr Kisumo was telling Litowa that the party had disbanded the Association and the party was to control all village growth, asked, "If you live where the branch of the party is not strong, would it not be right for one to oneself encourage people to come together?" Answer: "The party is strong everywhere."

There is also conflict as to what constitutes development. Part of Mr Kisumo's further argument as to why it was necessary to disband the RDA as stated to the people of Litowa, was that development was not rapid enough, and particularly did he compare it with the resettlement projects at Rufiji quoting size and number of villages as the criteria of development. Comparisons are rather odious things but the Association never expected to be able to work on a scale possible with government. However it seems a strange comparison in a country which possesses such a document as Freedom and Development which starts by putting in clear terms what constitutes development. As far as reported to me, the Rufiji settlements are not in a stage where one can begin to judge them, still being on a basis of government feeding, with no village self-government and being in an area abounding in witchcraft, which more than anything else perhaps prevents co-operation.

Similarly it appears that many think of development in terms of putting in much money so that at Njoomlole this is being done on a grand scale, partly I feel to "do better" than the RDA villages. In spite of the village membership being smaller than the larger of the RDA villages, which we are told by Mr Kisumo are too small, his ministry as well as the second VP's office are pouring money in.

I think this is a dangerous pretence and can make "development" look so easy whilst people's ability is not necessarily growing. At Litowa we have been assisting with the permanent school buildings with overseas money. But in spite of having roofing timber easily available at our own mill which we could purchase with this money, the Association has organized to build the maximum, and as hand sawing produces timber at half the price of machine sawing, all school roofing timbers are cut in the bush locally by the Litowa and Liweta villages, and I feel that this sort of thing is an essential part of an education for people with limited resources. Njoomlole however has just been supplied with a timber order from the Association mills of Shs 7000/–. Perhaps they learn less of organization, management and thrift.

I believe all this harder way of the Association pays handsomely in increased ability and I am rather impressed at the state of Litowa management at the time I left. There was much to be managed and things did get done. Above the usual village agricultural work, in itself now more complicated, there was considerable dispensary work for the surrounding district as well as a village and school, a very considerable building programme of village housing and village communal buildings and alterations at the dam for the installation of a larger ram, all progressing very well. Also the village on behalf of the Association was organizing the brick-making and building programme of the school, keeping well all records of days worked of outside labour, calculating wages due and paying out, etc., organizing timber sawing for roofing. No fuss and well done. On top of all of this many groups being sent in from other villages, many visitors, researchers and so on, all taking up the time of management, not to mention the worry of false stories and the knowledge that many were trying to cause trouble and break up the people's organization.

The Association was also at a very interesting and hopeful stage. During the time of Mr Ngairo being chairman there were many difficulties, as although he understood much of the policy of *ujamaa* and believed in it, he had several character defects which inevitably caused trouble. Particularly too much desire for the political limelight and to run things himself, a tendency to create factions within the organization and a not one hundred percent honesty.

Since the election of Wayakile Sangu as chairman, and an emphasis on the needs of the villages, one has been able to feel again the pull of the people.

To see this Association of the people destroyed is to me a very sad thing but does not surprise me as we have attempted to discuss and co-operate with such people as Messrs Haule, Walwa and Barongo in the past, and never has it been possible to reach a level of real discussion; always this has been made impossible by what I can only describe as their basic despotism – always in the end this seems to come through. In the present central committee members it is difficult to see anything new learnt from your writings and speeches, and this "despotism" still seems to me the basic drive. I hear now from someone just arrived from Tanzania that the whole staff of the school has been dispersed throughout the country – Kigoma, Mara, Singida, Dodoma and Mbeya. That this should be felt necessary and be a step taken several weeks after disbanding the Association, during which time there have been no troubles, can only show a tremendous lack of confidence in those who control affairs, which is I believe a large part of the cause of despotism in people who in ordinary life are pleasant beings.

It would seem from this that the ideas of Socialism and Rural Development, Education for Self-Reliance and Freedom and Development are too far in advance of the times in Tanzania – but I do not accept this. One of the most encouraging things to me in this last year in particular was the number of people in various levels of government who were beginning to have a genuine understanding of and interest in the socialism as expressed in your speeches and writings. Meeting some of these again in Dar es Salaam before leaving, it was sad to see that they were all very worried men and all felt that very much more was at stake than the RDA.

This is also very much my own feeling. That it is basically a rejection of the doctrine of Ujamaa as expressed by you and even of the Arusha Declaration. Also such unwanted things as having to go out into the bush, which I think in their eyes is a plot hatched up between Millinga and yourself. The elected body of the party has exerted its authority according to the feelings of its members, and have by doing so created an atmosphere of fear amongst those who were understanding socialism. To me it is a question of either a true free development of the people under the leadership of a government with a slowly but steadily increasing enlightenment or else a rigid absolute party control – the latter appears to have won. If there was with it a real knowledge of the practical mechanics of rural development this would not be so sad, but with that missing . . . ?

Life in this world never has been an easy thing but I would like to say that with all these difficulties and disappointments, yet it has been a great time for us to have been able to work in Tanzania. We do not in any way regret it, and have seen much growth in ideas, which I feel is real growth.

Very sincerely yours,
Ralph Ibbott

APPENDIX III

Excerpt: Letter from Ntimbanjayo Millinga to Ralph Ibbott

18 December 1971

Dear Ralph,

I am still at Dar es Salaam at TANU HQ. So far the wicked efforts haven't managed to get me out of the headquarters in spite of their many attempts to do so behind the President's back. He is the one, I am sure, who has kept me there to the moment.

. . . Comrade, things are in the stage where no chances are allowed. Either the revolution wins or the counter-revolutionary forces win. I just hope that the President now takes the right steps to stop the bureaucrats from controlling the situation, or else we shall have had it. The peasants will soon stand together if they are undisturbed for the next two years. For the time being I feel being of more use to the revolution than if I left and allowed the reactionaries get Mhagama to this position. Although I am being centralized but my presence also neutralizes the neutralizers of people's effort through misleading people using such offices and positions. For Litowa and fellow villages I have been of some help here, and I believe I have so far been of the same to the rest of the villages in the country . . .

. . . The anti-RDA move was a move against peasants all over the country . . .

. . . Best regards to the Ibbotts . . .

Yours sincerely,

Ntimbanjayo

APPENDIX IV

In 1992 Noreen and Ralph Ibbott visited Ruvuma. This was the (translated) welcoming speech they were given in Matetereka on 18 April.

Short Historical Summary of *Ujamaa* Development in Matetereka Village

Matetereka Village was started by eight families farming the lands on the present site. The farm was known as Mahiwa Farm. By 1965, seventy-five families worked the land and settled on Mahiwa Farm. The name of the village was changed from Mahiwa Farm to Matetereka Village. The change in the name came after the villagers realized that there was a similar name in Lindi for an agricultural training centre.

On advice from the leadership of the Ruvuma Development Association (RDA), Matetereka Village became a member of the Association. Inside the Association, under the leadership and advice from Mr Ibbott and Millinga Ntimbanjayo, several villages of the Association were provided with facilities to promote the development. Being one of the several villages in the RDA, Matetereka was given a tractor with a trailer, plough, harrow and planter. Some members of the village got training in such skills as mechanics, spinning and weaving, animal husbandry, etc., after which the village was provided with spinning wheels, dairy cattle, etc. Matetereka Village children were provided with primary education at Litowa.

Following the achievements in the RDA villages, enemies of Ujamaa from the national level were angered and schemed vicious manoeuvres to wipe out Ujamaa. In 1969 the Nation destroyed the people's vehicle for development, the Ruvuma Development Association, and dispersed the leaders. Villagers' properties worth hundreds of thousands of shillings belonging to the labouring villagers were taken away from their rightful owners and given away to conmen, thus humiliating the people.

The humiliation took away from the members of the RDA villages (and others that were ready to join in *ujamaa* life) the hope for development.

In spite of the enemies' continual vices to wipe out *ujamaa*, we in Matetereka have continued with the struggle without despair. During this period our efforts have achieved the following:

1. Good utilization of the tractor and implements for cultivation and delivery of products to the markets for consumers.

2. Cultivation by hand hoe continued to the expansion of the fields.

3. Small industries strengthened the *ujamaa* development.

Proceeds accrued from our above mentioned efforts enabled us to fulfil the following:

1. Provide free primary and secondary education to our children.

2. Provide training to *ujamaa* village members in mechanics, health-care, soap making, fruit canning, tailoring, masonry, carpentry, driving and bookkeeping.

3. Give cash dividends to all members.

4. Give incentives by providing those who performed best their duties with such items as chairs and beds.

5. Provide free medical treatment to members.

6. Run a nursery.

7. Provide two mattresses to every family in the *ujamaa* community.

8. Became the first village in the country to buy seven-ton lorry in 1974 and another later on in 1978.

9. Became winners of the Regional Best Village Competition for three years consecutively and were once the sixth best village in the country.

In spite of the above mentioned achievements, national economic problems which have caused devaluation of the Tanzanian shilling, war, drought, enemies of *ujamaa* taking over the leadership of the village, etc., have contributed considerably to the deterioration of economic and social development.

For the time being we have the following projects run on a commercial basis:

1. Fifteen acres of coffee.
2. Carpentry workshop.
3. Three grinding and dehusking mills.
4. Thirty beef and milk cattle.
5. A lorry for transport.
6. Iron smith.
7. House renting in the village and towns.
8. Vegetable garden and orchard.
9. Beekeeping.
10. Timber cutting.
11. Tailoring.
12. Construction of good living homes.
13. Afforestation.
14. A provisions store.

Projections

The Matetereka *Ujamaa* Village community have the following aims in the future:

1. To make changes in the working methods i.e. from communal mode of life and economy to a co-operative way of running the economy.

2. To do everything possible to get a lorry in order to be able to provide reliable transport for villagers and for goods to and from the market.

3. Because most modern machinery depends on electric power for efficient performance, effort will be made to get a generator to provide power for the running of the carpentry, iron smith, grinding mills, welding, etc.

Further Reading

Uhuru na Umoja / Freedom and Unity – A Selection from Writings and Speeches 1952-1965, JK Nyerere, Oxford University Press, Dar es Salaam, 1966.

Uhuru na Ujamaa / Freedom and Socialism – A Selection from Writings and Speeches 1965-1967, JK Nyerere, OUP, Dar es Salaam, 1968.

Uhuru na Maendeleo / Freedom and Development – A Selection from Writings and Speeches 1968-1973, JK Nyerere, OUP, Dar es Salaam, 1973.

Ujamaa – Essays on Socialism, JK Nyerere's nine key essays 1962-1968, OUP, Dar es Salaam, 1968.

The Arusha Declaration – Rediscovering Nyerere's Tanzania, JK Nyerere, preface by Madaraka Nyerere, introduction by Selma James, Crossroads Books, London, 2008.

Shamba Letu, Kate Wenner, Houghton Mifflin Co, Boston, 1970.

Matetereka: Tanzania's Last Ujamaa Village, David M Edwards, Centre of African Studies, Occasional Papers No 77, Edinburgh University, 1998.

Tanzanian Ujamaa and Scientific Socialism, Walter Rodney, *African Review*, Dar es Salaam, 1:4, 1972.

The Critical Phase in Tanzania, 1945-1968, Cranford Pratt, Cambridge University Press, Cambridge, 1976.

False Start in Africa, René Dumont, Sphere Book, London, 1966.

The Wretched of the Earth, Frantz Fanon, Penguin Books, 1967.

Ralph Ibbott was born in 1924 in Hertfordshire, England. His generation was shaped by World War II and the widespread post-war determination for change that resulted in the Welfare State in the UK and elsewhere. He served in the Royal Engineers in Europe, and was demobbed in 1947, dedicated to working for a just world from the bottom up.

Portrait by Noreen Ibbott, 1971.

A grammar school boy, in 1950 he qualified as a quantity surveyor and met his future wife, Noreen Moriarty, who had been raised in Ireland and England. She agreed to go with him to Africa, with one proviso: they would have no more than four children.

From 1952, Ralph worked in apartheid Southern Rhodesia with Guy Clutton-Brock who had set up a multiracial co-operative farm at St Faith's Anglican Mission with its tenant farmers. Welcomed at first, in 1959 a new hostile priest urged the bishop to ask the Ibbotts to leave. With some of the tenant farmers, they started a new co-operative farming project at Nyafaru on a donated piece of land. The community created a school with simple housing for teachers, an open air facility for members of all faiths to worship together, and wool and rug-making workshops which Noreen helped to establish.

In 1961, while on holiday in Tanganyika (soon to become Tanzania), Ralph met Ntimbanjayo Millinga, "a very impressive young man" who with a group of men had just started the collective village of Litowa, in the south of the country. Ntimbanjayo asked Ralph to come to Litowa to give advice and technical assistance. After discussion and planning, in April 1963 the Ibbotts with their three children moved to Litowa which was to become the lead village of the seventeen *ujamaa* villages of the Ruvuma Development Association – the model of *ujamaa*,

President Nyerere's strategy for development. (A fourth child was born in Litowa.)

The RDA was banned by the ruling party in 1969.

The Ibbotts returned to the UK, where Ralph headed the international service at the UN Association in London.

In 1973 he became community development worker in one of the most deprived areas of Greenock, near Glasgow. He believed that, as in Africa, the people could solve their own problems. The local tenants association and youth club persuaded the council to build a sports centre and let the youth club run it. With Ralph's leadership much was accomplished by young people previously dismissed as troublemakers. He retired in 1989.

In 1992 Noreen and Ralph visited Ruvuma and met up again with their old friend and colleague Ntimbanjayo Millinga. He asked whether resources might be found if young village people were interested in development projects based on their 1960s experience. After Millinga's retirement, Ruvuma Development Aid (RUDA), a registered charity, was founded to develop a primary school to a high standard. After Millinga's death in 2008, the school became a memorial to him.

Noreen died in 2012. Ralph currently lives in East Lothian, Scotland.

www.rudatanzania.org.uk

Selma James is an anti-sexist, anti-racist campaigner and author, and editor of Crossroads Books. From 1958 to 1962, she worked with CLR James in the movement for the federation and independence of the English-speaking Caribbean. In 1972 she founded the International Wages for Housework Campaign, and in 2000 she helped launch the Global Women's Strike. She co-authored the classic *The Power of Women and the Subversion of the Community*. She is a founding member of the International Jewish Anti-Zionist Network. Her latest publication is *Sex, Race and Class – The Perspective of Winning*, 2012. She lives in London.

www.globalwomenstrike.net